THE CARMELITE TRADITION

SPIRITUALITY IN HISTORY SERIES

The Carmelite Tradition

Steven Payne, O.C.D.

Phyllis Zagano, Series Editor

LITURGICAL PRESS
Collegeville, Minnesota

www.litpress.org

Published by Order of Saint Benedict, Collegeville, Minnesota. All rights reserved. No part of this book may be reproduced in any form, by print, microfilm, microfiche, mechanical recording, photocopying, translation, or by any other means, known or yet unknown, for any purpose except brief quotations in reviews, without the previous written permission of Liturgical Press, Saint John's Abbey, PO Box 7500, Collegeville, Minnesota 56321-7500. Printed in the United States of America.

2   3   4   5   6   7   8   9

Library of Congress Cataloging-in-Publication Data

The Carmelite tradition / Steven Payne.
    p. cm. — (Spirituality in history series)
    Includes bibliographical references (p.   ).
    ISBN 978-0-8146-1912-4 — ISBN 978-0-8146-3953-5 (ebook)
 1. Carmelites—Spiritual life.   I. Payne, Steven, 1950–

    BX3203.C39   2011
    271'.73—dc22   2011002357

Contents

Acknowledgments

Rule of St. Albert, translated by Bede Edwards, from *The Rule of Saint Albert*, edited by Hugh Clarke and Bede Edwards (Aylesford and Kensington, 1973). Used with permission of the Anglo-Irish Province of Discalced Carmelite Friars.

Excerpts from Nicholas of Narbonne, "The Flaming Arrow," translated by Bede Edwards, *Sword* 39 (1979): 3–52. Used with permission of the Order of Carmelites, North American Province of the Most Pure Heart of Mary, Darien, Illinois.

Excerpt from Felip Ribot, O.CARM., *The Ten Books on the Way of Life and Great Deeds of the Carmelites (including The Book of the First Monks)*, translated into English by Richard Copsey, O.CARM. (Faversham: Saint Albert's Press & Rome: Edizioni Carmelitane, 2005, Second Edition 2007), *Early Carmelite Spirituality* Series Volume 1. © British Province of Carmelites (www.carmelite.org). Reprinted with permission; all rights reserved.

Excerpts from *The Book of Her Life*, in *The Collected Works of St. Teresa of Avila*, vol. 1, translated by Kieran Kavanaugh, O.C.D., and Otilio Rodriguez, O.C.D. Copyright © 1976 by Washington Province of Discalced Carmelites. ICS Publications, 2131 Lincoln Road, NE, Washington, DC 20002-1199. www.icspublications.org. Used with permission.

Excerpts from *The Way of Perfection* and *The Interior Castle*, in *The Collected Works of St. Teresa of Avila*, vol. 2, translated by Kieran Kavanaugh, O.C.D., and Otilio Rodriguez, O.C.D. Copyright © 1980 by Washington Province of Discalced Carmelites. ICS Publications, 2131 Lincoln Road, NE, Washington, DC 20002-1199. www.icspublications.org. Used with permission.

"Efficacy of Patience," in *The Collected Works of St. Teresa of Avila*, vol. 3, translated by Kieran Kavanaugh, O.C.D., and Otilio Rodriguez, O.C.D. Copyright © 1980 by Washington Province of Discalced Carmelites. ICS Publications, 2131 Lincoln Road, NE, Washington, DC 20002-1199. www.icspublications.org. Used with permission.

1953), chaps. 1, 5, 6, 8, 13. Used with permission of the Order of Carmelites, North American Province of St. Elias, Middletown, New York.

"Christmas Hymn by Sr. Teresa of St. Augustine" and "Song Composed in Prison by Sr. Julie-Louise," in Terrye Newkirk, o.c.d.s., *The Mantle of Elijah: The Martyrs of Compiègne as Prophets of the Modern Age.* Copyright © 1995 by Washington Province of Discalced Carmelites. ICS Publications, 2131 Lincoln Road, NE, Washington, DC 20002-1199. www.icspublications.org. Used with permission.

Excerpts from William Bush, *To Quell the Terror: The Mystery of the Vocation of the Sixteen Carmelites of Compiègne Guillotined July 17, 1794.* Copyright © 1999 by Washington Province of Discalced Carmelites. ICS Publications, 2131 Lincoln Road, NE, Washington, DC 20002-1199. www.icspublications.org. Used with permission.

Excerpts from *Story of a Soul: The Autobiography of Saint Thérèse of Lisieux*, translated by John Clarke, o.c.d. Copyright © 1975, 1976, 1996 by Washington Province of Discalced Carmelites. ICS Publications, 2131 Lincoln Road, NE, Washington, DC 20002-1199. www.icspublications.org. Used with permission.

"Prayer to the Trinity" and excerpt from "Heaven in Faith," in *Elizabeth of the Trinity: I Have Found God; Complete Works, Volume 1: Major Spiritual Writings*, translated by Aletheia Kane, o.c.d. Copyright © 1984 by Washington Province of Discalced Carmelites. ICS Publications, 2131 Lincoln Road, NE, Washington, DC 20002-1199. www.icspublications.org. Used with permission.

Excerpts from Letters 123 and 133, in *Elizabeth of the Trinity: I Have Found God; Complete Works, Volume 2: Letters from Carmel*, translated by Anne Englund Nash. Copyright © 1995 by Washington Province of Discalced Carmelites. ICS Publications, 2131 Lincoln Road, NE, Washington, DC 20002-1199. www.icspublications. org. Used with permission.

Excerpts from Titus Brandsma, *Carmelite Mysticism: Historical Sketches* (Darien, IL: Carmelite Press, 2002), 75–85. Used with permission of the Order of Carmelites, North American Province of the Most Pure Heart of Mary, Darien, Illinois.

Excerpt from the sermons of Titus Brandsma, in *Proper of the Liturgy of the Hours of the Order of the Brothers of the Blessed Virgin Mary of Mount Carmel and of the Order of the Discalced Carmelites* (Rome: Institutum Carmelitanum, 1993), 224–27. Used with permission of the Institutum Carmelitanum, Rome.

Titus Brandsma, "Before a Picture of Jesus in My Cell," translated by Gervase Toelle, in *Proper of the Liturgy of the Hours of the Order of the Brothers of the Blessed Virgin Mary of Mount Carmel and of the Order of the Discalced Carmelites* (Rome: Institutum Carmelitanum, 1993), 455–56. Used with permission of the Order of Carmelites, North American Province of the Most Pure Heart of Mary, Darien, Illinois.

Preface

The worldwide explosion of interest in "spirituality" has sent inquirers in several directions. One of the more fruitful is toward the traditional spiritualities that have enriched and nurtured the church for many hundreds of years. Among the oldest Christian spiritualities are those connected to particular foundations, charisms, or individuals. This series of spiritualities in history focuses on five distinct traditions within the history of the church, those now known as Benedictine, Carmelite, Dominican, Franciscan, and Ignatian.

Each volume in the series seeks to present the given spiritual tradition through an anthology of writings by or about persons who have lived it, along with brief biographical introductions of those persons. Each volume is edited by an expert or experts in the tradition at hand.

The present volume of Carmelite spirituality has been edited by Steven Payne, O.C.D., past editor of ICS Publications and of *Spiritual Life* magazine, and the author of several works in philosophy of religion, theology, and Carmelite spirituality. He is a member of the Carmelite Forum and of the Carmelite Institute in Washington, DC, of which he is a past president. Fr. Payne, of the Washington Province of Discalced Carmelite Friars, is a member of the Carmelite Friars' formation team at the Monastery of St. John of the Cross near Nairobi, Kenya, and director of the Institute of Spirituality and Religious Formation (ISRF) at Tangaza College, a constituent college of the Catholic University of Eastern Africa (CUEA) in Nairobi.

Fr. Payne's elegant presentation of the essentials of the Carmelite tradition traces the various paths followers of the original hermits of Mount Carmel have lived through the eight hundred years since Albert, the Latin patriarch of Jerusalem, handed them their simple plan of life. The remarkable contemplatives who move through these pages demonstrate the results of their belief in God's immanence, even in darkness. Each entry adds another layer to the unfolding mysteries of Carmelite spirituality, inserted in the history of the church and of the world. The lives of the thousands of men and women who sought and seek the living God in silence and solitude form the quiet background for the few whose writings are here so well represented. Their contemporary witness to Christian contemplation gives living witness to the writings of their predecessors.

My own work on this book and for this series has continued with the able assistance of librarians, particularly the reference and interlibrary loan staff of Hofstra University, Hempstead, New York, who have tirelessly met so many of my research needs. I am grateful as well for the congenial staff of Liturgical Press, and especially for the professional support and encouragement of Hans Christoffersen, editorial director, and Peter Dwyer, director of Liturgical Press.

Phyllis Zagano
September 8, 2010
Feast of the Nativity of the Blessed Virgin Mary

Introduction

B rief introductions to this or that spiritual tradition never seem entirely satisfactory, especially to those who know the tradition firsthand. When I was unexpectedly transferred to the Discalced Carmelite Community in Nairobi, Kenya, some years ago, for example, among the first tasks I was given was to teach a few introductory classes on *African* spirituality. Needless to say, the African students were amused at my early efforts to present systematically, from the few available texts I had read, what they knew far better from lifelong personal experience!

Yet even to clarify the scope of our topic was not easy. We recognized that the term "spirituality" itself is notoriously difficult to define. But to speak of "*African* spirituality," some argued, as if it were distinct from African religion, culture, ethics, politics, economics, and so on, is already to impose foreign categories on what Africans have traditionally experienced as part of a unified whole. Moreover, since the continent is home to hundreds of different peoples and cultures, each with its own traditional beliefs and practices, some wondered if we should speak instead of African *spiritualities* in the plural.

In the end, however, we came to admit the usefulness of the singular term. We could thereby refer collectively to certain distinctive ways of relating to the transcendent that, if not exclusive to Africa or exemplified in every African individual or society, are nevertheless found, in some form, virtually everywhere across the continent. In that sense, and with all the necessary qualifications, it seemed legitimate to us to talk of "African spirituality."

The issues are much the same when we turn to Carmelite spirituality, the focus of this volume. Carmelites typically do not distinguish their spirituality from their whole way of life, and no simple description can capture all the rich diversity of its symbols, themes, practices, and representative figures. The Carmelite tradition has been evolving for at least eight hundred years, and Carmelites have traditionally claimed spiritual (and sometimes even historical) roots going back much further, even to the biblical figures of Mary and Elijah. Over many centuries, the ancient "vine of Carmel" has sprouted many branches. Besides the friars and nuns of the two main groups (the Order of Carmelites and the Order of Discalced Carmelites), there are today the numerous "apostolic" congregations, secular institutes, and ecclesial movements that belong to the broader Carmelite family, as well as countless Lay and Secular Carmelites around the globe who live a Carmelite vocation "in the midst of the world."

Meanwhile, the classic spiritual texts of Carmel are now eagerly read by people of all faiths (and no faith). Surveys of Western spirituality invariably give great prominence to the Carmelite tradition. Three of the Carmelite saints (Teresa of Avila, John of the Cross, and Thérèse of Lisieux) have been named doctors of the church for their spiritual teaching. All of this suggests that "Carmelite spirituality" is not monolithic but has many expressions and can take many forms. Certainly it is no longer the private monopoly of any one group, but belongs to the entire church and world. One might argue, then, that today there are *many* Carmelite spiritualities, because there are so many different perspectives on the Carmelite heritage and so many ways of being Carmelite.

And yet to speak of "Carmelite spirituality" in the singular is to acknowledge that, down through the ages, these varied Carmelite expressions have returned again and again to certain images, themes, and spiritual models in pondering the mystery of divine-human friendship: the mountain, the garden, the spring, the hermit's cell, the journey, night, fire, the heart, allegiance to Jesus Christ, continual pondering of the Law of the Lord, radical availability to God, mystical union, self-transcending love, contemplative prayer, prophetic zeal, Elijah, Mary, Joseph, and so on. At first glance this list of characteristic emphases may seem disappointing, since each one can also be found in other Christian spiritual traditions. But, in fact, this is only to be expected if Carmelite spirituality is but one way of trying to live the Gospel with complete fidelity. Carmelite spirituality seeks nothing more nor less than to "stand before the face of the living God" and prophesy with Elijah, to "hear the word of God and keep it" with Mary, to grow in friendship with God through unceasing prayer with Teresa, to "become by participation what Christ is by nature" as John of the Cross puts it, and thereby to be made, like Thérèse of Lisieux, into instruments of God's transforming merciful love in the church and society. One of the striking features of the tradition's greatest saints and teachers is that the more thoroughly "Carmelite" they are, the more universal their message. They speak directly to hearts of those who may know little of religious orders but are somehow searching for meaning in life, yearning for a deep encounter with God. Perhaps the clearest example is Thérèse herself, dying at twenty-four in an obscure French Carmel; her simple yet profound reflections mainly on the ordinary struggles of convent life have inspired an audience of millions and helped make her the most popular saint of modern times.

The Carmelite tradition offers an abundance of spiritual "classics." We have chosen representative texts from the main periods of Carmel's history and from the main branches of the Carmelite family. Authors quoted here include men and women, ordained and lay, scholars and nonscholars, famous and little known. Inevitably, many favorite passages had to be omitted for lack of space, but the bibliography provides guidance for those who may want to explore further.

First in every sense is a work known as the Rule of St. Albert (ca. 1207), the earliest surviving document related to the Carmelites. Among the shortest of the classic rules, it is in fact a *formula vitae* composed by the Latin patriarch of Jerusalem, Albert of Vercelli, at the request of the original group of European hermits assembled in the *wadi-ain-es-Siah* on the western slopes of Mount Carmel. It sets out briefly the fundamental elements of the Carmelite vocation, and is the foundational text to which all later Carmelite reforms and renewal movements have turned for inspiration.

Next comes a selection from *The Flaming Arrow* (ca. 1270), which Thomas Merton once described as "representative of the pure and prophetic spirit of the early Carmelites."[1] Ostensibly written as he was retiring from office by Nicholas of France, a disillusioned prior general of the time, this highly rhetorical work laments that the Carmelites are already abandoning their original spirit by following the mendicant friars into urban life and ministry, and exhorts them to return to the prayerful solitude of the desert.

Medieval Carmelite spirituality, however, finds its fullest expression in the third work anthologized here, *The Book of the Institution of the First Monks*, first published in the late fourteenth century but long assumed to be much older. Written in the form of a lengthy allegorical commentary on the biblical account of Elijah in 1 and 2 Kings, this book brings together the Order's Elijan and Marian spirit, as well as the prophetic and contemplative dimensions of its spirituality.

Many scholars suggest that, in addition to the Carmelite Rule, this *Book of the Institution of the First Monks* may have helped inspire the ideal of a renewed Carmel in Teresa of Avila (1515–1582), one of history's most remarkable women. In a period when the church and society in Spain were deeply distrustful of feminine initiative, Teresa not only managed to inaugurate and oversee a large-scale reform movement within the Order but also, in her rare free moments, composed some of the most highly regarded mystical texts of all time, from which we have chosen a few key passages.

Twenty-seven years her junior, John of the Cross (1542–1591) became Teresa's friend and collaborator, helping to extend her reform movement to the Carmelite friars. Today John is ranked among the greatest poets of the Spanish language and among the greatest teachers of mystical spirituality. In recent times, both Christians and non-Christians alike turn especially to his treatment of the "dark night" for guidance in facing the mystery of human suffering and the experience of God's seeming silence.

An unusual selection from St. Teresa's favorite friar, the prolific Jerome Gracián (1545–1614), brings out an important aspect of Teresian spirituality too often overlooked, namely, her aversion to "sad-faced" sanctity and her insistence on balance and a sense of humor for a healthy spiritual life. Gracián's *Constitutions of the Cerro* offers a satiric body of legislation for "melancholy" friars and nuns set on destroying their own religious orders.

The passages in the next section are from Mary Magdalen de' Pazzi (1566–1607), a near contemporary of Teresa of Avila and John of the Cross. She entered the Carmelite convent of Florence in 1582 and soon began receiving almost daily visions, messages, and ecstasies. Her ecstatic utterances, transcribed by the other sisters in the community, fill five manuscript volumes and are noteworthy for their doctrinal content.

In seventeenth-century France, the Carmelites of the Ancient Observance (i.e., the Carmelite Order from which Teresa's Discalced Carmelites had become canonically separate) underwent their own renewal movement, known as the reform of Touraine. Its great spiritual figure is John of St. Samson (1571–1636), the blind lay brother whose dictated mystical texts are once more available in contemporary critical editions.

The most influential representative of the Teresian reform in the seventeenth century, as it began to spread beyond Spain, was not a prominent theologian or even a canonized saint. Nicolas Herman, better known as Br. Lawrence of the Resurrection (1614–1691), spent over fifty years in the Discalced Carmelite Monastery of Paris, working mainly as community cook and sandal maker. Because he found the formal meditation methods of his era too complex, he developed his own approach of simply remaining always in God's presence throughout the day, in good times and bad. After his death, his surviving letters, notes, and records of his conversations were gathered under the title *The Practice of the Presence of God*, which has gone through myriad editions in many languages.

In Belgium, the o.carm. Touraine reform produced a number of important spiritual writers, including the lay "tertiary" Maria Petyt (1623–1677) and her spiritual director, the Carmelite friar and theologian Michael of St. Augustine (1621–1684). As the passages included in this section show, their writings present Carmelite spirituality in an emphatically Marian form, yet firmly grounded in traditional Catholic doctrine rather than private devotions.

In the eighteenth century, the Discalced Carmelite nuns of Compiègne in France opened a new chapter in Carmelite spirituality, written not with pen and ink but in their own blood. The story of Teresa of St. Augustine and her companions, who offered their lives to "restore peace" and were martyred during the French Revolution's Reign of Terror, has been immortalized in the Poulenc opera, *Dialogues of the Carmelites*. This section includes a more historically accurate account of their dramatic final moments.

Among the many admirers of the Compiègne martyrs was Thérèse of Lisieux (1873–1897), whom Pope Pius X famously described as "the greatest saint of modern times." Known especially for her "little way," and represented here by passages from *Story of a Soul*, she remains one of the church's most appealing saints, and recently became the newest, and youngest, doctor of the church.

Seven years her junior, Elizabeth of the Trinity (1880–1906) has been called Thérèse's "sister in the spirit."[2] Her famous "Prayer to the Trinity," included below, is quoted in the *Catechism of the Catholic Church*, and she is remembered especially for having so deeply experienced and taught the fundamentally trinitarian character of the Christian spiritual life.

World War II and the rise of Nazi ideology produced a new wave of Carmelite martyrs. Titus Brandsma (1881–1942), a member of the Carmelite Order in Holland, was a leading scholar and educator who served for a time as rector magnificus of the Catholic University of Nijmegen. As ecclesiastical advisor to the Dutch Catholic journalists, he consistently urged them to resist printing Nazi materials and was accordingly arrested and later martyred at Dachau.

Even more prominent among the Carmelite victims of Nazism was Titus's contemporary, St. Teresa Benedicta of the Cross, better known as Edith Stein (1891–1942). Born into a Jewish family but abandoning her faith as an adolescent, Stein became a leading figure in the early phenomenological movement and personal assistant to the philosopher Edmund Husserl. Convinced of the truth of Christianity after a conversion experience in 1921, she sought admission to the Catholic Church and later to the Discalced Carmelite convent of Cologne, Germany. A transfer to the Carmel of Echt, Holland, provided only temporary safety. She was finally arrested by the Nazis and sent to her death at Auschwitz in 1942. More recently Pope John Paul II named her copatroness of Europe.

Closer to our own day, Jessica Powers (1905–1988) lived for nearly five decades as Sr. Miriam of the Holy Spirit, a nun of the Carmel of Pewaukee, Wisconsin. The subject of numerous books and articles, she is regarded as one of the great religious poets of our time. Her work reminds us that Carmelite spirituality, and indeed any profound spirituality, expresses itself most effectively in the language of imagery and symbol. Following a small sampling of her poems, we then close this volume with a few contemporary voices, sharing their reflections on what Carmelite spirituality can contribute to the church and world of the twenty-first century and beyond.

I wish to give special thanks to Liturgical Press and to series editor Phyllis Zagano for her unfailing patience and support. I am also deeply grateful to all the members of the Carmelite family who have advised and assisted me in this project or granted permission to use the texts quoted here, as well as those who, by their words and example over many years, have helped me better understand the practical significance of Carmelite spirituality in today's world. Finally, for each of the authors and works represented here, many others (e.g., John Baconthorpe, John Soreth, Baptist of Mantua, Anne of St. Bartholomew, Mary of Jesus Crucified, Francisco Palau, Teresa of the Andes) could also have been chosen. The Carmelite tradition offers an almost endless variety of spiritual treasures. These brief selections will have served their purpose if they whet the reader's appetite to explore further. But at the same time, it should be remembered that Carmelite spirituality is most fully expressed not on the written page but in the "living book" of day-to-day Carmelite life. Even within the Carmelite family, in different times and places, access to the "classics" of the tradition has often been limited for various reasons. Many exemplary Carmelites have lived and died without having had much opportunity for serious study of our great spiritual masters. Instead, they learned by faithfully living the life, by imbibing the wisdom and spiritual practices of the Carmelite men and women who handed on to them what they had received.

This volume, then, offers no formal definition of Carmelite spirituality but simply presents some of the major representative voices from the Carmelite tradition. Further resources are listed in the bibliography. But the most reliable guides to this heritage must be sought elsewhere, outside of books. What is Carmelite spirituality? Ask any Carmelite who knows what it is to "stand before the face of the living God."

The Carmelite Tradition

The story of the Carmelite tradition can be told in many ways. Some authors begin with the prophet Elijah, or with Mary under the title of "Our Lady of Mount Carmel." Others take Teresa of Avila as their point of reference. Still others work backward from the present to retrieve whatever in the Carmelite heritage seems useful for today.

Here we begin with the *place* from which this tradition takes its name. Mount Carmel is not, in fact, a single mountain but rather a range of high hills along the eastern shore of the Mediterranean Sea, in the northwestern part of what is now the modern state of Israel. From a high promontory above the city of Haifa, these hills stretch to the southeast for more than fifteen miles, and are dotted with woodlands and secluded valleys, bearing abundant and diverse vegetation. The town of Nazareth is visible in the distance to the east. Even today, despite the incursions of urban development, one can easily appreciate why the word "Carmel" is so often used in the Hebrew Scriptures to evoke natural beauty and fruitfulness (cf. Song 7:6; Isa 33:9; 35:1-2; Jer 2:7), a place to commune with God.

From antiquity, Mount Carmel has been regarded as sacred, even among the ancient pagans. Today it is home to several Druze communities and to the Bahá'í World Centre, with its spectacular Shrine of the Báb. But for Jews, Christians, and Muslims, Mount Carmel is forever linked with the memory of the prophet Elijah the Tishbite, whose mission was to summon the people away from their religious syncretism (including worship of the Canaanite rain-god), back to single-hearted fidelity to the one true God. Elijah suddenly bursts onto the pages of Scripture with the powerful declaration: "As the LORD the God of Israel lives, before whom I stand, there shall be neither dew nor rain these years, except by my word" (1 Kgs 17:1). Mount Carmel is identified as the site of his dramatic confrontation with the prophets of Baal (1 Kgs 18:19-40), and the subsequent end to the long drought after Elijah's servant returned from the top of Carmel and reported seeing a small white cloud rising over the sea (1 Kgs 18:42-46).

Many extrabiblical traditions portray Elijah (and his successor Elisha) spending long periods on Mount Carmel, in solitude or guiding the otherwise obscure "guild of prophets" occasionally mentioned in the Elijah/Elisha cycle. Several patristic authors imaginatively portray Elijah as a kind of model for the Christian monk and even as the "founder" of monasticism and the eremitical life. During the flowering of Palestinian monasticism in the fourth to seventh centuries, a number of Byzantine monastic settlements and *laurae* (loosely knit hermit communities) were established on Mount Carmel, no doubt attracted by its association with Elijah.

Yet the origins of the Carmelites as we know them today still remain somewhat mysterious. Perhaps this is altogether fitting for a tradition so closely associated with mystical spirituality. In any case, most contemporary historians trace their beginnings to some time after the Third Crusade (1189–1192), when it seems that a group of "Latin" (that is, European) hermits settled in the *wadi-ain-es-Siah* on the western slopes of Mount Carmel, in a strip of coastal territory recaptured from Saladin. It was a time of dramatic social and religious change in Europe, with the decline of the feudal system, the rise of city-states, and the corresponding emergence of an urban middle class whose spiritual needs, like those of the urban poor, were not being met by traditional ecclesiastical and monastic structures. Popular piety of the day was marked by increasing devotion to the humanity of Jesus Christ and a corresponding desire to imitate his way of life as closely as possible, according to the understanding of the period. Pilgrims were eager to reach the Holy Land and to walk, literally, in the footsteps of Christ. Many vowed to remain there, pursuing a life of penance and prayer.

This was also the era of the "vita apostolica" movement. Countless ordinary Christians were unimpressed by a monastic life grown too comfortable (at least according to their perceptions). They sought instead what was understood to be a more "apostolic life," not by undertaking more numerous "apostolates" in the contemporary sense, but rather by imitating the poor itinerant preaching life of Jesus and the apostles. The new mendicant groups, such as the Franciscans and Dominicans, who played such a key role in the renewal of the medieval church, grew out of this larger movement.

As far as we now know, the anonymous hermits who gathered together in the *wadi* on Mount Carmel would have shared many of these same aspirations. They had a "prior" rather than a monastic "abbot," for example, and consciously chose not to embrace any of the traditional monastic rules. Instead, they approached Albert of Vercelli, the papal legate and patriarch of Jerusalem, for a brief set of written norms "in keeping with [their] avowed purpose." The "formula of life" he provided (known to later generations as the Carmelite Rule or the Rule of St. Albert) outlines a simple fraternal life of "allegiance to Christ" in unceasing prayer and meditation, common ownership of goods, silence, manual labor, practice of the virtues, and mutual charity (Rule, pars. 2–4). It became the foundational document for the entire Carmelite spiritual tradition.

The original site also left its enduring imprint on Carmelite spirituality. The hermits had chosen to establish themselves "near the spring [of Elijah]" on the mountain sacred to his memory (Rule, par. 1). Little wonder, then, that later generations of Carmelites, pondering the group's obscure beginnings, would come to claim not only a spiritual but even a historical connection with this great prophet whom the Scriptures link with the coming of the Day of the Lord and the appearance of the Messiah (see Mal 3:23-24; Sir 48:10-12; Matt 17:1-13). Elijah gradually came to be seen as the "father" and model of Carmelites.

In addition, following one of the directives in Albert's "formula of life," the hermits in the *wadi* built "an oratory in the midst of the cells," which they dedicated to Mary (cf. Rule, par. 14). To the feudal mind, this choice meant that she was the "lady of the place," the one under whose patronage and protection the hermits would fight their spiritual battles. Gradually, Christian pilgrims and the church at large came to identify this little community of hermits, according to the name of their chapel, as the "brothers of Our Lady of Mount Carmel," and the Carmelites themselves came to identify Mary as their special patron, mother, and even sister, seeing in her life the pattern of their vocation.

Within a few decades, as the political situation in Palestine deteriorated, the Carmelites began migrating westward, making foundations in Cyprus, Sicily, southern France, England, and other parts of Europe. Yet they soon discovered that their eremitical lifestyle on Mount Carmel did not easily translate to the new European context. Moreover, as recent arrivals from the East, they were suspected of being in violation of the Fourth Lateran Council's ban of 1215 against the founding of any additional religious orders (although their "rule of life" predated the council's decision). Accordingly, in 1247, at the Carmelites' request, Pope

Innocent IV promulgated the "Innocentian" version of the Carmelite Rule, which included minor alterations to Albert's text. These brought out more clearly the communal dimension of their life and allowed the Carmelites to found houses not only in "solitary places" but wherever they were "given a site that is suitable and convenient for the observance proper to your Order" (Rule, par. 5).

Later tradition also held that it was at this critical juncture, in 1251, that St. Simon Stock, prior general of the Carmelites, received from Mary the brown scapular, together with weighty promises of special assistance at the time of death to those who would wear it devoutly. Modern scholars have raised many questions about the historical accuracy of these scapular traditions. (Among other difficulties, the earliest surviving testimonies come more than a century and a half after the vision was said to have occurred, and modern research indicates that the prior general in 1251 was a man named Godfrey, not Simon.) But what is beyond dispute is that the Carmelites soon began to thrive, for which they gave thanks to Our Lady of Mount Carmel. Moreover, in the centuries that have followed, the brown scapular has gradually become one of the most familiar expressions of Catholic Marian devotion, and has been repeatedly endorsed by the church as a way of symbolizing allegiance to Mary and her Son by wearing a part of the habit of the Order especially dedicated to her.

A more practical reason for their newfound success was that the Carmelites had begun assimilating themselves to the mendicants, who were attracting numerous vocations at the time. They followed the other mendicants in founding houses in the urban academic centers and sending their students to the universities to train them for scholarly and professional careers. With the Franciscans and Dominicans, the Carmelites and Augustinians came to be recognized as among the four principal mendicant orders of the Middle Ages (joined later by the Servites and others).

Not all were happy with these changes, however. The *Ignea Sagitta*, or *Flaming Arrow*, is a long lament about the decline of the Carmelites from their initial fervor, a critique of their new lifestyle in the cities, and a call to return to the contemplative life of the desert. The text was apparently composed around the year 1270 by the prior general of the Order, Nicholas the Frenchman (also known as Nicholas of Narbonne). This would make it the earliest surviving document of significant length originating from within the Order, and perhaps the earliest expression of a perennial yearning among dedicated Carmelites to recapture something of the original spirit of the first hermits.

In addition, because the Carmelites were unable to point to any saintly founder of recent memory when challenged about their legitimacy, they sought ever stronger ecclesiastical confirmation of their way of life, and became ever more insistent on their links with Elijah the prophet. A text known as the *Rubrica prima*, from the earliest surviving Carmelite *Constitutions*, has this to say:

> Since some of the younger brothers in our Order do not know how to satisfy according to the truth those who inquire from whom and in what way our Order had its origin, we wish to respond to them, giving them a written formula for such inquirers. For we say, bearing witness to the truth, that from the time of those devout inhabitants of Mount Carmel, the prophets Elijah and Elisha, holy fathers of both the Old Testament and the New have truly loved the solitude of that same mountain for the sake of contemplation of heavenly things; that they undoubtedly lived a praiseworthy life of holy penitence there next to the spring of Elijah; and that by a holy inheritance this life has been continuously maintained. In the time of Innocent III, Albert, patriarch of the church of Jerusalem, gathered their successors into one college, writing a Rule for them which Pope Honorius, Innocent's successor, and many of his successors, approving this Order, have most devoutly confirmed with the testimony of their bulls. In this profession we, their followers, serve the Lord in various parts of the world until the present day.[1]

With the collapse of the Latin kingdom of Jerusalem in 1291, the Carmelites lost all physical contact with their original home. The hermits were finally driven from their *wadi* (Carmelite tradition has them martyred) and were unable to return until hundreds of years later. Yet even as their external lifestyle became less and less distinguishable from that of other mendicant friars, Mount Carmel itself remained for them a "dangerous memory," and Carmelites continued to see themselves as somehow still "sons of the prophets" and hermits at heart. In the last decades of the fourteenth century, the Carmelite provincial of Catalonia, Philip Ribot, published a collection of documents that included a remarkable text known as *The Book of the Institution of the First Monks*, allegedly written for the Carmelites in AD 412, though now generally thought to have been composed by Ribot himself, perhaps drawing on earlier materials. Insisting on Elijah as founder of the Order, the work takes the form of a detailed allegorical reading of the Elijan cycle from 1 and 2 Kings. Though no longer regarded as a reliable historical account, *The Book of the Institution of the First Monks* is appreciated today as perhaps the finest synthesis of medieval Carmelite spirituality, blending the Order's ascetical and mystical doctrine, and explaining the spiritual significance of various elements in the Carmelite way of life. Most important, Ribot neatly ties together the earlier Elijan and Marian heritage. Thus, in an interpretation that would have an enormous impact on later Carmelite art and literature, Ribot suggests that the small white cloud rising over the sea (1 Kgs 18:44), ending the drought after the battle with the prophets of Baal, was a foreshadowing, for Elijah, of the torrent of grace that would come through the Blessed Virgin and her Son.

Meanwhile, throughout the fourteenth and fifteenth centuries the Carmelites had their great saints (such as Peter-Thomas, papal legate and Latin patriarch of Constantinople), eminent scholars (such as John Baconthorpe), and national heroes (such as Nuno Alvares Pereira, who led the fight for Portuguese independence). Yet in the wake of the Black Plague, the Western Schism, the Hundred Years' War, and other calamities, they suffered the same general decline in religious observance as the other Orders and the rest of the European church.

Perhaps the best known Carmelite example is the career of Fra Filippo Lippi (1406–1469), subject of a famous poem by Robert Browning. According to some sources, he was orphaned in infancy and entrusted to the care of the friars at the Carmine in Florence, where he was professed at the age of fifteen. Florence at this time had become the cultural center of the Italian Renaissance, and the Carmine played its part. Thus, as a young friar, "Lippo" was able to observe the masters Masolino and Masaccio painting their famed frescoes in the Carmine's Brancacci Chapel. Encouraged by the prior to develop his own artistic skills, Fra Filippo went on to become one of the most outstanding painters of the *quattrocento*. But as his fame grew and the number of commissions increased, he spent less and less time in the monastery, setting up his own studio in the city and obtaining his own property. Despite the patronage of Cosimo de' Medici, Filippo seems to have been chronically short of money and was even taken to court for forgery. In 1456 he was appointed chaplain to the Augustinian nuns of Prato, where he met an attractive younger boarder, Lucretia Buti. Their relationship produced a son, Filippino Lippi, who went on to become an important painter in his own right. Fra Lippo Lippi is perhaps the greatest visual artist that Carmel has so far produced. His paintings hang in major galleries around the world, and his Madonnas, in particular, remain perennial favorites. But unlike his near contemporary, the saintly Dominican Fra Angelico, Lippi's mode of living his vocation left much to be desired.

In 1432 Pope Eugene IV granted further modifications of the Rule, relaxing somewhat the requirement of abstinence from meat and allowing the friars to move about more freely. Modest though the changes were, rejection of this "mitigation" became one of the rallying points for those who sought to renew the spirit of Carmel, such as members of the Mantuan and Albi reforms. The most important contribution to the renewal efforts in this period, however, came from John Soreth, prior general of the Carmelites for twenty years (1451–1471). Besides encouraging more faithful religious observance, he obtained papal approval in 1452 to formally accept laity into the Order as "tertiaries," and communities of women as Carmelite nuns. The permission was worded broadly, and the lifestyle of the tertiaries and nuns took different forms in different parts of Europe, but Soreth clearly hoped that the addition of these new members would have a beneficial influence on the friars as well.

Indeed, it was from the first such community of Carmelite women in the Castilian region of Spain that the Order's most influential renewal movement would eventually emerge. In 1535 a lively and outgoing twenty-year-old by the name of Teresa de Ahumada y Cepeda reluctantly left her father's home to join the nearby Carmelite Monastery of the Incarnation in Avila. It was a large and busy religious community that reflected the economic and class divisions of Spanish society, with many visitors to entertain and long hours spent in elaborate liturgical prayers. At first Teresa found the life surprisingly congenial, and she began to grow in prayer, but a complete breakdown in health and long convalescence found her settling into a life of religious routine. After a "second conversion" at the age of thirty-nine, however, Teresa rededicated herself to faithfully living the Carmelite Rule, especially what she called its "most important aspect," namely, "unceasing prayer" (*Way*, 4.2), which she understood in terms of "an intimate sharing between friends" and "taking time frequently to be alone with the one whom we know loves us" (*Life*, 8.5).[2] As her spiritual life deepened and her extraordinary religious experiences raised concerns among confessors and superiors, Teresa began writing, both to clarify her own path and to teach others the ways of contemplative prayer. From her pen would eventually flow such spiritual classics as *The Book of Her Life*, *The Way of Perfection*, and *The Interior Castle*.

Seeking to create a more conducive environment for "unceasing prayer," Teresa established the new monastery of San José in Avila in 1562. Everything was arranged according to her ideal of a small austere community of enclosed Carmelite women, living together as friends and supporting one another in a vocation of intense contemplative prayer for the sake of the church. The Teresian reform had begun. Visiting five years later, the Carmelite prior general approved what he saw, and Teresa eagerly took up his challenge to establish as many similar foundations as she could. At her invitation, Juan de Yepes, a young Carmelite priest, also joined her project, taking the name "John of the Cross" and helping her to spread this reform to the Carmelite friars. John himself was an outstanding poet, and his poems "The Dark Night," "The Spiritual Canticle," and "The Living Flame of Love," together with their prose commentaries, are considered among the greatest works of Western mystical literature. For many today, the message of Teresa of Avila and John of the Cross, for which both were named doctors of the church, is virtually synonymous with Carmelite spirituality. More successfully than previous authors, they offer a detailed analysis of requirements, pitfalls, and progressive stages in the journey toward transforming mystical union, and their writings provide a dynamic synthesis of major Carmelite themes and symbols. They teach, among other things:

- that the spiritual life is a process (like climbing a mountain, watering a garden in different ways, traveling by night, journeying through an enormous castle, changing from a silkworm to a butterfly, or searching for a beloved who, it turns out, was always near) through predictable stages toward an outcome beyond all expectation;

- that the goal is nothing less than intimate loving union with the Trinity and an ever-deepening friendship with Christ that transforms us into his likeness, by dying and rising with him who heals all our brokenness (one might call it a "christification" that includes both "divinization" and "humanization," yet without ever losing our creaturely identity);

- that faithful friends, a loving community, wise spiritual guides, liturgy and sacraments, good books (especially Scripture), learning, "determined determination," silence, solitude, humility, healthy asceticism, affability, fidelity to regular times of quiet prayer, and so on can be great helps along the way, but must never become idols;

- that the purpose is not self-satisfaction but service of others. (Indeed, it has sometimes been said that Teresa was the first founder of a contemplative community to fully grasp the essentially apostolic nature of an authentic contemplative vocation, that a life dedicated to contemplative prayer may, in some mysterious way, be the greatest service of all that one can render.)

Though initially the prior general preferred the term "contemplative Carmelites" for Teresa's followers, they soon became popularly known as "discalced" (because members typically wore sandals or went barefoot as a sign of greater austerity). After the death of Teresa (in 1582) and John of the Cross (in 1591), the movement they had begun separated from the original Carmelite Order (sometimes called the "Ancient Observance" and identified by the religious initials O.CARM.) to become the Order of Discalced Carmelites (sometimes called, a bit misleadingly, the "Primitive Observance," and identified by the initials O.C.D.). Soon the Discalced Carmelites themselves had divided further into a Spanish and Italian Congregation, with the latter embracing Teresa's enthusiasm for the missions and carrying the Carmelite presence to many parts of Europe, the Middle East, and beyond.

Teresa's writings were also enormously popular throughout Europe in the seventeenth century, and especially in France, influencing Francis de Sales, Vincent de Paul, and many members of the French school of spirituality. During that same time period, a lay brother of the Discalced Carmelite community in Paris, Lawrence of the Resurrection, developed a simple and appealing approach to prayer by "keeping God always present"; a collection of his letters, notes, and conversations, published posthumously under the title *The Practice of the Presence of God*, remains a perennial favorite among many Protestant Christians, who are often unaware of the implicitly Carmelite origins and orientation of Lawrence's spirituality. Meanwhile, seventeenth-century France also gave birth to a new renewal movement among the Carmelites of the Ancient Observance. Known as the reform of Touraine, it likewise featured outstanding mystical and spiritual authors such as John of St. Samson. This Touraine reform included, among other points, a stronger emphasis on well-celebrated liturgy, and its influence eventually spread throughout the Carmelite Order.

But the papal condemnations of Quietism and semi-Quietism in 1687 and 1699 had a chilling effect on Catholic interest in mysticism, and for the next two centuries mainstream Catholic spirituality tended to focus on more "active" expressions of piety, such as personal devotions and structured methods of meditation. Carmelite spirituality became closely associated with Marian devotions, especially the brown scapular. Teresa's influence helped spread devotion to St. Joseph, about whom she had written so warmly. From Carmelite communities in Beaune (France) and Prague came widely popular forms of devotion to the Infant Jesus, just as devotion to the Holy Face would later emerge from the

Carmel of Tours. But even among Carmelites the works of Teresa and John were approached with some caution, and their more mystical texts were not ordinarily considered suitable reading for the laity or those in early religious formation. Meanwhile, Carmelite spiritual theologians of this period spent considerable effort trying to squeeze the doctrine of Teresa and John into scholastic categories, and wrote at length on increasingly technical issues such as the nature and possibility of "acquired contemplation." Among Catholics, in other words, popular interest in Carmelite mysticism had gone into temporary decline.

Along with the whole church, Carmel was deeply shaken by the political revolutions that swept through Europe in the eighteenth and nineteenth centuries. She continued to produce saintly members but they were typically noted more for the example of their holy and heroic lives rather than for any memorable spiritual writings. The best example, perhaps, is that of the sixteen Discalced Carmelite nuns of the community of Compiègne, France, who collectively offered their lives "to restore peace to the church and to the state" and died at the guillotine in 1794 during the Reign of Terror. The inspiring story of their martyrdom has become widely known, albeit in a somewhat fictionalized form, through the novelette *Song at the Scaffold* and the opera *Dialogues of the Carmelites*.

Verging on extinction after so much persecution and so many losses, the Carmelites of the Ancient and Primitive Observances, like other religious orders, experienced an astounding resurgence in numbers and vitality as the nineteenth century progressed. Once again, they enthusiastically embraced the work of the missions. And just when it seemed as if Carmelite spirituality had nothing more to offer the modern world beyond the recycling of its rich spiritual heritage, a fresh flowering of the "vine of Carmel" occurred in the unlikeliest of places, an obscure Carmelite community in Normandy. There in 1897 Sr. Thérèse of the Child Jesus and of the Holy Face died of tuberculosis in the Lisieux Carmel at the age of twenty-four, virtually unknown. Yet her spiritual autobiography, published a year later under the title *Story of a Soul*, quickly captured the hearts of the Catholic faithful everywhere, with its account of "ordinary" holiness through her "little way" of confidence and love, and its promise of a "shower of roses" through her intercession. Once described by Pope Pius X as "the greatest saint of modern times," Thérèse is certainly among the best known and most popular, cherished even far beyond the bounds of Roman Catholicism for her message of childlike confidence in God's merciful love. Numerous religious congregations and lay movements have based themselves on her message, and she has been the subject of more films, books, and articles than almost any other modern Catholic figure. In 1997 she was named doctor of the church, by far the youngest—the third Carmelite and only the third woman—to receive this recognition.

With the general resurgence of interest in mysticism and spirituality at the beginning of the twentieth century, the new chapter in Carmelite spirituality opened by the "Little Flower" was soon followed by others. Influenced by Thérèse and following a similar course, Elizabeth of the Trinity died of Addison's disease in the Carmel of Dijon (France) in 1906 at the age of twenty-six, leaving behind a trove of letters and retreat notes testifying to her intense focus on the reality of the indwelling Trinity, of which Teresa and John had written so eloquently. Meanwhile, inspired by *both* Thérèse and Elizabeth, nineteen-year-old Teresa of the Andes professed her religious vows on her deathbed in 1920 at the Carmel of "los Andes" in Chile, subsequently becoming the first Chilean to be canonized and Carmel's youngest canonized saint. Her shrine draws thousands of pilgrims each year, especially among the youth, who are attracted by her theme of God as "the joy of my life."

Two twentieth-century examples of Carmel's Elijan spirit of prophetic witness are Titus Brandsma, O.CARM., and Sr. Teresa Benedicta of the Cross, O.C.D., better known as Edith Stein. Both were scholars and teachers, both wrote extensively on Carmelite topics, both strongly opposed the ideology and actions of the National Socialists, especially their persecution of Jews, and both died in 1942 in Nazi concentration camps (Brandsma at Dachau and Stein at Auschwitz). Brandsma was a professor of philosophy and history of mysticism at the Catholic University of Nijmegen in the Netherlands. At the time of his arrest he was serving as ecclesiastical advisor to the Dutch Catholic journalists, urging them to refuse publication of Nazi propaganda. Jewish-born Edith Stein was a noted philosopher and leading member of the Göttingen Circle of early phenomenologists before her conversion to Catholicism and eventual entry into the Discalced Carmelite community of Cologne. In 1933 she had already written to Pius XI urging the pope to speak out more forcefully against the anti-Semitic policies of the Nazis. Transferred to the Carmel of Echt in the Netherlands, she was completing a major text on St. John of the Cross when she was arrested, along with her sister Rosa and other Catholics of Jewish descent, in retaliation for a pastoral letter of the Dutch bishops critical of National Socialism. The example of Stein and Brandsma helps remind contemporary Carmelites that their spiritual heritage has social implications, and that the mystical and prophetic dimensions of Carmelite spirituality are inseparable.

The twentieth century also brought a fresh flowering of Carmelite spirituality in the Anglophone world, with new English-language translations and studies of the Carmelite classics, new Carmelite authors, and new initiatives to interpret the Carmelite tradition for contemporary English-speaking audiences. Carmelite themes pervade the work of American author Sr. Miriam of the Holy Spirit, o.c.d., better known as Jessica Powers (1905–1988), who is increasingly recognized as among the best of modern religious poets.

In our own day, Carmelite spirituality is more popular than ever, and the Carmelite classics are read by men and women of every religious background. It could be said, in fact, that during its long journey through history, Carmelite spirituality has become ever more "democratized." A heritage once viewed as the special preserve of medieval hermits and cloistered nuns is now seen as speaking profoundly to the universal human longing for self-transcendence and integral liberation. John of the Cross's description of the "dark night," Thérèse's "trial of faith," and the honest witness of so many Carmelites to their own spiritual trials and struggles strike a responsive chord with people today facing a world of massive suffering and injustice, where God often seems silent and hidden. Nor has it escaped notice that over the centuries, in varying degrees, Carmel has provided a significant space for women's religious experience and testimony, even when these were not always sufficiently respected in the broader church and world. And busy Christians today, who cannot withdraw to the silence and solitude of a cell in the *wadi* on Mount Carmel, still look to the Carmelite tradition for guidance on how to cultivate the far more important *interior* silence and solitude essential for spiritual growth, how to center themselves in the *hermitage of the heart*, where the living God is encountered.

And what of the future? Since the nineteenth century, many new "apostolic" congregations, secular institutes, and ecclesial movements have associated themselves in some way with Carmel and embraced at least some aspects of Carmelite spirituality as part of their charism. The Lay and Secular Carmelites have experienced a phenomenal upsurge in numbers in the wake of the Second Vatican Council, and are increasingly assuming roles of greater leadership and responsibility. Today Carmelite vocations seem to be most plentiful in the developing world, where the different branches of Carmel are experiencing their most dramatic growth. Thus the Carmelite family is becoming increasingly diverse and "global," facing the exciting challenge of inculturating its spirituality in new and varied contexts. Perhaps the next great representative of

Carmelite spirituality will come from Africa, Latin America, or Asia, and may not come from the ranks of the Carmelite friars, nuns, and sisters. Given the surprising turns in Carmel's rich spiritual heritage, however, it is risky at best to predict its future, except to affirm that Carmelite spirituality will continue to nourish people of goodwill throughout the world for many generations to come.

The Carmelite Rule (ca. 1207)

Apart from the Bible itself, no text is more fundamental for Carmelite spirituality than what has come to be known as the Rule of St. Albert. It has shaped generation after generation of Carmelites, and is the original articulation of the spiritual ideal to which all Carmelite renewal movements have attempted to return. Yet at least in its earliest form it is not technically a "rule" at all in the strict canonical sense, but a simple *formula vitae* (formula of life), composed for a single community of medieval hermit-penitents on Mount Carmel in Crusader Palestine, by someone who was not himself a member.

St. Albert of Jerusalem, as he is called by Carmelites, was born around 1150 in the diocese of Parma, and later joined the canons regular of Mortara before being chosen as bishop of Bobbio in 1184. A year later he was named bishop of Vercelli, a post he ably filled during the next two decades. In 1205 he was elected patriarch of Jerusalem and subsequently took up official residence in Acre, near Mount Carmel, because Jerusalem itself remained under Muslim control. During his distinguished career he played a role in drawing up rules for several religious groups, including the Humiliati, and carried out many important diplomatic missions for the pope.

Much about the first recipients of the Rule of St. Albert remains obscure. We do not even know their names. Tradition has given the name "Brocard" to their leader, though only his first initial, "B," appears in the earliest manuscripts. Most scholars today would at least agree that they were a group of "Latin" hermits who assembled sometime around the beginning of the thirteenth century in the *wadi-ain-es-Siah* near the "spring of Elijah" on the western slopes of Mount Carmel, already sacred to the memory of the prophet Elijah as the site of his contest with the prophets of Baal (1 Kgs 18:20–46). Europe was in the midst of a religious revival and devout Christians everywhere were seeking a more "apostolic" life (that is, one more closely imitating the poor and simple lifestyle of Jesus and his apostles) in contrast to the perceived complacency and wealth of the traditional monastic orders. At the same time, as noted earlier, a deepening spiritual focus on Christ's humanity inspired many to go on pilgrimage to the Holy Land to visit the sites associated with Jesus, and sometimes even to remain, dedicating themselves to prayer and penance.

Such were the first Carmelites. We do not know precisely when they settled on Mount Carmel. Presumably it was some time after the Third Crusade (1189–1192), that is, after Richard the Lionhearted had recaptured from Saladin's Muslim troops the narrow coastal strip that included Acre, Mount Carmel, and the *wadi-ain-es-Siah*. Presumably also the hermits had been living on Mount Carmel for some time before they requested Albert's intervention. The Rule of St. Albert bears no date, but we know that it must have been delivered to the Carmelites between 1206, when Albert first arrived in Acre, and 1214, when he was assassinated.

The text is in the form of a letter from the patriarch of Jerusalem to "his beloved sons in Christ, B. and the other hermits under obedience to him, who live near the spring on Mt Carmel" (par. 1). Albert notes at the outset that there are already "many and varied" approved ways of living "a life of allegiance to Jesus Christ . . . pure in heart and steadfast in conscience, . . . unswerving in the service of [one's] Master" (par. 2). Indeed, at the time, new groups like the Carmelites were being pressured to conform to more familiar models of religious life by adopting one of the classic Rules, of Benedict or Augustine. But Albert evidently approves of what he observes in this hermit community, and wishes to grant their request for a particular *formula vitae* "in keeping with your avowed purpose" (par. 3), which suggests to many commentators that there had been some kind of consultation process. The hermits may even have presented him with a preliminary draft indicating what they hoped would be included. In any case, the fact that this document differs so dramatically from other legislation Albert helped to write seems to imply that it was based on what the hermits were already living, or aspiring to live, rather than on some alien model.

Thus despite many points of contact with the earlier desert and monastic traditions, and traces of the influence of Cassian throughout the document, these first Carmelites consciously opted for an alternative to the Benedictine model, at least as it was being lived at that time. Albert requires first of all that they have a "prior, one among yourselves, to be chosen by common consent, or that of the greater or maturer part" (par. 4). Unlike the traditional monastic abbot who served for life as the supreme authority and spiritual father of his community, the Carmelite "prior" is simply the "first among equals," chosen for a set term of office, and making decisions in regular consultation with the brethren he serves. Again, in contrast with the Benedictine tradition of dormitory living, each Carmelite hermit is to have his own "cell," presumably to better support a life of intense personal prayer.

Albert goes on to offer a few general guidelines regarding the duties of the prior, the daily schedule, community prayer, common ownership, fraternal correction, fasting, abstinence, and so on. He instructs the hermits, as they prepare for their spiritual battles, to "clothe yourselves in God's armor" (par. 18), which includes chastity, holy meditations, holiness of life, faith, and the word of God. The longest paragraphs in this *formula vitae* are devoted to work and silence.

Particularly notable throughout is the spirit of freedom and balance. Albert is content to lay down a few key points, and leave the rest to the ongoing discernment of the group. His use of many qualifying phrases ("if necessary," "if it can be done without difficulty," "unless bodily sickness, or feebleness, or some other good reason, demand a dispensation") allows for great flexibility (cf. pars. 14–16). And though, in closing, Albert encourages the brothers to ever greater generosity of spirit, he reminds them to use holy *discretio*, which is "the guide of the virtues" (par. 24). Thus the text reveals far more about the original spirit of the thirteenth-century hermits in the *wadi-ain-es-Siah* than about the details of their daily life, which is why it has proved so durable an inspiration for generation after generation of their successors living in vastly different times and circumstances.

Nevertheless, the hermits themselves soon felt the need for some adaptations as they began returning West in the face of mounting Muslim pressures in Palestine. They quickly discovered that the eremitical lifestyle they had followed in the *wadi* did not easily translate to the very different climate and culture of western Europe, where they also were suspected of violating the Fourth Lateran Council's 1215 ban against the further founding of new religious orders. Accordingly, they were eager to seek papal approval as well as certain "clarifications" and "mitigations" of their *formula vitae*. Responding to their request, Innocent IV promulgated a slightly revised version in 1247. The changes he approved included meals and canonical office in common, some moderating of the requirements regarding silence and abstinence, and most important, permission to establish foundations "where you are given a site suitable and convenient for the observance proper to your Order" (par. 5). The Carmelites interpreted this clause as allowing houses in the towns and cities, where they soon began assimilating themselves to the ranks of the mendicants (Franciscans, Dominicans) and began sending their students to the universities. In 1432 Pope Eugene IV granted further dispensations, which many saw as symptomatic of a decline in religious observance.

Thus when Teresa of Avila in the sixteenth century called for a return to the spirit of the "Primitive Rule" of Carmel, she actually had in mind the Innocentian version, which Carmelites of her time described as "primitive" when contrasted with the mitigation of Eugene IV. In fact, with its stronger emphasis on the communal dimension of Carmelite life, the Innocentian version, though not the earliest, was better suited to her reform efforts. Today it is Albert's *formula vitae* with the Innocentian modifications that stands at the head of most Carmelite legislation. The following pages, therefore, present the reconstructed original version of Albert's Rule, with the Innocentian modifications and additions indicated in italics.

What, then, is this Rule all about? Many authors of the past have insisted that its "heart" lies in the precept that "each one of you is to stay in his own cell or nearby, pondering the Lord's law [i.e., Scripture] day and night and keeping watch at his prayers unless attending to some other duty" (par. 10). Thus in *The Way of Perfection* St. Teresa writes that "our primitive rule states that we must pray without ceasing. If we do this with all the care possible—for unceasing prayer is the most important aspect of the rule—the fasts, the disciplines, and the silence that the order commands will not be wanting" (*Way*, 4.2). Some more recent commentators, however, would also insist on the centrality (both in the text and in the life of the first hermits) of the "oratory" where the Carmelites are "to gather each morning to hear Mass" (par. 14), and of the elements of life in common sketched out in the surrounding paragraphs. But however one interprets the balance between personal prayer and community life in Albert's *formula vitae*, certainly both are crucial in the Carmelite tradition.

More surprising are the apparent omissions. Albert's text says nothing directly about the apostolate, although we know the first hermits had established themselves near a source of fresh water along the main pilgrim route, and so presumably attracted many visitors. Moreover, the two biblical figures who would assume such importance in the later Carmelite tradition, Elijah and Mary, are not even mentioned by name.

Their presence must be found "between the lines." Albert addresses his text to the hermits living "near the spring," known to the locals as the "spring of Elijah"; thus the first Carmelites had founded at a site resonant with memories of the great prophet. Likewise, the "oratory" that Albert had directed them to build they dedicated to Mary, who thus became the "lady of the place" and their adopted patron. Such seemingly small details had a decisive impact in shaping Carmelite spirituality ever after.

The Carmelite Rule

(Albert's "formula of life," with the AD 1247 additions and modifications by Innocent IV indicated in italics. In cases where Innocent IV replaced some of Albert's text, the two versions are indicated by "[Alb.]" or "[Inn.].")

1. Albert, called by God's favor to be Patriarch of the Church of Jerusalem, bids health in the Lord and the blessing of the Holy Spirit to his beloved sons in Christ, B. and the other hermits under obedience to him, who live near the spring [of Elijah] on Mt Carmel.

2. Many and varied are the ways in which our saintly forefathers laid down how everyone, whatever his station or the kind of religious observance he has chosen, should live a life of allegiance to Jesus Christ—how, pure in heart and stout in conscience, he must be unswerving in service of his Master.

3. It is to me, however, that you have come for a rule of life [*formula vitae*] in keeping with your avowed purpose, a rule you may hold fast to henceforward: and therefore:

4. The first thing I require is for you to have a Prior, one of yourselves, who is to be chosen for the office by common consent, or that of the greater and maturer part of you; each of the others must promise him obedience—of which, once promised, he must try to make his deeds the true reflection—[Inn.] *and also chastity and the renunciation of ownership.*

5. [Inn.] *If the Prior and brothers see fit, you may have foundations in solitary places, or where you are given a site that is suitable and convenient for the observance proper to your Order.*

6. Next, each one of you is to have a separate cell, situated as the lie of the land you propose to occupy may dictate, and allotted by disposition of the Prior with the agreement of the other brothers, or the more mature among them.

7. [Inn.] *However, you are to eat whatever may have been given you in a common refectory, listening together meanwhile to a reading from Holy Scripture where that can be done without difficulty.*

8. None of the brothers is to occupy a cell other than that allotted to him, or to exchange cells with another, without leave of whoever is Prior at the time.

9. The Prior's cell should stand near the entrance to your property, so that he may be the first to meet those who approach, and whatever has to be done in consequence may all be carried out as he may decide and order.

10. Each one of you is to stay in his own cell or nearby, pondering the Lord's law day and night and keeping watch at his prayers unless attending to some other duty.

11. [Alb.] Those who know their letters, and how to read the psalms, should for each of the hours, say those our holy forefathers laid down and the approved custom of the Church appoints for that hour. Those who do not know their letters must say twenty-five "Our Fathers" for the night office, except on Sundays and solemnities when that number is to be doubled so that the 'Our Father' is said fifty times; the same prayer must be said seven times in the morning in place of Lauds, and seven times too for each of the other hours, except for Vespers when it must be said fifteen times.

[Inn.] *Those who know how to say the canonical hours with those in orders should do so, in the way those holy forefathers of ours laid down, and according to the Church's approved custom. Those who do not know the hours must say twenty-five "Our Fathers" for the night office, except on Sundays and solemnities when that number is to be doubled so that the "Our Father" is said fifty times; the same prayer must be said seven times in the morning in place of Lauds, and seven times too for each of the other hours, except for Vespers when it must be said fifteen times.*

12. [Alb.] None of the brothers must lay claim to anything as his own, but your property is to be held in common; and of such things as the Lord may have given you each is to receive from the Prior—that is from the man he appoints for the purpose—whatever befits his age and needs. However, as I have said, each of you is to stay in his allotted cell, and live, by himself, on what is given out to him.

[Inn.] *None of the brothers must lay claim to anything as his own, but you are to possess everything in common; and each is to receive from the Prior—that is from the brother he appoints for the purpose—whatever befits his age and needs.*

13. [Inn.] *You may have as many asses and mules as you need, however, and may keep a certain amount of livestock or poultry.*

14. An oratory should be built as conveniently as possible among the cells, where if it can be done without difficulty, you are to gather each morning to hear Mass.

15. On Sunday too, or other days if necessary, you should discuss matters of discipline and your spiritual welfare: and on this occasion the indiscretions and failings of the brothers, if any be found at fault, should be lovingly corrected.

16. You are to fast every day, except Sundays, from the feast of the Exaltation of the Holy Cross until Easter Day, unless bodily sickness or feebleness, or some other good reason, demand a dispensation from the fast; for necessity overrides every law.

17. [Alb.] You are always to abstain from meat, unless it has to be eaten as a remedy for sickness or great feebleness.

[Inn.] *You are to abstain from meat, except as a remedy for sickness or feebleness. But as, when you are on a journey, you more often than not have to beg your way, outside your own houses you may eat foodstuffs that have been cooked with meat, so as to avoid giving trouble to your hosts. At sea, however, meat may be eaten.*

18. Since man's life on earth is a time of trial, and all who would live devotedly in Christ must undergo persecution, and the devil your foe is on the prowl like a roaring lion looking for prey to devour, you must use every care to clothe yourselves in God's armour so that you may be ready to withstand the enemy's ambush.

19. Your loins are to be girt with chastity, your breast fortified by holy meditations, for, as Scripture has it, holy meditation will save you. Put on holiness as your breastplate, and it will enable you to love the Lord your God with all your heart and soul and strength, and your neighbour as yourself. Faith must be your shield on all occasions, and with it you will be able to quench all the flaming missiles of the wicked one: there can be no pleasing God without faith; [and the victory lies in this—your faith]. On your head set the helmet of salvation, and so be sure of deliverance by our only Saviour, who sets his own free from their sins. The sword of the spirit, the word of God, must abound in your mouths and hearts. Let all you do have the Lord's word for accompaniment.

20. You must give yourselves to work of some kind, so that the devil may always find you busy; no idleness on your part must give him a chance to pierce the defenses of your souls. In this respect you have both the teaching and the example of Saint Paul the Apostle, into whose mouth Christ put his own words. God made him preacher and teacher of faith and truth to the nations: with him as your leader you cannot go astray. We lived among you, he said,

labouring and weary, toiling night and day so as not to be a burden to any of you; not because we had no power to do otherwise but so as to give you, in your own selves, an example you might imitate. For the charge we gave you when we were with you was this: that whoever is not willing to work should not be allowed to eat either. For we have heard that there are certain restless idlers among you. We charge people of this kind, and implore them in the name of our Lord Jesus Christ, that they earn their own bread by silent toil. This is the way of holiness and goodness; see that you follow it.

21. The Apostle would have us keep silence, for in silence he tells us to work. As the Prophet also makes known to us: Silence is the way to foster holiness. Elsewhere he says: Your strength will lie in silence and hope.

[Alb.] For this reason I lay down that you are to keep silence from Vespers until Terce the next day, unless some necessary or good reason, or the Prior's permission, should break the silence.

[Inn.] *For this reason I lay down that you are to keep silence from after Compline until after Prime the next day.*

At other times, although you need not keep silence so strictly, be careful not to indulge in a great deal of talk, for, as Scripture has it—and experience teaches us no less—Sin will not be wanting where there is much talk, and He who is careless in speech will come to harm; and elsewhere: The use of many words brings harm to the speaker's soul. And our Lord says in the Gospel: Every rash word uttered will have to be accounted for on judgement day. Make a balance then, each of you, to weight his words in; keep a tight rein on your mouths, lest you should stumble and fall in speech, and your fall be irreparable and prove mortal. Like the Prophet, watch your step lest your tongue give offense, and employ every care in keeping silent, which is the way to foster holiness.

22. You, brother B., and whoever may succeed you as Prior, must always keep in mind and put into practice what our Lord said in the Gospel: Whoever has a mind to become a leader among you must make himself servant to the rest, and whichever of you would be first must become your bondsman.

23. You other brothers too, hold your Prior in humble reverence, your minds not on him but on Christ who has placed him over you, and who, to those who rule the Churches, addressed the words: Whoever pays you heed pays heed to me, and whoever treats you with dishonour dishonours me; if you remain so minded you will not be found guilty of contempt, but will merit life eternal as fit reward for your obedience.

24. Here then are the few points I have written down to provide you with a standard of conduct to live up to: but our Lord, at his second coming, will reward anyone who does more than he is obliged to do. See that the bounds of common sense [*discretio*] are not exceeded, however, for common sense is the guide of the virtues.[1]

Ignea Sagitta (*The Flaming Arrow*) (ca. 1270)

Within a few decades of their beginnings, the Latin hermits of Mount Carmel had already begun migrating westward, where they had to adapt themselves to an environment very different from what they had known in the *wadi*. To some in Europe, these newcomers appeared to be in violation of the Fourth Lateran Council's ban on new religious orders. To others, their claims to a special affiliation with Mary, and even the striped mantle they wore, seemed problematic. Most of all, making their foundations in "solitary places" without the benefit of owning large tracts of land made it difficult for the Carmelites to support themselves or recruit new vocations.

Faced with such challenges, the Carmelites began seeking a series of ecclesiastical confirmations and concessions to ensure their survival. Chief among them were the modifications to Albert's "formula of life" approved by Pope Innocent IV in 1247, which drew them significantly closer to the category of the mendicant friars, a process that continued throughout the 1200s. Broadly interpreting Innocent's permission to found in places "suitable and convenient for the observance proper to your Order," they began following the Franciscans and Dominicans into the cities and engaging in preaching and sacramental ministry. By the end of the century, they had changed the striped mantle for a white one (hence the nickname "Whitefriars") and had become largely urban and clerical (since only those ordained were allowed to preach).

Their choice to join the ranks of the friars was certainly understandable, for the mendicant movement was one of the great "success stories" of that era, particularly in the case of the Franciscans and Dominicans. Mendicant vocations were plentiful, and their ministries were much in demand. Nor did medieval Christians necessarily see an intrinsic incompatibility between the calling of a hermit and that of a friar. Francis of

Assisi, after all, had written a "Rule for Hermits," and the mendicant order of Augustinian friars (the Order of Hermit Friars of St. Augustine) was created through the union of various hermit communities that were following the Rule of Augustine. Still, it is also understandable that such developments would also provoke a profound uneasiness among some of those aware of how much the daily lifestyle of the Carmelites had changed in a few short years.

The only surviving major literary work from the thirteenth century originating from within the Order, the *Ignea Sagitta* (translated as *Fiery Arrow* or *Flaming Arrow*) gives the name of its author as "Brother Nicholas, sometime Prior General of the Order of the Brothers of the Blessed Mary of Mount Carmel," and bears a date of February, 1270. It takes the form of an elaborate lament over the decline of the Carmelites from their original ideal, and a call to return to their desert origins. The overall tone is highly critical, and one might rightly call it a "jeremiad," especially since Jeremiah and Lamentations are among the biblical books most often cited. Yet "looking at the work objectively and free from administrative concern," Thomas Merton once wrote, "we feel it is permitted to admire the author and sympathize with his ideals."[1]

Nicholas Gallicus (Nicholas the Frenchman, also known as Nicholas of Narbonne) had served as prior general of the Carmelites from 1266 to 1271, and in that capacity would have had the opportunity to gauge the state of the Order as he visited its scattered and rapidly multiplying communities. He writes that he "sailed the seas and journeyed from country to country" as he "made the round of the Provinces and [became] acquainted with their members." Little is known about him beyond a few matters of administration and what is contained in the *Ignea Sagitta* itself, which reveals him to be a well-educated man, able to quote from Scripture, patristic and medieval writers, canon law, and even classical philosophy. Tradition holds that the text was written as he was resigning from office, disillusioned and discouraged. More recently it has been suggested, however, that he may simply have died in 1271, with this letter still unpromulgated (or even written later and pseudonymously attributed to him). This would help explain, in fact, why the *Ignea Sagitta* seems to have passed unnoticed by Carmelites of his time. Still, the evidence is not strong enough to draw any certain conclusion. What *is* certain, however, is that the author is deeply dissatisfied by what he sees as the Order's abandonment of its original spirit.

The work is divided into a prologue and fourteen chapters. Nicholas first addresses the Order as "devoted Mother of mine," "most religious of Mothers," and "tenderest of Mothers," calling her to mourn the loss of her former glory. He then turns accusingly to her "unfaithful" offspring, whom he calls "stepsons," who have abandoned the desert for the city, before addressing the "true sons" and exhorting them not to stand idly by as the Order falls into ruin. Without rejecting active ministry as such, he rejects the excuse of Carmel's "stepsons," that living in the cities enables them to better serve the people of God, by arguing instead that they are poorly equipped for apostolic works, and that in any case they performed a far greater service, and more effectively inspired others to holiness, when they remained alone in their cells, "pondering God's law day and night." (Indeed, one of his complaints against urban Carmelites is that their cramped accommodations in the city allow only for contiguous individual rooms, not the freestanding "separate" cells specified by the Rule.)

Repetitive, verbose, rambling, at times intemperate and highly rhetorical, the *Ignea Sagitta* as a whole may strike contemporary readers as overwrought and overwritten. Nicholas, for example, finds absolutely nothing favorable to say about the city (which he dismisses as a "cesspool of vices"), and seems inordinately suspicious of women (who "turn wise men into fools, strong men into weaklings, and saintly men into apostates"). His use of Scripture is highly selective, simply ignoring passages that run counter to his argument, such as the warning of Ecclesiastes: "Do not say, 'Why were the former days better than these?' For it is not from wisdom that you ask this" (Eccl 7:10). Yet it is the perennial privilege of age, perhaps, to recall the past as a golden era. And there is a kind of paradoxical consolation for discouraged Carmelites today in knowing that, so shortly after the Order's beginnings, there were already complaints of its decline, even though its best (and worst!) days still lay far in the future.

In any case, it is clear that Nicholas's stern language is motivated by a genuine love of hermit vocation and an authentic concern for the welfare of his Carmelite brethren. Moreover, *The Flaming Arrow* also includes passages of great beauty, as when Nicholas recalls biblical models of solitude, or praises the beauty of the desert. For Carmelites, the text represents, in a sense, one of the earliest commentaries on the Rule and the Order's primitive spirit. For Christians in general, it remains an eloquent defense of the perennial value of the eremitical life.

From the *Ignea Sagitta*

Here begins the Letter called THE FLAMING ARROW, by Brother Nicholas, sometime Prior General of the Order of the Brothers of Blessed Mary of Mount Carmel; in which Letter he mourns the Order's primitive spirit, utterly passed away.

Prologue

Nicholas, in his poverty, bids all his fellow-prisoners [cf. Rom 16:7] health and the counsel of the Holy Spirit for ever.

The sight of that devoted Mother of mine [i.e., the Carmelite Order] who conceived me as one dead and brought me forth before my time [cf. 1 Cor 15:8], between her degenerate stepsons [i.e., Carmelites who have embraced life in the city] on the one hand and those wrongful prisoners who are her true children [i.e., Carmelites who still long for the desert] on the other, moves me to minister to each, with the help of God's grace, what each stands in need of.

Our Mother I shall do my best to awaken, with my sobs of lament, from her heedless slumber, so that she may take account of her deformed condition and mend it. . . .

In this desire of mine it is my heart's love that goes out to every one of you without exception, for it is a shame common to all of us that I want to do away with. But I know—and although I would spare myself this burden if I could, I cannot—that this letter, fittingly named *The Flaming Arrow* for its bright, sharp truthfulness, welcomed as it may be by the lawful sons whose faces are towards the light [cf. 1 John 1:7], will seem hateful to the stepsons, whose ill deeds it will show to be the deeds of those who hate the light [cf. John 3:20].

Chapter I

"How the gold has grown dim, the finest of colours is changed, the stones of the sanctuary lie scattered at the head of every street!" [see Lam 4:1]. . . .

Have you forgotten that you were rightly counted as 'gold,' in your former state, for the excellence of your devotion? For just as gold is more precious than other metals, so were you distinguished among all the Orders for the greater sureness of your secret contemplation. . . .

. . . Those 'stones' your true sons were, while, mortared together in unfeigned charity [cf. 2 Cor 6:6] they held aloof from the least violation of what they had vowed when they made profession; while yet they strove (at home in their cells, not wandering the streets) to "ponder God's law" and "watch at their prayers" [cf. Rule of St. Albert] not because they were compelled to, but happily, moved by joy of spirit. Alas! Now, torn loose from the mortar of charity by discord and instability, pitifully "scattered at the head of every street," they are "stones of the sanctuary" no longer. . . .

Chapter III

. . . [The stepsons] will perhaps reply, only too ready to give birth to the arrogance they have conceived, in some such deceitful manner as this:

> We have not the least intention of resisting the divine will, but of conforming to it; for our purpose is to edify the people of God, preaching his word, hearing confessions, giving advice, and performing other good works to our own profit and that of our neighbours. This, rightly and properly, is our wholehearted desire. This is the reason—and a very good one—why we left the desert's solitude to come and carry out these works amid the throngs of the cities.

See, Mother, see the pride of your stepsons! Never a thought do they give to you, to spare you confusion and shame . . .

Fools! What use is this veneer of apparent truth with which you try to gloss over your protestations? . . . You falsely assure anyone who is ready to believe you that it is so as to be able to profit both yourselves and your neighbours, by putting into act what in times past you were privileged to experience, that you have abandoned your desert life and come into the cities. Let me point out to you that you achieve neither of these aims in the city, while both were fully accomplished in the solitude of your former days.

As long as you persevered in solitude in your contemplations, your prayers and holy exercises, with profit to yourselves, the renown of your holiness, wafted abroad like a perfume, far and wide, over city and town, brought wonderful comfort to all those it reached; and it attracted many, in those days, to the solitude of the desert, edified by its fragrance, and drawn, as though by a cord of tenderness, to repent of their misdeeds.

But now, conducting yourselves as worldlings among worldlings, you profit neither yourselves nor them. Indeed in not profiting you lose, and you offend the people, the very ones you are so anxious to please, by inflicting on them the poisonous stench of your ill fame. . . .

. . . Though like seeks like, as the saying goes, it is when they know them to be different from themselves in the holiness of their lives that those in the world truly love and honour religious. When they see that they are no different from themselves in their vicious ways, they may sometimes praise them to their faces, but behind their backs they deride them and hold them up to ridicule, for they rightly deem them of little worth.

Chapter IV

Where among you, tell me, are to be found preachers, well versed in the word of God, and fit to preach as it should be done?

Some there are, indeed, presumptuous enough, in their craving for vain glory, to attempt it, and to trot out to the people such scraps as they have been able to cull from books, in an effort to teach others what they themselves know neither by study nor by experience. They prate away before the common folk—without understanding a word of their own rigmarole—as bold-faced as though all theology lay digested in the stomach of their memory, and any tale will serve their turn if it can be given a mystical twist and made to redound to their own glory. Then, when they have done preaching—or rather tale-telling—there they stand, ears all pricked up and itching to catch the slightest whisper of flattery. But not a vestige do they show of the endowments for which, in their appetite for vain glory, they long to be praised. . . .

. . . It is no less a matter for wonder that these same illiterates I speak of are breathlessly eager to be appointed physicians—useless ones though they make—of spiritual wounds and maladies, in the hearing of confessions. Ignorant alike of theology and law, they are unable to distinguish between one form of leprosy and another, loose what should not be loosed, and bind what should not be bound. A fine doctor indeed who thinks he can cure everyone's ills, every sort of disorder, with one and the same medicine—and what medicine! . . .

. . . Make the round of the Provinces, examine all their members, and tell me, on your return, how many there are in the Order who are worthy and capable of preaching, hearing confessions, and giving counsel, as befits those who dwell in cities. If you say there are many you will be wide indeed of the truth. I who have made the round of the Provinces and become acquainted with their members must sadly admit how very few there are who have knowledge enough or aptitude for these offices. . . .

Chapter V

. . . What is this new Order that has appeared in the cities, tell me? Answer me—though you must surely blush as you do so—in what useful occupation are you engaged there? I will spare you the embarrassment of telling the truth, and will answer more truthfully than you would yourselves. Two by two you roam the streets of the city from morning to night, you scurry hither and thither; and your master is he who "prowls about like a roaring lion seeking someone to devour" [cf. 1 Pet 5:8]. Thus, in you, to your utter disgrace, is the prophecy truly fulfilled: "On every side the wicked prowl" [see Ps 12:9]. . . .

. . . The main reason for your wanderings is to visit not orphans but young women, not widows in their adversity but silly girls in dalliance, beguines, nuns, and highborn ladies. Once in their company you gaze into each other's eyes and utter words fit for lovers, the downfall of right conduct and a snare to the heart. . . .

. . . But now raise your eyes and see how, in the desert, the Lord delivers and defends those who dwell there by the might of his arms from the snares of the enemy, casting an impregnable wall about them.

In the desert heavenly guardians stand with us in battle array; in the desert the angels, our fellow-citizens, posted as sentinels on the ramparts of our desert-founded city, never cease, as they faithfully keep watch night and day, to praise the name of the Lord; and thus we may boldly proclaim with the Prophet: "Blessed be the Lord, for he has shown his wondrous mercy to us in a fortified city" [see Ps 31:22].

We could be happy there together, hidden in the desert, in the possession of a true city—a true fellowship, that is, of citizens. But you, not content with that, are doing your best to divide and destroy our fellowship, in your hankering after another kind of city. . . .

Chapter VI

Was it not our Lord and Saviour who led us into the desert, as a mark of his favour, so that there he might speak to our hearts with special intimacy? It is not in public, not in the market place, not amid noise or bustle that he shows himself to his friends for their consolation and reveals his secret mysteries to them, but behind closed doors. . . .

. . . You who flee solitude and spurn the consolation it has to offer, would you hear how the Lord has shown by his works the high esteem in which he holds it?

To the solitude of the mountain did Abraham, unwavering in faith and discerning the issue from afar in hope, ascend at the Lord's command, ready for obedience's sake to sacrifice Isaac his son [cf. Gen 22:1-12; Rom 4:16-22]; under which mystery the passion of Christ—the true Isaac—lies hidden.

To the solitude of the mountain was it also that Abraham's nephew, Lot, was told to flee for his life in haste from Sodom [cf. Gen 19:15-30].

In the solitude of Mount Sinai was the Law given to Moses, and there was he so clothed with light that when he came down from the mountain no one could look upon the brightness of his face [cf. Exod 34:28-35; 2 Cor 3:7].

In the solitude of Mary's chamber, as she conversed with Gabriel, was the Word of the Father Most High in very truth made flesh [Luke 1:26-38].

In the solitude of Mount Thabor it undoubtedly was, when it was his will to be transfigured, that God made man revealed his glory to his chosen intimates of the Old and New Testaments [Matt 17:1-18; Mark 9:2-8; Luke 9:28-36].

To a mountain solitude it was that our Saviour ascended alone, in order to pray [cf. Matt 14:23; Mark 6:46; Luke 6:12; John 6:13].

In the solitude of the desert did he fast forty days and forty nights together, and there did he will to be tempted by the devil, so as to show us the most fitting place for prayer, penance and victory over temptation [cf. Matt 4:1-11; Mark 1:12-13; Luke 4:1-13].

To the solitude of mountain or desert it was, then, that our Saviour retired when he desired to pray; although we read that he came down from the mountain [cf. Luke 6:17] when he wished to preach to the people or manifest his works. He who planted our fathers in the solitude of the mountain thus gave himself to them and their successors as a model, and desired them to write down his deeds, which are never empty of mystical meaning, as an example.

It was this rule of our Saviour, a rule of utmost holiness, that some of our predecessors followed of old. They tarried long in the solitude of the desert, conscious of their own imperfection. Sometimes, however, though rarely, they came down from their desert, anxious, so as not to fail in what they regarded as their duty, to be of service to their neighbours, and sowed broadcast of the grain, threshed out in preaching, that they had so sweetly reaped in solitude with the sickle of contemplation. . . .

Chapter VII

. . . We have undertaken by our profession to live according to a Rule that abounds with observances. A brief consideration of that Rule is therefore not out of place.

There are three general practices to which our profession obliges us: obedience, chastity and the renunciation of ownership. These are common to the profession of all Orders. . . .

. . . But in our Order, as in every other, these general practices are reinforced by others that are more particular, and by these the Orders are distinguished one from another, some being stricter than others . . .

. . . For the Lord, whose providence is unerring in its dispositions, designedly set some in the desert with Mary, when it was his purpose to array the garden of the Church militant with a diversity of Orders, and others with Martha in the city. Those endowed with learning, industrious in the study of the Scriptures, and of adequate moral probity, he established in the city, so that they could exercise their zeal in nourishing the people with his word. Those of a simpler cast, however, those with whom he holds secret colloquy, he marked out to be sent into the desert. . . .

With such special care has the Lord provided for the guidance of all religious, whether in the desert or in the city, that in his infinite wisdom he has given them all, through those best qualified to draw up their Rules, their own distinct ways of life—the ways he knew to be best suited to each of the Orders in the circumstances its members would find themselves in.

Chapter VIII

Let us then examine carefully our own form of life, the form we profess to follow. Let us apply our minds to a close scrutiny of it, to find out whether our salvation demands that we live in the desert or in the city.

The Holy Spirit knows what is best for each man. Was it not for a purpose that he laid down in our Rule that "each one is to have a separate cell"? It does not say "contiguous," but "separate," in order that the heavenly Bridegroom and his Bride, the contemplative soul, might converse the more secretly as they repose therein. . . .

. . . For this is the command he gave us in our Rule: "Each of you is to stay in his cell or nearby, pondering God's law day and night, and keeping watch at his prayers unless some other duty claims his attention." Do you not see? If we mean to live up to our profession, as I said, we must have separate cells. Regular observance necessarily obliges us to have them, so that we may stay in them, pondering God's law day and night, and keeping watch at our prayers unless some other duty claims our attention.

But you city dwellers, who have exchanged your separate cells for a common house, what spiritual task do you perform, there in full view of one another, what are your holy occupations? When do you ponder God's law and watch at your prayers? Does not all the vanity you see or hear, say or do, as you wander hither and thither all day long, come back to your memories at night? Do you not busy those memories of yours with lawless and unclean thoughts, so that your distracted minds can ponder nothing else? . . .

. . . I know that when you come home from your rovings and ramblings, there and then the rumours begin to fly. The hubbub grows louder, disagreement makes its appearance, quarrels arise, offence is taken, envy springs up, hatred is conceived, plots are hatched, and often these words of strife end in fisticuffs and blows. "Behold how good and pleasant it is for brethren to dwell together in unity" [cf. Ps 133:1]—idle brethren in a single house! But just as that house divides those it unites in body from the love of God and neighbour, and scatters them, so do the separate cells unite by bodily separation those they shelter from strife, and bind them together in that love.

Perhaps some of you will say: "Although we live in the city, we have separate cells, or mean to have them by and by." "Why this waste?" I reply. What use to you in the city are cells that none enters except at bedtime, so that he might sleep and rest in greater security? As I said, you scurry about the lanes and streets of the city at random all day—do you not?—and as soon as you get home, down you sit, cheek by jowl, to exchange rumours and gossip. Why, your whole day's labour is vanity! You reserve your empty cells for sleep alone—do you not?—and spend a third of the night, if not half, in foolish chatter and immoderate tippling. Cells are of no use to those whose thoughts and pastimes are vain. They are for those who make prayer their business. . . .

Chapter XI

And now that you have heard the things that lead to damnation, I will tell you some of the wonderful privileges which are ours in the desert. It is unbelievable how much consolation, outward and inward, they bring.

In the desert all the elements conspire to favour us. The heavens, resplendent with the stars and planets in their amazing order, bear witness by their beauty to mysteries higher still. The birds seem to assume the nature of angels, and tenderly console us with their gentle carolling. The mountains too, as Isaiah prophesied, "drop down sweetness" incomparable upon us, and the friendly hills "flow with milk and honey" such as is never tasted by the foolish lovers of this world. When we sing the praises of our Creator, the mountains about us, our brother conventuals, resound with corresponding hymns of praise to the Lord, echoing back our voices and filling the air with strains of harmony as though accompanying our song upon stringed instruments. The roots in their growth, the grass in its greenness, the leafy boughs and trees—all make merry in their own ways as they echo our praise [cf. Isa 55:12]; and the flowers in their loveliness, as they pour out their delicious fragrance, smile their best for the consolation of us solitaries. The sunbeams, though tongueless, speak saving messages to us. The shady bushes rejoice to give us shelter. In short, every creature we see or hear in the desert gives us friendly refreshment and comfort; indeed, for all their silence they tell forth wonders, and move the interior man to give praise to the Creator—so much more wonderful than themselves. . . .

Chapter XIV

. . . But I have been complaining of you, Mother, when it is myself I should have been complaining of, myself I should have been impugning. How could I have presumed, how dared to govern you, I who have never learned to govern myself? . . .

. . . Spare your penitent son then, Mother, and be merciful; forgive him. For although, through stupidity and weakness, he may have offended you in some matters, you must not, I beg of you, impute this to his will, which has always been devoted to you.

GIVEN AND EXECUTED in the year of our Lord one thousand two hundred and seventy, in the month of February, on Mount Enatrof, terrible to enemies; there is the house of God and the gate of Paradise.[2]

The Book of the Institution of the First Monks (ca. 1380)

B y the closing decades of the fourteenth century, church and society in Europe were reeling from the impact of multiple calamities. By some estimates, the Black Death (ca. 1348–1350) claimed the lives of over half of the European population. The church was split by the Western Schism (1378–1417) with two rival claimants to the papacy each offering dispensations and privileges to win the allegiance of followers. The on-again-off-again Hundred Years' War (1337–1453) left large parts of France devastated.

Religious life was seriously affected. To fill up their depleted ranks, orders began recruiting anyone they could find, including many who were underage or otherwise unsuitable. Dispensations from community acts or the obligations of the vow of poverty were easily obtained. Priests were able to accumulate multiple benefices and salaried chaplaincies that guaranteed a sizeable income with few pastoral responsibilities (e.g., a Mass said annually on the anniversary of the donor's death). Among religious, private ownership and administration of finances and property (including one's own rooms in the monastery!) had become widespread. And as with the "diploma mills" of today, money placed in the right hands could obtain documents giving one the title of "doctor" or even "bishop," with all of the rights and exemptions, and none of the responsibilities, ordinarily attached to such positions.

Remarkably, however, in the midst of this decline appeared the most important and influential text of medieval Carmelite spirituality apart from the Carmelite Rule itself. Sometime between the years 1379 (when he was appointed to office) and 1391 (the year of his death), the Carmelite provincial of Catalonia, Felip Ribot, brought out *The Way of Life and Great Deeds of the Carmelites*, purporting to be an anthology of four earlier Carmelite works. The first, longest, and most important bears the title

The Book of the Institution of the First Monks and, according to Ribot, was originally written for the Greek-speaking Carmelites in AD 412 by John, the forty-fourth patriarch of Jerusalem. Addressed to a certain monk of Mount Carmel named Caprasius, and relying on an imaginative and highly allegorical reading of certain biblical passages, especially the Elijan cycle, the work traces the "history" of the Carmelites from their founding by the prophet Elijah until the coming of Christ. (The other works in this collection discuss the significance of Albert's Rule and the modifications approved by Innocent IV, and bring the story of the Carmelites down to the time of their migration to Europe and subsequent expulsion from the Holy Land in 1291.)

Divided into seven "books" of eight chapters each, *The Book of the Institution of the First Monks* describes the nature and origin of the Carmelite vocation to prayer; the significance of the Order's habit, customs, and titles; and especially its Marian orientation. Book 6, for example, includes a lengthy allegorical analysis of 1 Kings 18:41-46, arguing that God revealed to Elijah and his followers the future coming of the sinless Virgin Mother and her Savior Son through the symbol of the "small white cloud" rising above the sea. Carmel's two great scriptural paradigms, Mary and Elijah, were thus ingeniously linked through an interpretation of this biblical scene in a way that powerfully influenced later Carmelite art, liturgy, and spirituality.

Although *The Book of the Institution of the First Monks* draws upon earlier sources (including patristic authors), scholars today agree that it is substantially a medieval work, most probably composed by Ribot himself. Nevertheless, for centuries after its publication this text powerfully influenced the spirituality of Carmelite men and women, who took its claims to antiquity at face value and regarded it as a kind of earlier "rule" by which their predecessors had lived before receiving Albert's "formula of life." St. Teresa's Monastery of the Incarnation in Avila possessed a copy, for example, and it may have helped to shape her understanding of the early life of the hermits on Mount Carmel. Contemporary Carmelites, no longer concerned with defending its historical accuracy, are now better able to appreciate *The Book of the Institution of the First Monks*, not as an accurate account of Carmelite origins, but rather as an inspiring reflection of the spirituality and self-understanding of medieval Carmelites.

From *The Book of the Institution of the First Monks*

Chapter 1: *What were the beginnings of the first founder of this Order, at what time did he live, from whom was he born, where did he grow up, and when in his youth did he decide to live a dedicated way of life.*

John XLIV bishop of Jerusalem in his book on the way of life of the first monks who began under the Old Law and continue under the New, to the monk Caprasius.

With good reason, beloved Caprasius, you inquire about the beginning of the Order and how and from whom it came forth, for these are things that should be examined before anything else. For although an understanding of this way of life consists in experience alone—and this understanding cannot be given fully in words alone unless from someone who is experienced, nor can it be completely grasped by you unless with equal application and toil you strive to learn it through experience—nevertheless, you will be able to follow the teaching of this way of life much better and be encouraged to practise it more fervently if you understand the worthiness of its members and founders, and are acquainted with the original pattern of life of the Order.

So that we may proceed in due order, we shall begin to speak for a while of the supreme founder of this Order and its first way of life. Then we shall describe briefly some of the holy deeds, glorious virtues and the habit worn by the founder himself, and then of his first disciples and the other early members of the Order, as the ancient followers of this—our way of life—understood all these things before us, and taught them to us both in the Old law and in the New, by their teachings and their example. From all this you may learn how our Order's way of life is confirmed by the authority of outstandingly holy men, and how we, following a form of life which is founded not on novelties or empty fables but on the original approved example of the complete monastic life, make a way in our hearts for the Lord, and we "make straight the paths for our God" to come to us, so that "when he comes and knocks we may open immediately" to him who says "Behold, I stand at the door and knock. If anyone hears my voice and opens the door, I will come in to him and dine with him and he with me."

Know this, therefore, and remember: From the beginning of the reign of Ahab, king of Israel, until the coming of Christ in the flesh, there passed about 940 years. It was this length of time, as recorded by the chroniclers, that Ahab began to rule before the incarnation of our Lord Jesus. In these days of Ahab, king of Israel, and in his kingdom, there was a certain great prophet of the tribe of Aaron whose name was Elijah, born in the city of Tishbe in the region of Gilead, of a father named Sabach, and from this Tishbe Elijah was called the Tishbite. Later Elijah was an inhabitant of the city of Gilead, which was built on Mount Gilead, and which took its name from the mountain, as did the region surrounding the mountain, which lay across the Jordan, and was allotted to the half-tribe of Manasseh.

Chapter 2: *How Elijah was the first man, under the inspiration of God, to lead the monastic and prophetic eremitical life, and how God communicated to him the way of reaching this goal and the perfection of this life, partly openly and partly in a mystical fashion.*

This prophet of God, Elijah, was the first leader of monks, from whom this holy and ancient way of life took its origin. For he, having reached divine contemplation and filled with the desire for higher things, withdrew far from the cities, and laying aside all earthly and worldly things, was the first to begin to devote himself to following the religious and prophetic eremitical life, which, under the inspiration and command of the Holy Spirit, he initiated and formulated. Then God appeared to him and commanded him to flee from normal human habitation and hide himself in the desert away from the crowds, and thereafter live like a monk in the desert according to the way of life made known to him.

This is all proved by the clear testimony of Holy Scripture, for we read about this in the book of *Kings*, Chapter 3: "The word of the Lord came to Elijah saying, 'Depart from here and go towards the East, and hide yourself in the wadi Carith, which is over against the Jordan, and there you will drink of the torrent, and I have commanded the ravens to feed you there'" [1 Kgs 17:2-4].

Now these salutary commands which the Holy Spirit inspired Elijah to fulfil, and these welcome promises which he encouraged him to strive for, should be meditated upon by us hermit monks word for word, not only for their historical sense but even more for their mystical sense; because our way of life is contained in them so much more fully, that is, the way of arriving at prophetic perfection and the goal of the religious eremitical life.

The goal of this life is twofold. One part we acquire by our own effort and the exercise of the virtues, assisted by divine grace. This is to offer God a pure and holy heart, free from all stain of sin. We attain this goal when we are perfect and "in Carith," that is, hidden in that love of which the Wiseman speaks: "love covers all offences" [Prov 10:12]. Wishing Elijah to reach this goal, God said to him, "Hide in the wadi Carith."

The other goal of this life is granted to us as the free gift of God, namely, to taste somewhat in the heart and to experience in the mind the power of the divine presence and the sweetness of heavenly glory, not only after death but already in this mortal life. This is to "drink of the torrent" of the pleasure of God. God promised this to Elijah in the words: "And there you shall drink of the torrent."

It is to achieve both these goals that the prophetic eremitical life is adopted by the monk, as the prophet bears witness: "In a desert land" he says, "where there is no way and no water, so in the sanctuary have I come before you, O God, to see your power and your glory" [Ps 63:1-2]. And so, by choosing to remain "in a desert land where there is no way and no water," and so to come before God "in the sanctuary," that is, with a heart purified of sin, he indicates that the first goal of the solitary life which he has chosen is to offer God a holy heart, that is, purified of all actual sin. By adding "to see your power and your glory," he indicates quite clearly the second goal of this life, which is, whilst in this life, to experience or to see mystically in the heart something of the power of the divine presence and to taste the sweetness of heavenly glory.

Through the first of these, that is, through purity of heart and perfection of love, one comes to the second, that is, to an experiential knowledge of the divine power and heavenly glory. As the Lord says in *John* Chapter 14: "He who loves me will be loved by my Father, and I will love him and will show myself to him" [John 14:21]. And so God, by what he had proposed to the holy prophet Elijah in all the above words, wanted greatly to persuade him—the first and outstanding leader of monks—and us his followers, that we should "be perfect as our heavenly Father is perfect," "having above all things love, which is the bond of perfection" [Matt 5:48; Col 3:14]. Therefore, in order that we may be worthy of the perfection urged on us and the promised vision of glory, let us seek attentively to understand clearly and logically, and to fulfil in our actions, the form of life given by God in the above words to blessed Elijah as a way to achieve them.

For, speaking to the holy Elijah, the Lord also says, both in the Old Law and the New, to every hermit monk: "Depart from here," that is, from the perishable and transitory things of this world, and "go towards the East," that is, against the natural desires of your flesh, "and hide in the wadi Carith," so that you do not live in the cities with their crowds, "which is over against the Jordan," that is, so that through love you are cut off from all sins. By these four steps you will ascend to the height of prophetic perfection, and "there you will drink of the torrent." And so that you may be able to persevere in this: "I have commanded the ravens to feed you there."

All this you will understand better if, going through each part separately, we explain them clearly and in order.[1]

Teresa of Avila (1515–1582)

One striking feature of the Carmelite spiritual tradition is that its most prominent representative came not from among the hermits on Mount Carmel but centuries later, from the feminine branch in Spain. Although women had long been associated in various ways with the Carmelite friars, it was only in 1452 that the reforming prior general John Soreth, as part of his effort to renew the Order, obtained papal permission (through the bull "Cum nulla") to grant formal membership as Carmelite nuns to groups of "pious virgins, widows, beguines, mantellates or others who wear the habit." The first such community in Castile was established in 1479 in Avila, later moving outside the city walls to its present site of the Monastery of the Incarnation, which was officially dedicated in 1515.

That same year, Avila's most famous citizen, Teresa de Ahumada y Cepeda, was born into a large family that had bought its way into the minor nobility, partly in order to cover up Jewish ancestry on the father's side in an era of rising anti-Semitism. (At that time the Spanish monarchs regarded themselves as responsible for the church in Spain, and considered a common Catholic faith one of the most important factors uniting the diverse regions of the Iberian Peninsula; the Spanish Inquisition that they established thus gradually assumed the task of investigating anyone suspected of heterodoxy, Protestant sympathies, or ancestral links with other religions.)

By her own account, Teresa was a pious child, affectionate and outgoing, with a lively intelligence and imagination. Like most women of her era and social class, she received a modest education at home, where she learned reading, writing, and other domestic skills. As a teenager, after the death of her mother, Teresa came under the influence of more "worldly" and frivolous young relatives, until her father decided to send her to a nearby Augustinian convent boarding school to protect her "honor." There, guided by an older nun, she became more serious about her prayer and began to ponder her future. In 1535, after a great interior struggle, she finally left her home and father to enter the Carmelite Monastery of the Incarnation, where she was professed a year later.

Teresa acknowledges that she found convent life more congenial than she expected, and yet after a short time, her health broke down completely. She was taken to a healer for treatments that proved nearly fatal and left her partially paralyzed for several years. She attributed her cure in 1542 to the intercession of St. Joseph, and for the rest of her life promoted special devotion to him.

Teresa had already begun making progress in contemplative prayer and recollection before her illness, but during and after her long convalescence, she settled into what she later regarded as a state of comfortable mediocrity, fulfilling her religious obligations but spending long hours gossiping in the parlor with the monastery's numerous visitors. In fact, life at the Incarnation posed other challenges as well. The community was too large to provide adequately for its members, who were often forced to go out to their families in search of a decent meal. Wealthy sisters lived in suites of rooms, often with servants, and were addressed by their formal social titles, while the poorer ones huddled together in dormitories. The daily schedule was filled with liturgical obligations and vocal prayers required by the monastery's benefactors, so that there was little time to pursue quiet personal prayer, even if the sisters had felt so inclined. In addition, Teresa acknowledges that she was badly misled for a time by the notion that spiritual progress required setting aside all concepts and images of created things, even those of the human Jesus; she would later become an eloquent defender of the indispensability of Christ's humanity for Christian prayer.

After a profound "conversion" experience in Lent of 1554 before a representation of the wounded Christ, Teresa recommitted herself to the practice of "mental prayer." Soon she began having extraordinary spiritual experiences that alarmed her friends and confessors, who suspected that they might be the work of the devil, until they were reassured by more qualified spiritual advisors. In the meantime, learning of turmoil occurring elsewhere in Europe because of the Protestant Reformation, and pondering what she could do to help within the limitations imposed on women of her day, Teresa concluded that her first obligation "was to follow the call to the religious life, . . . by keeping my rule as perfectly as I could" (*Life*, 32.9).[1] For her, this meant especially a commitment to unceasing prayer. Not long afterward, she felt inspired to found a small austere community of similarly minded Carmelite women, living together simply as equals, in mutual friendship, dedicated to an intense life of contemplative prayer for the sake of the church and the world (cf. *Way*, 1.2). The project was particularly problematic in the strongly patriarchal culture of her time, which stressed social status and honor, and in which those interested in contemplative prayer (especially women) often fell under the suspicious eye of the Inquisition.

Overcoming many obstacles and great opposition, Teresa was able to bring her dream to fulfillment with the founding of the Monastery of St. Joseph in Avila in 1562, the first community of her reform. As a sign of her new way of life, she set aside the formal title "Doña Teresa de Ahumada" and began identifying herself by her religious subtitle, as "Teresa of Jesus." Five years later, during a visit to Avila, the Carmelite general encouraged her to establish more such foundations, subsequently granting permission for similar communities of Carmelite men; among her first male recruits was John of the Cross. Thus at the age of fifty-two Teresa began a career as the leader and driving force behind not just a single monastery but an entire renewal movement within the Carmelite family, which would become known as the "discalced." (Literally, the term "discalced" means "without shoes," and was popularly used at the time to refer to certain reform groups among religious congregations, because of their custom of wearing sandals or going barefoot as a sign of greater austerity.) By the time of her death in 1582, seventeen foundations of the nuns of the Teresian reform were already established, along with numerous communities of her friars. Later on, the movement she began would evolve into a new juridically independent religious order, the Discalced Carmelites (or more officially, the Discalced Nuns and Friars of the Blessed Virgin Mary of Mount Carmel).

Even more important than Teresa's work as a reformer and founder, however, is her lasting impact as a spiritual teacher, especially through her many writings. Despite many other demands on her time, Teresa took up her pen frequently and for a variety of reasons: to satisfy the wishes of superiors and confessors, to give an account of her inner journey, to clarify her own thoughts, to guide the members of her reform movement and all who sought her advice, to provide a historical record of how her communities had been established, to insist on women's capacity for a deep and vibrant interior life, to share her wisdom regarding the ways of God with human beings, and to sing the mercies of the Lord. Though she lacked any formal literary training and often complained about the burden of writing, she was an exceptionally gifted author, among the first to describe the progressive stages in the Christian spiritual journey so clearly and in such detail, with such a wealth of memorable images. Her writings are full of warmth, humor, and common sense even when discussing the most sublime topics. Besides numerous letters, poems, and other shorter texts she left behind, Teresa is particularly remembered for three major works, now regarded as spiritual classics. In *The Book of Her Life*, Teresa recounts her spiritual journey from childhood to the time of establishing her first foundation in 1562; in the midst of her account she inserts a dozen chapters famously comparing the degrees of prayer to four ways of watering a garden. In *The Way of Perfection*, written at the request of her own nuns, Teresa explains the nature of their vocation and three qualities she considers necessary for anyone seeking "to follow the way of prayer" (love for one another, detachment, and true humility), before demonstrating, through an extended commentary on the Our Father, how to pursue "mental prayer." *The Interior Castle*, her masterpiece, compares the soul to a great crystalline castle of seven progressively more interior sets of rooms, through which one journeys in prayer toward the center, where the Lord dwells. (A fourth major work, *The Book of Foundations*, continues Teresa's account of her foundations down to the final community she established in Burgos in 1582, in her last months.)

Teresa's writings were first published in 1588, only six years after her death, in an edition edited by Luis de Leon, and quickly spread throughout Europe and beyond. Her works have remained in print ever since, and have been translated into most major languages. Teresa's influence on Catholic spiritual theology has been incalculable, and she is regarded as one of the foremost mystics of the Christian tradition. In 1970 she was declared doctor of the church by Pope Paul VI, the first woman to be honored with this title. Today her works are avidly read by spiritual seekers of all sorts. She is admired even by those of no particular religious affiliation as someone who dramatically overcame the prejudices of her time—against women, those of Jewish ancestry, and those interested in deeper interior prayer—in order to accomplish great things.

From *The Book of Her Life*[2]

(Numbers indicate chapter and section in the Kavanaugh/Rodriguez edition.)

8.5. The good that one who practices prayer possesses has been written of by many saints and holy persons; I mean mental prayer—glory be to God for this good! If it were not for this good, even though I have little humility, I should not be so proud as to dare speak about mental prayer.

I can speak of what I have experience of. It is that in spite of any wrong they who practice prayer do, they must not abandon prayer since it is the means by which they can remedy the situation; and to remedy it without prayer would be much more difficult. May the devil not tempt them, the way he did me, to give up prayer out of humility. May those persons believe that God's words cannot fail. For if we are truly repentant and resolve not to offend God, He will return to the former friendship and bestow the favors He previously did, and sometimes more if the repentance merits it.

Whoever has not begun the practice of prayer, I beg for the love of the Lord not to go without so great a good. There is nothing here to fear but only something to desire. Even if there be no great progress, . . . at least a person will come to understand the road leading to heaven. And if one perseveres, I trust then in the mercy of God, who never fails to repay anyone who has taken Him for a friend. For mental prayer in my opinion is nothing else than an intimate sharing between friends; it means taking time frequently to be alone with Him who we know loves us. In order that love be true and the friendship endure, the wills of the friends must be in accord. The will of the Lord, it is already known, cannot be at fault; our will is vicious, sensual, and ungrateful. And if you do not yet love Him as He loves you because You have not reached the degree of conformity with His will, you will endure this pain of spending a long while with one who is so different from you when you see how much it benefits you to possess His friendship and how much He loves you. . . .

9.4. This is the method of prayer I then used: since I could not reflect discursively with the intellect, I strove to picture Christ within me, and it did me greater good—in my opinion—to picture Him in those scenes where I saw Him more alone. It seemed to me that being alone and afflicted, as a person in need, He had to accept me. I had many simple thoughts like these.

The scene of His prayer in the garden, especially, was a comfort to me; I strove to be His companion there. . . . I remained with Him as long as my thoughts allowed me to, for there were many distractions that tormented me. Most nights, for many years before going to bed when I commended myself to God in preparation for sleep, I always pondered for a little while this episode of the prayer in the garden. . . . I believe my soul gained a great deal through this custom because I began to practice prayer without knowing what it was; and the custom became so habitual that I did not abandon it, just as I did not fail to make the sign of the cross before sleeping. . . .

11.5. Speaking now of the initial stages of those who are determined to seek out this good [i.e., prayer] and embark on this enterprise (for I shall speak afterward of the other stages I began to mention in regard to mystical theology, which I believe it is called), the greatest labor is in the beginning because it is the beginner who works while the Lord gives the increase. In the other degrees of prayer the greatest thing is enjoying; although whether in the beginning, the middle, or the end, all bear their crosses even though these crosses be different. For all who follow Christ, if they don't want to get lost, must walk along this path that He trod. And blessed be the trials that even here in this life are so superabundantly repaid.

— says some of the greatest of doctors

11.6. . . . It seems now to me that I read or heard of this comparison—for since I have a bad memory, I don't know where or for what reason it was used, but it will be all right for my purposes. Beginners must realize that in order to give delight to the Lord they are starting to cultivate a garden on very barren soil, full of abominable weeds. His Majesty pulls up the weeds and plants good seed. Now let us keep in mind that all of this is already done by the time a soul is determined to practice prayer and has begun to make use of it. And with the help of God we must strive like good gardeners to get these plants to grow and take pains to water them so that they don't wither but come to bud and flower and give forth a most pleasant fragrance to provide refreshment for this Lord of ours. Then He will often come to take delight in this garden and find His joy among these virtues.

11.7. But let us see now how it must be watered so that we may understand what we have to do, the labor this will cost us, whether the labor is greater than the gain, and for how long it must last. It seems to me the garden can be watered in four ways. You may draw water from a well (which is for us a lot of work). Or you may get it by means of a water wheel and aqueducts in such a way that it is obtained by turning the crank of the water wheel. (I have drawn it this way sometimes—the method involves less work than the other, and you get more water.) Or it may flow from a river or a stream. (The garden is watered much better by this means because the ground is more fully soaked, and there is no need to water so frequently—and much less work for the gardener.) Or the water may be provided by a great deal of rain. (For the Lord waters the garden without any work on our part—and this way is incomparably better than all the others mentioned.)

11.8. Now, then, these four ways of drawing water in order to maintain this garden—because without water it will die—are what are important to me and have seemed applicable in explaining the four degrees of prayer in which the Lord in His goodness has sometimes placed my soul. . . .

11.9. Beginners in prayer, we can say, are those who draw water from the well. This involves a lot of work on their own part, as I have said. They must tire themselves in trying to recollect their senses. Since they are accustomed to being distracted, this recollection requires much effort. They need to get accustomed to caring nothing at all about seeing or hearing, to practicing the hours of prayer, and thus to solitude and withdrawal—and to thinking on their past life. . . . They must strive to consider the life of Christ—and the intellect grows weary in doing this. . . .

14.1. It has been explained now how the garden is watered by labor and the use of one's arms, drawing the water up from the well. Let us speak now of the second manner, ordained by the Lord of the garden, for getting water; that is, by turning the crank of a water wheel and by aqueducts, the gardener obtains more water with less labor; and he can rest without having to work constantly. Well, this method applied to what they call the prayer of quiet is what I now want to discuss.

14.2. Here the soul begins to be recollected and comes upon something supernatural because in no way can it acquire this prayer through any efforts it may make. . . .

In this prayer the faculties are gathered within so as to enjoy that satisfaction with greater delight. But they are not lost, nor do they sleep. Only the will is occupied in such a way that, without knowing how, it becomes captive; it merely consents to God allowing Him to imprison it as one who well knows how to be the captive of its lover. O Jesus and my Lord! How valuable is Your love to us here! It holds our love so bound that it doesn't allow it the freedom during that time to love anything else but You.

14.3. The other two faculties [i.e., memory and intellect] help the will to be capable of enjoying so much good—although sometimes

it happens that even though the will is united, they are very unhelp-
ful. But then it shouldn't pay any attention to them; rather it should
remain in its joy and quietude. . . .

16.1. Let us come now to speak of the third water by which this
garden is irrigated, that is, the water flowing from a river or spring.
By this means the garden is irrigated with much less labor, although
some labor is required to direct the flow of the water. The Lord so
desires to help the gardener here that He Himself becomes practically the gardener and the one who does everything.

This prayer is a sleep of the faculties: the faculties neither fail
entirely to function nor understand how they function. The consolation, the sweetness, and the delight are incomparably greater than
that experienced in the previous prayer. The water of grace rises up
to the throat of this soul since such a soul can no longer move forward; nor does it know how; nor can it move backward. It would
desire to enjoy the greatest glory. . . . This experience doesn't seem
to me to be anything else than an almost complete death to all
earthly things and an enjoyment of God.

I don't know any other terms for describing it or how to explain
it. . . . This prayer is a glorious foolishness, a heavenly madness
where the true wisdom is learned; and it is for the soul a most delightful way of enjoying. . . .

18.1. May the Lord teach me the words necessary for explaining
something about the fourth water. Clearly His favor is necessary,
even more so than for what was explained previously. In the previous prayer, since the soul was conscious of the world, it did not feel
that it was totally dead. . . .

In all the prayer and modes of prayer that were explained, the
gardener does some work, even though in these latter modes the
work is accompanied by so much glory and consolation for the soul
that it would never want to abandon this prayer. As a result, the
prayer is not experienced as work but as glory. In this fourth water
the soul isn't in possession of its senses, but it rejoices without
understanding what it is rejoicing in. It understands that it is enjoying a good in which are gathered together all goods, but this good
is incomprehensible. All the senses are occupied in this joy in such
a way that none is free to be taken up with any other exterior or
interior thing. . . .

In the previous degrees, the senses are given freedom to show
some signs of the great joy they feel. Here in this fourth water the

soul rejoices incomparably more; but it can show much less since no power remains in the body, nor does the soul have any power to communicate its joy. . . .

From *The Way of Perfection*

(Numbers indicate chapter and section in the Kavanaugh/Rodriguez edition.)

1.1. When I began to take the first steps toward founding this monastery . . . , it was not my intention that there be so much external austerity or that the house have no income; on the contrary, I would have desired the possibility that nothing be lacking. . . .

1.2. At that time news reached me of the harm being done in France and of the havoc the Lutherans had caused. . . . The news distressed me greatly, and, as though I could do something or were something, I cried to the Lord and begged Him that I might remedy so much evil. It seemed to me that I would have given a thousand lives to save one soul out of the many that were being lost there. I realized I was a woman and wretched and incapable of doing any of the useful things I desired to do in the service of the Lord. All my longing was and still is that since He has so many enemies and so few friends that these friends be good ones. As a result I resolved to do the little that was in my power; that is, to follow the evangelical counsels as perfectly as I could and strive that these few persons who live here do the same. I did this trusting in the great goodness of God, who never fails to help anyone who is determined to give up everything for Him. My trust was that if these Sisters matched the ideal my desires had set for them, my faults would not have much strength in the midst of so many virtues; and I could thereby please the Lord in some way. Since we would all be occupied in prayer for those who are the defenders of the Church and for preachers and for learned men who protect her from attack, we could help as much as possible this Lord of mine who is so roughly treated by those for whom He has done so much good. . . .

1.3. O my Redeemer, my heart cannot bear these thoughts without becoming terribly grieved. What is the matter with Christians nowadays? Must it always be those who owe You the most who afflict You? Those for whom You performed the greatest works, those You have chosen for Your friends, with whom You walk and commune by means of Your sacraments? Aren't they satisfied with the torments You have suffered for them? . . .

1.5. O my Sisters in Christ, help me beg these things of the Lord. This is why He has gathered you together here. This is your vocation. These must be the business matters you're engaged in. These must be the things you desire, the things you weep about; these must be the objects of your petitions—not, my Sisters, the business matters of the world. For I laugh at and am even distressed about the things they come here to ask us to pray for: to ask His Majesty for wealth and money—and this is done by persons who I wish would ask Him for the grace to trample everything underfoot. They are well intentioned, and in the end we pray for their intentions because of their devotion—although for myself I don't think the Lord ever hears me when I pray for these things. The world is all in flames; they want to sentence Christ again, so to speak, since they raise a thousand false witnesses against Him; they want to ravage His Church—and are we to waste time asking for things that if God were to give them we'd have one soul less in heaven? No, my Sisters, this is not the time to be discussing with God matters that have little importance. . . .

[handwritten margin note: "these" – i.e. the salvation of souls and unity of Church, in context of 1.4]

26.1. Now then let us return to our vocal prayer that it may be so recited that, without our being aware of the fact, God may grant us everything together and also enable us to say vocal prayers as we should, as I have mentioned.

As is already known, the examination of conscience, the act of contrition, and the sign of the cross must come first. Then, daughters, since you are alone, strive to find a companion. Well what better companion than the Master Himself who taught you this prayer [i.e., the Our Father]? Represent the Lord Himself as close to you and behold how lovingly and humble He is teaching you. Believe me, you should remain with so good a friend as long as you can. If you grow accustomed to having Him present at your side, and He sees that you do so with love and that you go about striving to please Him, you will not be able—as they say—to get away from Him; He will never fail you; He will help you in all your trials; you will find Him everywhere. Do you think it's some small matter to have a friend like this at your side?

26.2. O Sisters, those of you who cannot engage in much discursive reflection with the intellect or keep your mind from distraction, get used to this practice! Get used to it! See, I know that you can do this; for I suffered many years from the trial—and it is a very great one—of not being able to quiet the mind in anything. But I know that the Lord does not leave us so abandoned; for if we humbly ask Him for this friendship, He will not deny it to us. And if we cannot succeed in one year, we will succeed later. Let's not regret the time that is so well spent. Who's making us hurry? I am speaking of acquiring this habit and of striving to walk alongside this true Master.

26.3. I'm not asking you now that you think about Him or that you draw out a lot of concepts or make long and subtle reflections with your intellect. I'm not asking you to do anything more than look at Him. . . .

26.4. . . . If you are joyful, look at Him as risen. Just imagining how He rose from the tomb will bring you joy. The brilliance! The beauty! The majesty! How victorious! How joyful! Indeed, like one coming forth from a battle where he has gained a great kingdom! And all of that, plus Himself, He desires for you. . . .

26.5. If you are experiencing trials or are sad, behold Him on the way to the garden: what great affliction He bore in His soul; for having become suffering itself, He tells us about it and complains of it. Or behold Him bound to the column, filled with pain, with all His flesh torn in pieces for the great love He bears you; so much suffering, persecuted by some, spit on by others, denied by His friends, abandoned by them, with no one to defend Him, frozen from the cold, left so alone that you can console each other. Or behold Him burdened with the cross, for they didn't even let Him take a breath. He will look at you with those eyes so beautiful and compassionate, filled with tears; He will forget His sorrows so as to console you in yours, merely because you yourselves go to Him to be consoled, and you turn your head to look at Him.

26.6. O Lord of the world, my true Spouse! (You can say this to Him if He has moved your heart to pity at seeing Him thus, for not only will you desire to look at Him but you will also delight in speaking with Him, not with ready-made prayers but with those that come from the sorrow of your own heart, for He esteems them highly.) Are You so in need, my Lord and my Love, that You would want to receive such poor company as mine, for I see by Your expression that You have been consoled by me? . . . If it's true, Lord, that You want to endure everything for me, what is this that I suffer for

You? Of what am I complaining? . . . Let us walk together, Lord. Wherever You go, I will go; whatever you suffer, I will suffer. . . .

26.9. What you can do as a help in this matter is try to carry about an image or painting of this Lord that is to your liking, not so as to carry it about on your heart and never look at it but so as to speak often with Him; for He will inspire you with what to say. . . .

26.10. It is also a great help to take a good book written in the vernacular in order to recollect one's thoughts and pray well vocally, and little by little accustom the soul with coaxing and skill not to grow discouraged. . . .

From *The Interior Castle*

(Numbers indicate dwelling place, chapter, and section in the Kavanaugh/Rodriguez edition.)

1.1.1. Today while beseeching our Lord to speak for me because I wasn't able to think of anything to say nor did I know how to begin to carry out this obedience, there came to my mind what I shall now speak about, that which will provide us with a basis to begin with. It is that we consider our soul to be like a castle made entirely out of a diamond or of very clear crystal, in which there are many rooms, just as in heaven there are many dwelling places. For in reflecting upon it carefully, Sisters, we realize that the soul of the just person is nothing else but a paradise where the Lord says He finds His delight. So then, what do you think that abode will be like where a King so powerful, so wise, so pure, so full of all good things takes His delight? I don't find anything comparable to the magnificent beauty of a soul and its marvelous capacity. Indeed, our intellects, however keen, can hardly comprehend it, just as they cannot comprehend God; but He Himself says that He created us in His own image and likeness.

Well if this is true, as it is, there is no reason to tire ourselves in trying to comprehend the beauty of this castle. Since this castle is a creature and the difference, therefore, between it and God is the same as that between the Creator and His creature, His Majesty in saying that the soul is made in His own image makes it almost impossible for us to understand the sublime dignity and beauty of the soul. . . .

1.1.3. Well, let us consider that this castle has, as I said, many dwelling places: some up above, others down below, others to the sides; and in the center and middle is the main dwelling place where the very secret exchanges between God and the soul take place. . . .

1.1.5. Well getting back to our beautiful and delightful castle we must see how we can enter it. It seems I'm saying something foolish. For if this castle is the soul, clearly one doesn't have to enter it since it is within oneself. How foolish it would seem were we to tell someone to enter a room he is already in. But you must understand that there is a great difference in the ways one may be inside the castle. For there are many souls who are in the outer courtyard—which is where the guards stay—and don't care at all about entering the castle, nor do they know what lies within that most precious place, nor who is within, nor even how many rooms it has. You have already heard in some books on prayer that the soul is advised to enter within itself; well that's the very thing I'm advising. . . .

1.1.7. Insofar as I can understand the door of entry to this castle is prayer and reflection. I don't mean to refer to mental more than vocal prayer, for since vocal prayer is prayer it must be accompanied by reflection. A prayer in which a person is not aware of whom he is speaking to, what he is asking, who it is who is asking and of whom, I do not call prayer however much the lips move. . . .

6.7.5. It will also seem to you that anyone who enjoys such lofty things will no longer meditate on the mysteries of the most sacred humanity of our Lord Jesus Christ. Such a person would now be engaged entirely in loving. This is a matter I wrote about at length elsewhere. . . . Nonetheless, they will not make me admit that such a road is a good one . . .

6.7.6. . . . To be always withdrawn from corporeal things and enkindled in love is the trait of angelic spirits not of those who live in mortal bodies. It's necessary that we speak to, think about, and become the companions of those who having had a mortal body accomplished such great feats for God. How much more is it necessary not to withdraw through one's own efforts from all our good and help which is the most sacred humanity of our Lord Jesus Christ. I cannot believe that these souls do so, but they just don't understand; and they will do harm to themselves and to others. . . . The Lord Himself says that He is the way; the Lord says also that

He is the light and that no one can go to the Father but through Him, and "anyone who sees me sees my Father.". . .

7.1.5. . . . Now then, when His Majesty is pleased to grant the soul this divine marriage that was mentioned, He first brings it into His own dwelling place [i.e., the seventh]. He desires that the favor be different from what it was at other times when He gave the soul raptures. I really believe that in rapture he unites it with Himself, as well as in the prayer of union that was mentioned. But it doesn't seem to the soul that it is called to enter into its center. . . .

7.1.6. In this seventh dwelling place the union comes about in a different way: our good God now desires to remove the scales from the soul's eyes and let it see and understand, although in a strange way, something of the favor He grants it. When the soul is brought into that dwelling place, the Most Blessed Trinity, all three Persons, through an intellectual vision, is revealed to it through a certain representation of the truth. First there comes an enkindling in the spirit in the manner of a cloud of magnificent splendor; and these Persons are distinct, and through an admirable knowledge the soul understands as a most profound truth that all three Persons are one substance and one power and one knowledge and one God alone. It knows in such a way that what we hold by faith, it understands, we can say, through sight—although the sight is not with the bodily eyes nor with the eyes of the soul, because we are not dealing with an imaginative vision. Here all three Persons communicate themselves to it, speak to it, and explain those words of the Lord in the Gospel: that He and the Father and the Holy Spirit will come to dwell with the soul that loves Him and keeps His commandments.

7.1.7. Oh, God help me! How different is hearing and believing these words from understanding their truth in this way! Each day this soul becomes more amazed, for these Persons never seem to leave it any more, but it clearly beholds, in the way that was mentioned, that they are within it. In the extreme interior, in some place very deep within itself, the nature of which it doesn't know how to explain, because of a lack of learning, it perceives this divine company.

7.1.8. You may think that as a result the soul will be outside itself and so absorbed that it will be unable to be occupied with anything else. On the contrary, the soul is much more occupied than before with everything pertaining to the service of God; and once its duties are over it remains with that enjoyable company. If the soul does not fail God, He will never fail, in my opinion, to make His presence clearly known to it. It has strong confidence that since God has granted this favor He will not allow it to lose the favor. Though the soul thinks this, it goes about with greater care than ever not to displease Him in anything. . . .

7.4.6. O my Sisters! How forgetful this soul, in which the Lord dwells in so particular a way, should be of its own rest, how little it should care for its honor, and how far it should be from wanting esteem in anything! For if it is with Him very much, as is right, it should think little about itself. All its concern is taken up with how to please Him more and how or where it will show Him the love it bears Him. This is the reason for prayer, my daughters, the purpose of this spiritual marriage: the birth always of good works, good works. . . .

7.4.8. Keep in mind that I could not exaggerate the importance of this. Fix your eyes on the Crucified and everything will become small for you. If His Majesty showed us His love by means of such works and frightful torments, how is it you want to please Him only with words? Do you know what it means to be truly spiritual? It means becoming the slaves of God. Marked with His brand, which is that of the cross, spiritual persons, because now they have given Him their liberty, can be sold by Him as slaves of everyone, as He was. . . .

7.4.9. I repeat, it is necessary that your foundation consist of more than prayer and contemplation. If you do not strive for the virtues and practice them, you will always be dwarfs. And, please God, it will be only a matter of not growing, for you already know that whoever does not increase decreases. I hold that love, where present, cannot possibly be content with remaining always the same. . . .

7.4.12. This is what I want us to strive for, my Sisters; and let us desire and be occupied in prayer not for the sake of our enjoyment but so as to have this strength to serve. Let's refuse to take an unfamiliar path, for we shall get lost at the most opportune time. It would indeed be novel to think of having these favors from God through a path other than the one He took and the one followed by all His saints. May the thought never enter our minds. Believe me, Martha and Mary must join together in order to show hospitality to the Lord and have Him always present. . . .

7.4.15. . . . In sum, Sisters, what I conclude with is that we shouldn't build castles in the air. The Lord doesn't look so much at the greatness of our works as at the love with which they are done. And if we do what we can, His Majesty will enable us each day to do more and more, provided that we do not quickly tire. But during the little while this life lasts—and perhaps it will last a shorter time than each one thinks—let us offer the Lord interiorly and exteriorly the sacrifice we can. His Majesty will join it with that which He offered on the cross to the Father for us. Thus even though our works are small they will have the value our love for Him would have merited had they been great. . . .

The Bookmark of St. Teresa

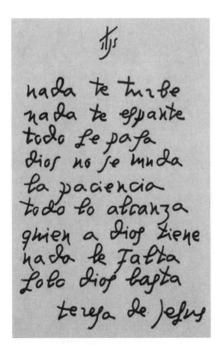

Efficacy of Patience

Let nothing trouble you,
Let nothing scare you,
All is fleeting,
God alone is unchanging.
Patience
Everything obtains.
Who possesses God
Nothing wants.
God alone suffices.[3]

John of the Cross (1542–1591)

Over the past one hundred years or so, John of the Cross has gradually emerged from the shadow of his more popular older contemporary, Teresa of Avila. Once read almost exclusively by Catholic spiritual theologians, his works are now eagerly studied by popes and diplomats, poets and artists, feminists and philosophers, psychologists and spiritual directors, Hindus and Buddhists, and countless numbers of ordinary Christians who find in him a wonderful guide for the spiritual journey. Today he is recognized in his own right as one of the most important figures in Carmelite spirituality and among the greatest mystics of the Western church.

Juan de Yepes was born in 1542 in Fontiveros (Spain), the youngest of three sons of Gonzalo de Yepes and Catalina Alvarez. His parents earned a meager living as humble weavers. Within a few years after John's birth, Gonzalo died, along with the middle brother, leaving the widowed mother to care for her two remaining sons. In search of employment, she moved the family to Medina del Campo, where John received his early education in a catechism school for the children of the poor. Later, as a teenager, John began working as a kind of nurse-orderly at Medina's so-called Plague Hospital, whose patients included many suffering from venereal diseases, and where he developed a lifelong concern for the sick. The hospital administrator was so impressed by this young man that he allowed him, in his spare time, to attend the new Jesuit *colegio* nearby, where John received a basic grounding in the humanities. Later on, the same administrator offered to sponsor John's seminary studies if he would return to the hospital afterward as permanent chaplain, a major career opportunity for this poor youth. But John declined the offer and instead chose to enter the Carmelites in 1563, taking the name of John of St. Matthias. After a year of novitiate, he was sent for studies to the University of Salamanca, one of the great institutions of learning at that time. After three years in the arts program, he was ordained to the priesthood in 1567 and returned to Medina del Campo to celebrate his first Mass. There he had a life-changing encounter with Teresa of Avila, who was in Medina at the time establishing the second foundation for the nuns of her reform, and looking for possible candidates to begin a similar initiative among the friars.

Although an outstanding student, John was apparently yearning for a lifestyle with a greater focus on contemplative prayer. In her account of their first meeting, Teresa notes that

> when I spoke with this young friar, he pleased me very much. I learned from him how he also wanted to go to the Carthusians. Telling him what I was attempting to do, I begged him to wait until the Lord would give us a monastery and pointed out the great good that would be accomplished if in his desire to improve he were to remain in his own order and that much greater service would be rendered to the Lord. He promised me he would remain as long as he wouldn't have to wait too long. (*Foundations*, 3.17)[1]

John then returned to Salamanca for a final year of theological studies. The following year, Teresa obtained a run-down farm property in the remote village of Duruelo for her project. She then took John with her while making another foundation of the nuns in Valladolid, in order "to teach [him] about our way of life so that he would have a clear understanding of everything, whether it concerned mortification or the style of both our community life and the recreation we have together" (*Foundations*, 13.5). Thus trained by Teresa herself, on November 28, 1568, John (along with two other friars) formally renounced Eugene IV's mitigation of the Carmelite Rule and established the first foundation of the Discalced Carmelite friars at Duruelo. As a sign of his new way of life, John also changed his religious subtitle at this time, becoming known thereafter as "John of the Cross." He was appointed the subprior and novice master of this new community.

For the rest of his life, John was entrusted with a variety of pastoral and administrative responsibilities among the discalced. He was especially valued as a wise and compassionate superior, confessor, and spiritual director. After Teresa was sent back in 1571 to be prioress of the Incarnation in Avila, the monastery she had left years before to begin her reform, she arranged to have John of the Cross assigned there as vicar and confessor to the nuns, because she believed he was the one best suited to assist in their spiritual growth. In early December 1577, some of John's own Carmelite confreres who were not part of the discalced movement, and who believed that John was defying his superiors by remaining at the Incarnation, arranged to have him abducted and taken to the Carmelite monastery in Toledo, where he was held under appalling conditions for close to nine months. Biographers have described the physical hardships he endured in lurid detail. Far more difficult for John, however, was his ordeal of interior darkness, the temptations to despair, and the fear that he had been abandoned not only by his friends and companions but by God as well. Yet in the nothingness (*nada*) of his Toledo cell John found the All (*Todo*), and when he escaped dramatically in mid-August of 1578, he brought with him some mystical verses composed during his imprisonment, including the first thirty-one stanzas of "The Spiritual Canticle," now ranked among the most sublime poetic compositions of all time.

In later years, it seems that John would often use his poems as the starting point for spiritual talks to the nuns and friars, and as they requested further clarifications, he began to develop his major prose commentaries. Toward the end of his life, John found himself once again the subject of persecution, this time by friars of his own reform movement, after he had spoken out against the heavy-handed policies of the rigorist leadership that had assumed power among the discalced. He was left without office and was preparing for assignment to a new mission in Mexico when he took ill. He spent his final days in the monastery of Ubeda, where the resentful prior treated him harshly, until finally won over by John's graciousness. John died on December 14, 1591.

Like Teresa, John of the Cross is remembered today primarily as a spiritual author and teacher, and he was honored with the title doctor of the church in 1926. Unlike Teresa, however, he left no "spiritual autobiography" as such. Nevertheless, John of the Cross is a poet of the first rank, and it is especially through his poetry, with its "strange figures and likenesses" (*Canticle*, prologue, 1), that readers catch a glimpse of the profound depths of his own mystical experience. His four classic prose treatises—*The Ascent of Mount Carmel*, *The Dark Night*, *The Spiritual Canticle*, and *The Living Flame of Love*—are all structured as commentaries on his poems, and (as John himself indicates) barely begin to uncover "in a general way" the inexhaustible riches contained in the verses.

In contrast to Teresa, John received a first-rate philosophical and theological education, which he does not hesitate to draw upon in his prose works. However, the same scholastic principles and distinctions that endeared him to past generations of Catholic spiritual theologians can prove daunting to a contemporary audience unfamiliar with the terminology. First-time readers of his prose sometimes find John "extreme," especially in light of certain radical statements ("endeavor to be inclined always not to the easiest, but to the most difficult . . ." [*Ascent*, 1.13.6]) and the fact that his early biographers tried to present him as a model of "strict observance." Yet if John is extreme, it is the extremism not of the grim ascetic but of the lover yearning for union with the Beloved as quickly as possible.

Because all of John's surviving texts were written after he had already developed his basic insights, the teaching throughout his commentaries is remarkably consistent. In the *Spiritual Canticle* treatise, John presents the successive stages of the mystical life through the image of a bride searching for, and finding, her bridegroom. The *Living Flame* commentary focuses on the deeper levels of mystical union once lover and beloved have been united. In the *Ascent* and *Dark Night* treatises, John describes the journey toward union with God in terms of a series of active and passive "nights" of sense and spirit, aligning these with the classic distinctions of the three "ages" (beginners, proficients, and the perfect) and three "ways" (purgative, illuminative, and unitive) of the spiritual life (see *Ascent*, 1.1.1–3; 2.1.2–3; *Night*, 1.1.1; 1.14.1; 2.1.1; see also *Canticle*, Theme 1–2; 22.3). According to John, we start the journey as spiritual beginners, "fired with love's urgent longings" for God (see *Ascent*, 1.14.1–3) but still troubled by our disordered desires for other satisfactions. Our efforts at self-discipline are crucial but must be completed by the "passive night of sense," in which our early fervor starts to wane and we learn to serve God for God's own sake, not for the consoling feelings our religious practices used to bring. Becoming "proficients" once the initial honeymoon phase has passed, we move into a quieter, deeper, and more stable "contemplative" approach to prayer and life, although accessing new levels of awareness may give rise to extraordinary experiences of various sorts. John advises caution toward visions, voices, and other paranormal phenomena that may occur, noting that they are not sure signs of holiness and may often simply be indicators of unresolved issues in the depths of the soul, still in need of purification. If God so chooses, we will undergo a second and far more radical crisis, which John calls the "passive night of spirit," where all hidden (and even unconscious) resistance is purged and we are prepared for "spiritual marriage" or "transforming union" with God. According to John, in this blissful "unitive way" of the "perfect" all inner turmoil ceases, as our human capacities are integrated and focused on God, and we "become by participation what Christ was by nature" (see *Canticle*, 39.5–6). For those who reach this goal, only a "thin veil" still separates this life from the eternal beatitude of heaven (see *Flame*, 1.29–35).

Nevertheless, despite his exalted view of human destiny and the unmatched beauty of his poetry, John remains best known for his description of the "dark night" experience. As Pope John Paul II has noted, this phrase is now used everywhere in speaking of overwhelming "physical, moral, or spiritual suffering, such as illness, the scourge of hunger, war, injustice, loneliness, the meaninglessness of life, the very fragility of human existence, the sad awareness of sin, the apparent absence of God," and so many other tragedies and struggles of our contemporary world. "All such moments have led to a better understanding of this expression of his, giving it moreover the character of a collective experience, applicable to the very reality of life and not just to a stage along a spiritual path. The Saint's teaching is invoked today in the face of the immeasurable mystery of human suffering."[2] After more than four centuries, John continues to point to the cross of Christ and remind us of its message of hope: that the One beyond all our imaginings is somehow with us in the midst of our anguish, mysteriously transforming our darkness into light, our death into new life.

From *Sayings of Light and Love*[3]

(*Sayings* are numbered according to the Kavanaugh/Rodriguez translation.)

27. Mine are the heavens and mine is the earth. Mine are the nations, the just are mine, and mine the sinners. The angels are mine, and the Mother of God, and all things are mine; and God himself is mine and for me, because Christ is mine and all for me. What do you ask, then, and seek, my soul? Yours is all of this, and all is for you. Do not engage yourself in something less or pay heed to the crumbs that fall from your Father's table. Go forth and exult in your Glory! Hide yourself in it and rejoice, and you will obtain the supplications of your heart.

34. Well and good if all things change, Lord, provided we are rooted in you.

60. When evening comes, you will be examined in love. Learn to love as God desires to be loved and abandon your own ways of acting.

100. The Father spoke one Word, which was his Son, and this Word he speaks always in eternal silence, and in silence must it be heard by the soul.

"The Dark Night"

1. One dark night,
fired with love's urgent longings
—ah, the sheer grace—
I went out unseen,
my house being now all stilled.

2. In darkness and secure,
by the secret ladder, disguised,
—ah, the sheer grace!—
in darkness and concealment,
my house being now all stilled.

3. On that glad night,
in secret, for no one saw me,
nor did I look at anything,
with no other light or guide
than the one that burned in my heart.

4. This guided me
more surely than the light of noon
to where he was awaiting me
—him I knew so well—
there in a place where no one appeared.

5. O guiding night!
O night more lovely than the dawn!
O night that has united
the Lover with his beloved,
transforming the beloved in her Lover.

6. Upon my flowering breast
which I kept wholly for him alone,
there he lay sleeping,
and I caressing him
there in a breeze from the fanning cedars.

7. When the breeze blew from the turret,
as I parted his hair,

it wounded my neck
with its gentle hand,
suspending all my senses.

8. I abandoned and forgot myself,
laying my face on my Beloved;
all things ceased; I went out from myself,
leaving my cares
forgotten among the lilies.

From *The Ascent of Mount Carmel* and *The Dark Night* (John's commentaries on "The Dark Night" poem)

(Sections are numbered according to the Kavanaugh/Rodriguez translation.)

The Ascent of Mount Carmel, Prologue

1. A deeper enlightenment and wider experience than mine is necessary to explain the dark night through which a soul journeys toward that divine light of perfect union with God that is achieved, insofar as possible in this life, through love. The darknesses and trials, spiritual and temporal, that fortunate souls ordinarily undergo on their way to the high state of perfection are so numerous and profound that human science cannot understand them adequately. Nor does experience of them equip one to explain them. Only those who suffer them will know what this experience is like, but they won't be able to describe it. . . .

4. . . . Some spiritual fathers are likely to be a hindrance and harm rather than a help to these souls that journey on this road. . . .
It will happen to individuals that while they are being conducted by God along a sublime path of dark contemplation and aridity, in which they feel lost and filled with darknesses, trials, conflicts, and temptations, they will meet someone who, in the style of Job's comforters [Job 4:8-11], will proclaim that all of this is due to melancholia, depression, or temperament, or to some hidden wickedness, and that as a result God has forsaken them. Therefore the usual verdict is that these individuals must have lived an evil life since such trials afflict them.

5. Other directors will tell them that they are falling back since they find no satisfaction or consolation as they previously did in

the things of God. Such talk only doubles the trial of a poor soul. . . . And when this soul finds someone who agrees with what it feels (that these trials are all its own fault), its suffering and distress grow without bounds. And this suffering usually becomes worse than death. Such a confessor is not satisfied with this but, in judging these trials to be the result of sin, he urges souls who endure them to go over their past and make many general confessions— which is another crucifixion. The director does not understand that now perhaps is not the time for such activity. Indeed, it is a period for leaving these persons alone in the purgation God is working in them, a time to give comfort and encouragement that they may desire to endure this suffering as long as God wills, for until then no remedy—whatever the soul does, or the confessor says—is adequate. . . .

The Ascent of Mount Carmel, book I, chapter 1

1. . . . [One] should know that a soul must ordinarily pass through two principal kinds of night—which spiritual persons call purgations or purifications of the soul—in order to reach the state of perfection. Here we will term these purgations nights because in both of them the soul journeys in darkness as though by night.

2. The first night or purgation . . . concerns the sensory part of the soul. The second night . . . concerns the spiritual part. . . .

3. This first night is the lot of beginners, at the time God commences to introduce them into the state of contemplation. . . . The second night or purification takes place in those who are already proficients, at the time God desires to lead them into the state of divine union. This purgation, of course, is more obscure, dark, and dreadful, as we will subsequently point out.

The Dark Night, book I, chapter 8

1. This night, which as we say is contemplation, causes two kinds of darkness or purgation in spiritual persons according to the two parts of the soul, the sensory and the spiritual. . . . The sensory night is common and happens to many. These are the beginners of whom we will treat first. The spiritual night is the lot of very few, those who have been tried and are proficient, and of whom we will speak afterward.

2. The first purgation or night is bitter and terrible to the senses. But nothing can be compared to the second, for it is horrible and frightful to the spirit. . . .

3. Since the conduct of these beginners in the way of God is lowly and not too distant from love of pleasure and of self, . . . God desires to withdraw them from this base manner of loving and lead them on to a higher degree of divine love. . . . God does this after beginners have exercised themselves for a time in the way of virtue and have persevered in meditation and prayer. For it is through the delight and satisfaction they experience in prayer that they have become detached from worldly things and have gained some spiritual strength in God. This strength has helped them somewhat to restrain their appetites for creatures, and through it they will be able to suffer a little oppression and dryness without turning back. Consequently, it is at the time they are going about their spiritual exercises with delight and satisfaction, when in their opinion the sun of divine favor is shining most brightly on them, that God darkens all this light and closes the door and the spring of sweet spiritual water they were tasting as often and as long as they desired. . . . God now leaves them in such darkness that they do not know which way to turn in their discursive imaginings. They cannot advance a step in meditation, as they used to, now that the interior sense faculties are engulfed in this night. He leaves them in such dryness that they not only fail to receive satisfaction and pleasure from their spiritual exercises and works, as they formerly did, but also find these exercises distasteful and bitter. . . . [When] God sees that they have grown a little, he weans them from the sweet breast so that they might be strengthened, lays aside their swaddling bands, and puts them down from his arms that they may grow accustomed to walking by themselves. This change is a surprise to them because everything seems to be functioning in reverse.

The Dark Night, book I, chapter 10

1. . . . Spiritual persons suffer considerable affliction in this [passive] night [of sense], owing not so much to the aridities they undergo as to their fear of having gone astray. Since they do not find any support or satisfaction in good things, they believe there will be no more spiritual blessings for them and that God has abandoned them. . . .

2. If there is no one to understand these persons, they either turn back and abandon the road or lose courage, or at least they hinder their own progress because of their excessive diligence in treading the path of discursive meditation. They fatigue and over-work themselves, thinking that they are failing because of their negligence or sins. Meditation is now useless for them because God is conducting them along another road, which is contemplation and is very different from the first. . . .

4. The attitude necessary in the night of sense is to pay no attention to discursive meditation since this is not the time for it. They should allow the soul to remain in rest and quietude even though it may seem obvious to them that they are doing nothing and wasting time, and even though they think this disinclination to think about anything is due to their laxity. Through patience and perseverance in prayer, they will be doing a great deal without activity on their part.

All that is required of them here is freedom of soul, that they liberate themselves from the impediment and fatigue of ideas and thoughts, and care not about thinking and meditating. They must be content simply with a loving and peaceful attentiveness to God, and live without the concern, without the effort, and without the desire to taste or feel him. All these desires disquiet the soul and distract it from the peaceful, quiet, and sweet idleness of the contemplation that is being communicated to it. . . .

The Dark Night, book II, chapter 1

1. If His Majesty intends to lead the soul on, he does not put it in this dark night of spirit immediately after its going out from the aridities and trials of the first purgation and night of sense. Instead, after having emerged from the state of beginners, the soul usually spends many years exercising itself in the state of proficients. In this new state, as one liberated from a cramped prison cell, it goes about the things of God with much more freedom and satisfaction of spirit and with more abundant interior delight than it did in the beginning before entering the night of sense. . . .

The Dark Night, book II, chapter 2

3. Not all of these proficients fall into actual imperfections in the same way. . . . Some encounter greater difficulties. . . . They

receive an abundance of spiritual communications and apprehensions in the sensory and spiritual parts of their souls and frequently behold imaginative and spiritual visions. All of this as well as other delightful feelings are the lot of those who are in this state, and a soul is often tricked through them by its own phantasy as well as by the devil. . . . As a result, these proficients are easily charmed and beguiled if they are not careful to renounce such apprehensions and feelings and energetically defend themselves through faith. . . .

The Ascent of Mount Carmel, book II, chapter 22

3. . . . [The] chief reason in the old law that the inquiries made of God were licit, and the prophets and priests appropriately desired visions and revelations from him, was that at that time faith was not yet perfectly grounded, nor was the Gospel law established. It was necessary for them to question God, and for him to respond sometimes by words, sometimes through visions and revelations, now in figures and likenesses, now through many other kinds of signs. All his answers, locutions, and revelations concerned mysteries of our faith or matters touching on or leading up to it. . . .

But in this era of grace, now that the faith is established through Christ and the Gospel law made manifest, there is no reason for inquiring of him in this way, or expecting him to answer as before. In giving us his Son, his only Word (for he possesses no other), he spoke everything to us at once in this sole Word—and he has no more to say. . . .

5. Those who now desire to question God or receive some vision or revelation are guilty not only of foolish behavior but also of offending him by not fixing their eyes entirely on Christ and by living with the desire for some other novelty.

God could answer as follows: If I have already told you all things in my Word, my Son, and if I have no other word, what answer or revelation can I now make that would surpass this? Fasten your eyes on him alone because in him I have spoken and revealed all and in him you will discover even more than you ask for and desire. You are making an appeal for locutions and revelations that are incomplete, but if you turn your eyes to him you will find them complete. For he is my entire locution and response, vision and revelation, which I have already spoken, answered, manifested, and revealed to you by giving him to you as a brother, companion, master, ransom, and reward. . . . Hear him because I have no more faith to reveal or truths to manifest. If I spoke before, it was to promise Christ. If they questioned me, their inquiries were related to their petitions and longings for Christ in whom they were to obtain every good, as is now explained in all the doctrine of the evangelists and apostles. But now those who might ask me in that way and desire that I speak and reveal something to them would somehow be requesting Christ again and more faith, yet they would be failing in faith because it has already been given in Christ. Accordingly, they would offend my beloved Son deeply because they would not merely be failing him in faith, but obliging him to become incarnate and undergo his life and death again. You will not find anything to ask or desire of me through revelations and visions. Behold him well, for in him you will uncover all of these already made and given, and many more. . . .

19. It ought to be noted in this regard that, even though we have greatly stressed rejection of these communications and the duty of confessors to forbid souls from making them a topic of conversation, spiritual fathers should not show severity, displeasure, or scorn in dealing with these souls. With such an attitude they would make them cower and shrink from a manifestation of these experiences, would close the door to these souls, and cause them many difficulties . . . The spiritual father should instead proceed with much kindness and calm. . . .

Spiritual directors should guide them in the way of faith by giving them good instructions on how to turn their eyes from all these things. . . . They should explain how one act done in charity is more precious in God's sight than all the visions and communications possible—since these imply neither merit nor demerit—and how it is that many individuals who have not received these experiences are incomparably more advanced than others who have received many.

The Dark Night, book II, chapter 3

1. These souls, then, are now proficients. Their senses have been fed with sweet communications so that, allured by the gratification flowing from the spirit, they could be accommodated and united to the spirit. . . . In this purgation [of the passive night of spirit], these two portions of the soul will undergo complete purification, for one part is never adequately purged without the other. The real purgation of the senses begins with the spirit. . . .

3. . . . [In the passive night of spirit] God divests the faculties, affections, and senses, both spiritual and sensory, interior and exterior. He leaves the intellect in darkness, the will in aridity, the memory in emptiness, and the affections in supreme affliction, bitterness, and anguish by depriving the soul of the feeling and satisfaction it previously obtained from spiritual blessings. . . .

The Lord works all of this in the soul by means of a pure and dark contemplation. . . .

The Dark Night, book II, chapter 10

1. For the sake of further clarity in this matter, we ought to note that this purgative and loving knowledge, or divine light we are speaking of, has the same effect on a soul that fire has on a log of wood. The soul is purged and prepared for union with the divine light just as the wood is prepared for transformation into the fire. Fire, when applied to wood, first dehumidifies it, dispelling all moisture and making it give off any water it contains. Then it gradually turns the wood black, makes it dark and ugly, and even causes it to emit a bad odor. By drying out the wood, the fire brings to light and expels all those ugly and dark accidents that are contrary to fire. Finally, by heating and enkindling it from without, the fire transforms the wood into itself and makes it as beautiful as it is itself. Once transformed, the wood no longer has any activity or passivity of its own. . . . It possesses the properties and performs the actions of fire: It is dry and it dries; it is hot and it gives off heat; it is brilliant and it illumines; it is also much lighter in weight than before. It is the fire that produces all these properties in the wood.

2. Similarly, we should philosophize about this divine, loving fire of contemplation. Before transforming the soul, it purges it of all contrary qualities. It produces blackness and darkness and brings to the fore the soul's ugliness; thus one seems worse than before and unsightly and abominable. This divine purge stirs up all the foul and vicious humors of which the soul was never before aware; never did it realize there was so much evil in itself, since these humors were so deeply rooted. And now that they may be expelled and annihilated they are brought to light and seen clearly through the illumination of this dark light of divine contemplation. Although the soul is no worse than before, either in itself or in its relationship with God, it feels clearly that it is so bad as to be not only unworthy that God see it but deserving of his abhorrence. In fact, it feels that

God now does abhor it. This comparison illustrates many of the things we have been saying and will say.

3. First, we can understand that the very loving light and wisdom into which the soul will be transformed is what in the beginning purges and prepares it, just as the fire that transforms the wood by incorporating it into itself is what first prepares it for this transformation.

4. Second, we discern that the experience of these sufferings does not derive from this wisdom . . . but from the soul's own weakness and imperfection. Without this purgation it cannot receive the divine light, sweetness, and delight of wisdom, just as the log of wood until prepared cannot be transformed by the fire that is applied to it. And this is why the soul suffers so intensely. . . .

5. . . . These imperfections are the fuel that catches on fire, and once they are gone there is nothing left to burn. So it is here on earth; when the imperfections are gone, the soul's suffering terminates, and joy remains.

"The Spiritual Canticle"

Stanzas between the Soul and the Bridegroom

Bride
1. Where have you hidden,
Beloved, and left me moaning?
You fled like the stag
after wounding me;
I went out calling you, but you were gone.

2. Shepherds, you who go
up through the sheepfolds to the hill,
if by chance you see
him I love most,
tell him I am sick, I suffer, and I die.

3. Seeking my Love
I will head for the mountains and for watersides,
I will not gather flowers,
nor fear wild beasts;
I will go beyond strong men and frontiers.

4. O woods and thickets,
planted by the hand of my Beloved!
O green meadow,
coated, bright, with flowers,
tell me, has he passed by you?

5. Pouring out a thousand graces,
he passed these groves in haste;
and having looked at them,
with his image alone,
clothed them in beauty.

6. Ah, who has the power to heal me?
now wholly surrender yourself!
Do not send me
any more messengers,
they cannot tell me what I must hear.

7. All who are free
tell me a thousand graceful things of you;
all wound me more
and leave me dying
of, ah, I-don't-know-what behind their stammering.

8. How do you endure
O life, not living where you live,
and being brought near death
by the arrows you receive
from that which you conceive of your Beloved?

9. Why, since you wounded
this heart, don't you heal it?
And why, since you stole it from me,
do you leave it so,
and fail to carry off what you have stolen?

10. Extinguish these miseries,
since no one else can stamp them out;
and may my eyes behold you,
because you are their light,
and I would open them to you alone.

11. Reveal your presence,
and may the vision of your beauty be my death;

for the sickness of love
is not cured
except by your very presence and image.

12. O spring like crystal!
If only, on your silvered-over faces,
you would suddenly form
the eyes I have desired,
which I bear sketched deep within my heart.

13. Withdraw them, Beloved,
I am taking flight!

Bridegroom
Return, dove,
the wounded stag
is in sight on the hill,
cooled by the breeze of your flight.

Bride
14. My Beloved, the mountains,
and lonely wooded valleys,
strange islands,
and resounding rivers,
the whistling of love-stirring breezes,

15. the tranquil night
at the time of the rising dawn,
silent music,
sounding solitude,
the supper that refreshes, and deepens love.

16. Catch us the foxes,
for our vineyard is now in flower,
while we fashion a cone of roses
intricate as the pine's;
and let no one appear on the hill.

17. Be still, deadening north wind;
south wind, come, you that waken love,
breathe through my garden,
let its fragrance flow,
and the Beloved will feed amid the flowers.

18. You girls of Judea,
while among flowers and roses
the amber spreads its perfume,
stay away, there on the outskirts:
do not so much as seek to touch our thresholds.

19. Hide yourself, my love;
turn your face toward the mountains,
and do not speak;
but look at those companions
going with her through strange islands.

Bridegroom
20. Swift-winged birds,
lions, stags, and leaping roes,
mountains, lowlands, and river banks,
waters, winds, and ardors,
watching fears of night:

21. By the pleasant lyres
and the siren's song, I conjure you
to cease your anger
and not touch the wall,
that the bride may sleep in deeper peace.

22. The bride has entered
the sweet garden of her desire,
and she rests in delight,
laying her neck
on the gentle arms of her Beloved.

23. Beneath the apple tree:
there I took you for my own,
there I offered you my hand,
and restored you,
where your mother was corrupted.

Bride
24. Our bed is in flower,
bound round with linking dens of lions,
hung with purple,
built up in peace,
and crowned with a thousand shields of gold.

25. Following your footprints
maidens run along the way;
the touch of a spark,
the spiced wine,
cause flowings in them from the balsam of God.

26. In the inner wine cellar
I drank of my Beloved, and, when I went abroad
through all this valley
I no longer knew anything,
and lost the herd that I was following.

27. There he gave me his breast;
there he taught me a sweet and living knowledge;
and I gave myself to him,
keeping nothing back;
there I promised to be his bride.

28. Now I occupy my soul
and all my energy in his service;
I no longer tend the herd,
nor have I any other work
now that my every act is love.

29. If, then, I am no longer
seen or found on the common,
you will say that I am lost;
that, stricken by love,
I lost myself, and was found.

30. With flowers and emeralds
chosen on cool mornings
we shall weave garlands
flowering in your love,
and bound with one hair of mine.

31. You considered
that one hair fluttering at my neck;
you gazed at it upon my neck
and it captivated you;
and one of my eyes wounded you.

32. When you looked at me
your eyes imprinted your grace in me;

for this you loved me ardently;
and thus my eyes deserved
to adore what they beheld in you.

33. Do not despise me;
for if, before, you found me dark,
now truly you can look at me
since you have looked
and left in me grace and beauty.

> *Bridegroom*

34. The small white dove
has returned to the ark with an olive branch;
and now the turtledove
has found its longed-for mate
by the green river banks.

35. She lived in solitude,
and now in solitude has built her nest;
and in solitude he guides her,
he alone, who also bears
in solitude the wound of love.

> *Bride*

36. Let us rejoice, Beloved,
and let us go forth to behold ourselves in your beauty,
to the mountain and to the hill,
to where the pure water flows,
and further, deep into the thicket.

37. And then we will go on
to the high caverns in the rock
which are so well concealed;
there we shall enter
and taste the fresh juice of the pomegranates.

38. There you will show me
what my soul has been seeking,
and then you will give me,
you, my life, will give me there
what you gave me on that other day:

39. the breathing of the air,
the song of the sweet nightingale,

the grove and its living beauty
in the serene night,
with a flame that is consuming and painless.

40. No one looked at her,
nor did Aminadab appear;
the siege was still;
and the cavalry,
at the sight of the waters, descended.

From *The Spiritual Canticle* (John's commentary on "The Spiritual Canticle" poem)

Prologue

1. . . . I do not plan to expound these stanzas in all the breadth and fullness that the fruitful spirit of love conveys to them. It would be foolish to think that expressions of love arising from mystical understanding, like these stanzas, are fully explainable. The Spirit of the Lord, who abides in us and aids our weakness, as St. Paul says [Rom 8:26], pleads for us with unspeakable groanings in order to manifest what we can neither fully understand nor comprehend.

Who can describe in writing the understanding he gives to loving souls in whom he dwells? And who can express with words the experience he imparts to them? Who, finally, can explain the desires he gives them? Certainly, no one can! Not even they who receive these communications. As a result these persons let something of their experience overflow in figures, comparisons and similitudes, and from the abundance of their spirit pour out secrets and mysteries rather than rational explanations.

If these similitudes are not read with the simplicity of the spirit of knowledge and love they contain, they will seem to be absurdities rather than reasonable utterances, as will those comparisons of the divine Song of Solomon and other books of Sacred Scripture where the Holy Spirit, unable to express the fullness of his meaning in ordinary words, utters mysteries in strange figures and likenesses. The saintly doctors, no matter how much they have said or will say, can never furnish an exhaustive explanation of these figures and comparisons, since the abundant meanings of the Holy Spirit cannot be caught in words. . . .

The Spiritual Canticle, stanza 39

2. In this stanza the soul declares with five expressions the "what" she says the Bridegroom will bestow on her in that beatific transformation. First, she says it is the breath or spiration of the Holy Spirit from God to her and from her to God. . . .

3. This breathing of the air is an ability that the soul states God will give her there in the communication of the Holy Spirit. By his divine breath-like spiration, the Holy Spirit elevates the soul sublimely and informs her and makes her capable of breathing in God the same spiration of love that the Father breathes in the Son and the Son in the Father. This spiration of love is the Holy Spirit himself, who in the Father and the Son breathes out to her in this transformation in order to unite her to himself. There would not be a true and total transformation if the soul were not transformed in the three Persons of the Most Holy Trinity in an open and manifest degree.

And this kind of spiration of the Holy Spirit in the soul, by which God transforms her into himself, is so sublime, delicate, and deep a delight that a mortal tongue finds it indescribable, nor can the human intellect, as such, in any way grasp it. Even what comes to pass in the communication given in this temporal transformation [on earth] is unspeakable, for the soul united and transformed in God breathes out in God to God the very divine spiration that God—she being transformed in him—breathes out in himself to her.

4. In the transformation that the soul possesses in this life, the same spiration passes from God to the soul and from the soul to God with notable frequency and blissful love, although not in the open and manifest degree proper to the next life. Such I believe was St. Paul's meaning when he said: Since you are children of God, God sent the Spirit of his Son into your hearts, calling to the Father [Gal 4:6]. This is true of the Blessed in the next life and of the perfect in this life according to the ways described.

One should not think it impossible that the soul be capable of so sublime an activity as this breathing in God through participation as God breathes in her. For, granted that God favors her by union with the Most Blessed Trinity, in which she becomes deiform and God through participation, how could it be incredible that she also understand, know, and love—or better that this be done in her—in the Trinity, together with it, as does the Trinity itself! Yet God accomplishes this in the soul through communication and participation. This is transformation in the three Persons in power and wisdom and love, and thus the soul is like God through this transformation. He created her in his image and likeness that she might attain such resemblance.

5. No knowledge or power can describe how this happens, unless by explaining how the Son of God attained and merited such a high state for us, the power to be children of God, as St. John says [John 1:12]. Thus the Son asked of the Father in St. John's Gospel: Father, I desire that where I am those you have given me may also be with me, that they may see the glory you have given me [John 17:24], that is, that they may perform in us by participation the same work that I do by nature; that is, breathe the Holy Spirit. . . .

6. Accordingly, souls possess the same goods by participation that the Son possesses by nature. As a result they are truly gods by participation, equals and companions of God. . . . Although this participation will be perfectly accomplished in the next life, still in this life when the soul has reached the state of perfection, as has the soul we are here discussing, she obtains a foretaste and noticeable trace of it in the way we are describing, although as we said it is indescribable.

Jerome Gracián (1545–1614)

Despite the differences in their ages and backgrounds, Teresa of Avila and John of the Cross shared a deep mutual respect and friendship. Yet when "la Madre" needed someone to help lead her growing Carmelite reform, she turned not to the man she had once acknowledged as "the father of my soul" but to an even younger friar whom she glowingly describes, in chapter 23 of *The Book of Foundations*, as a "man of much learning, intelligence, and modesty," able to "organize all the things pertaining to the order in these initial stages."

Jerónimo de la Madre de Dios, better known today as Jerome Gracián, came from a large and well-connected family. His father had served as secretary for Charles V and Philip II, and his mother was daughter of the Polish ambassador to Spain. At the age of fifteen he went to the University of Alcalá, where he studied law and theology and was ordained to the priesthood. At Alcalá he came into contact with the nuns and friars of the Teresian reform, and decided to enter the novitiate. Then in 1573, only a few months after Gracián's profession of vows, the apostolic visitor Francisco Vargas delegated him to serve as visitor of the Carmelites of the Observance in Andalusia, charged with the task of implementing reforms. Soon after, he was named vicar of *all* Carmelites in Andalusia. Subsequently the papal nuncio Ormaneto confirmed and even expanded Gracián's responsibilities. Not surprisingly, however, there was strong opposition, especially among the Andalusian friars of the Observance and their superiors, to the appearance on the scene of this freshly minted Carmelite claiming authority to impose new regulations. The general administration of the Carmelite Order sought to have Gracián's appointments revoked. Indeed, after the death of Ormaneto, a new nuncio, less favorable to the Teresian reform, deposed Gracián and had him confined for a time to a monastery.

Eventually, however, Pope Gregory XIII granted permission for the discalced to form their own province, and in 1581 Gracián was elected its first provincial by a slim margin. Gracián shared Teresa's enthusiasm for the apostolate, especially the missions, and remained close to the Teresian nuns, but his critics among the discalced friars regarded him as lax and his policies as too "soft." The administration of his rival and successor, Nicholas Doria, who stressed physical austerity and strict observance, eventually decided to expel Gracián from the Order in 1592. Gracián spent many years appealing the decision (including two terrible years as a prisoner of Turkish pirates) until finally receiving a papal brief authorizing him to return to the Carmelites. Because of the opposition in Spain, however, he accepted an invitation to live with the Italian Carmelites of the Observance while retaining his discalced habit. Later he moved to the Spanish Netherlands and assisted the Discalced Carmelites in establishing a presence there.

In recent decades there has been a renewed interest in, and reevaluation of, this complex and somewhat tragic figure of the early Teresian reform. In 1999, after a thorough review, the Discalced Carmelite Order officially lifted Gracián's decree of expulsion. His cause for canonization has been introduced in Rome.

A man of boundless energy, Gracián was a prolific author whose writings enjoyed a large readership in their day, though most are now out of print. His *Summary of the Excellencies of St. Joseph* (1597), for example, was translated into several languages and became "a European best-seller," representing "a watershed in the development of the saint's cult."[1] Here, however, we have chosen a selection of a different sort, one that clearly illustrates a striking characteristic of Teresian spirituality, namely, its lively appreciation of wit and humor as teaching tools and aids to spiritual growth. The *Constitutions of the Cerro* takes the form of a parody of typical religious legislation, in this case intended for an imaginary congregation of ill-tempered, troublesome, and neurotic friars and nuns (here described under the umbrella term, "melancholic"). Members of this fictional "Cerro" order are put under obligation to do precisely those things most likely to destroy religious life and make community living unbearable! The prologue suggests that this work could be useful for both amusement and edification at recreation times, by holding up a kind of mirror to readers in which they can examine their own dysfunctional behaviors.

Some have speculated that this work may have originated from humorous conversations between Gracián and Teresa herself in 1582, during their struggles in Teresa's last months to establish her final foundation in Burgos. Whatever the case, the final section on the importance of loving those who offend us is especially poignant in light of what Gracián would later suffer at the hands of others.

From *Constitutions of the Cerro*

Jesus + Mary

Provincial Chapter of the *Cerro*

Which Deals with the Imperfections and Faults of the Melancholy,

Which Arise from Sadness, Anger, Bitterness of Heart,

Disobedience, Despondency and a Wounded Spirit

Written in the form of Constitutions,

Commanding Everything Contrary to What is Proper,

so as to Serve as Recreation for the Religious

as well as an Examination of Conscience

[Letter of convocation]

We, Fray Melanco Cerruno, Provincial of all the melancholy, the sad and bitter-hearted, the vexed, restless, scrupulous, ill-tempered, insufferable and agitated, etc.:

Since the term of our office has now come to an end, we must have a Chapter and elect a Provincial. We order our subjects upon receipt of this patent and convocation letter, to gather in chapter and elect a delegate. Then, leaving behind a vicar for the convent, come as quickly as possible to our convent of La Culpa to deal with matters for the good governance of the Order and to plot how, in the houses of the Discalced friars and nuns, to break the Rule and Constitutions, introduce abuses, ruin the good spirit and perfection they seek, as well as the fruit they wish to give the Church by their example; and how to introduce at the beginning such imperfections and relaxations as may later cause notable harm, and many souls be condemned and—after laboring in this life—lose any reward and go to the dwelling of our great friend *Pedro Botero* [i.e., the devil].

Because we are so concerned about your health, we advise you always to travel at a bad time: in the summer from 8 AM until 6 PM so that you might enjoy the sun (this pertains to those coming by way of La Mancha and Andalusia [where the heat is excessive]); and in the winter, before dawn, in order to enjoy the cool. If there has been a lot of rain, you must go by way of the *Paso de los Pontones* and path of Gumiel, on the Burgos road [where the roads become nearly impassible]. Always and in every case, lose your way, even if it seems impossible to err. In every inn, forget and leave some of your baggage behind. Your pack animals should be very thin or seedy. Try to give bad example in everything while on the way, so that those who see you may despise religious. Because of you, the servants of God who stay in the monastery, keeping cloister and doing penance, may lose.

Meeting of the Priors and Delegates and Examination of the Patent Letters

On the date designated for the Chapter, the following religious met together with the Very Rev. Fr. Fray Melanco Cerruno:

From the convent of Disobedience, Prior Disobedient Backtalk and his companion, Fray Rigid Stiffneck; from the convent of Sensuality, Fray Sensual Softy, prior, and Fray Relaxed Meddler, his companion, the enemy of chastity; from the convent of La Avaricia, Fray Greedy Sharp, prior, and Fray Attached Toad, his companion, opponents of poverty; from the convent of Inattention, Fray Inattentive Bozo, prior, and Fray Hernando Dozer, his companion, opponents of the Divine Office and spiritual things; from the convent of La Gula, Fray Nabuzardan Glutton, prior, and Fray Sardanapal Discontent, socius, opposed to fast and abstinence; from the house of Little Discipline and Bad Confession, Fray Pious Bamba, prior, and Fray Shameful Excuses, socius; from the convent of Constant Chatter, Fray Goldfinch Talker, prior, and Fray Vociferous Self-seeking, socius, opponents of silence; from the convent of Sloth, Fray Lazy Goof-off, prior, and Fray Purse Beggar, socius, opponents of manual labor; from the convent of Dissension and Pride, Fray Nabucodonosor Proud, prior, and Master Moth of Corruption, socius, opponents of humility and peace; from the convent of Carelessness and Neglect of Responsibilities, the Bachelor Fray Ignorant Simpleton, prior, and the Presentado Fray Careless Deviator as socius.

The said priors and companions presented their letters and patents and the other messages they brought for the said Provincial Chapter and Fray Melanco Cerruno received and feasted them very well.

The next morning, before proceeding to the election of the Provincial and Definitors, the Very Rev. Fr. Fray Melanco Cerruno, Provincial, and the above mentioned Chapter members assembled and ordered the reading of the Rule and Constitutions of *el Cerro* and everyone noted what needed to be deleted or added to them that they might be confirmed before the election of the Provincial. Thus they read the chapters in the following order:

Constitutions of the Very Grave and Downcast
Fray Melanco Cerruno

We, Fray Melanco Cerruno, in our misfortune Provincial of all the *cerros*, the quarrelsome, and the difficult, wish poor health and misfortune to all the melancholics and the closed-minded and scrupulous who live in our convents.

Be it known that our Provincial Chapter petitioned that, since we live scattered among the Discalced convents without a rule or constitutions and without a way of life, that We, as a good shepherd, ought to gather you together and impose constitutions and rules; which we do by means of the constitutions that follow below, which will serve for the quarrelsome and unpraiseworthy mode of life of our servants.

Chapter I: *Concerning obedience*

1. First of all, let none of our subjects, in any case whatsoever, fail to object at least once or twice to that which obedience might demand of him or her. If they raise objections three or four or five times or even more, we will reward them when they appear before us. Use discretion, however, and maintain discipline. They must not only make their objection with disgust to what they are commanded, but so that the good and laudable custom of objecting not be lost, let them reply so rudely that all might see what obedience is. . . .

7. We ordain that, should the superior on some occasion mortify you or reprimand you, or say something harsh, you be disproportionately afflicted and become quite noticeably angry, gloomy and arrogant, so that the superior should be depressed and the other brothers or sisters feel it and be scandalized. Then get headaches and other illnesses so you can always go about complaining. Superiors from that point on will not dare reprimand or correct you, and

you can continue growing in your imperfections, vices and bad habits. . . .

Chapter II: *Concerning Chastity and the Cloister*

1. Let all our subjects be so chaste in everything that if by chance they see someone raise her eyes slightly or show some necessary courtesy to a secular, they think all is already lost. Let them always assume that things will come to a bad end, and say this, growling and murmuring. Let them never speak or mention this without exaggeration and malice, rash judging everything. . . .

Chapter III: *Concerning Poverty*

1. We decree and ordain for the perfect keeping of poverty that, though in the main they have put aside possessions, they should under the same claim to poverty become so attached to a patched habit or some broken sandals that they become notably annoyed and upset should the superior take them away. If on the other hand the superior take away a new habit and give an old one, let them become sad and upset and try to cover the holes by never taking off the mantle and hiding when seculars visit or things like this. . . .

Chapter IV: *Concerning Divine Office and Spiritual Exercises*

. . . 13. Touching the Divine Office and the canonical hours, the Fathers added that if on occasion for whatever reason one of our subject's attention wanders in the choir, however briefly, then it should seem to them that they have not prayed it satisfactorily. They should go back and recite the entire office, so that they are always short of time and full of scruples.

14. Let them be great friends of some old rubrics so that they think they do not meet their obligations by doing what is ordinarily recited unless the recitation is very burdensome. When chanting let them hold the final notes for a long time with great devotion, so that they slow things down and make choir hateful. . . .

When they got to this point in the constitutions, Rev. Fr. Fray Melanco asked for attention in order to treat of a very grave doctrine, which he had discussed with Rev. Fr. Fray Moth of Corruption, prior of the convent of Dissension, and he spoke in this manner:

"You already know, Reverend Fathers and my dear friends, how much I desire to destroy the convents of the discalced friars and nuns, to please my friend Satan, and for this reason I have given you constitutions and teaching as ingenious as I can; but it seems to me that in all these I have been beating about the bush and have not arrived at the root or the essence, which is what I want to say now, pointing out the steps by which one descends to hell by way of discord, anger and harshness and hatred.

"You know that a religious is obliged under pain of mortal sin to follow the way to perfection, although not obliged to be perfect. And that perfection is no other thing than perfect love of God and neighbor, as Jesus Christ, their Doctor and Teacher declared. Responding to the question of what is the greatest commandment of the law, that is, the highest perfection, Christ said, 'You shall love God with all your heart and all your soul and all your strength; and the second like it is this: you shall love your neighbor as yourself.' . . .

"What we must do with great diligence is get them to forget this high perfection and make it appear that everything consists in doing many penances, or going about outwardly composed, or having much delight and consolation in prayer and other things that they imagine, all the while going around with a heart full of hatred, rancor and animosity, sinking little by little towards hell, until they arrive there. . . ."

Having finished this speech, Fray Melanco said, "This, my comrades, is the plan by which all well-ordered communities and convents destroy themselves and in the same way we can destroy the discalced friars and nuns without any doubt. So take courage and be diligent, for they will not take perfection from us."

And having said this he began to weep bitterly and to say, "Woe is me! Woe is me! My soul escapes me when I think of a way to teach their superiors to undo this *Cerro*, which is the universal weapon before which everything falls and it is this:

Brief, Clear and Certain Plan for Attaining the Height of Perfection

"Devote yourself to being very humble and love God tenderly. And put that person who has hurt you the most, whether inside or outside the convent, in your heart and together with the Heart of Christ love that one greatly. Let this be the first person you pray for. Ask nothing good for yourself that you do not first ask for the other. Make many acts and promises to God that if for the glory and honor of God, it were necessary for you to lose honor, health and life and even your own glory for the honor, health and life and even glory of that person, then you are determined to give all that good.

"By making these promises and desires often and continually kissing their feet interiorly and even the ground on which they walk, and orienting all your acts and resolutions in prayer, you will by this single road rise to the highest grade of perfection and attain heroic virtue and pull up the *Cerro* by the roots."

The priors, when they saw Fray Melanco weeping so, consoled him saying that no one could understand such teaching. Then they called Srs. Ignorance, Passion and Malice and charged them to hide this secret thoroughly so that the *Cerro* might reach its greatest height.

* * *

These are the Constitutions of the *Cerro*, which we command be kept in all evil and disobedience so that, little by little, true religion be destroyed and intolerable abuses introduced. . . .[2]

Mary Magdalen de' Pazzi (1566–1607)

The Carmelite mystic and visionary Mary Magdalen de' Pazzi was born in 1566 into a noble and devout Florentine family and was given the baptismal name of Catherine. Even as a young child, Catherine felt drawn to God and strongly attracted to the Eucharist. Shortly after her first communion at the age of ten, she also made a personal vow of perpetual virginity. Trained in the practice of Ignatian meditation by Jesuit confessors and spiritual directors, Catherine entered the novitiate of the Carmelite Monastery of St. Mary of the Angels in Florence in 1583, where she was given the religious name of Sr. Mary Magdalen.

During her novitiate, the future saint became dangerously ill and so was allowed to profess her vows early, on May 27, 1584. Her sudden recovery was followed by a series of visions and ecstatic experiences lasting forty days, with two-hour ecstasies after Mass each morning as well as other "excesses of love" throughout the day. Such experiences continued into the following year, culminating in an almost continual eight-day trance in June 1585, from the vigil of Pentecost to Trinity Sunday, during which she is said to have "received the Holy Spirit in different forms" and entered into dialogue with the Persons of the Trinity. This was immediately followed by a period of great interior dryness and affliction lasting five years, as she was tormented by blasphemous thoughts, temptations against chastity, and terrible doubts about her religious vocation and her own salvation. At the same time, like Catherine of Siena, she felt inspired to write letters to religious leaders, even the pope, urging them to work for the renewal of the church.

Her five years in "the lion's den" of spiritual trials ended at Pentecost in 1590. Afterward her extraordinary experiences became less frequent, though during this time a famous incident occurred when she was overcome with the thought that God was not sufficiently loved and ran about the monastery ringing the bells, summoning her sisters to "love Love." She devoted herself increasingly to the care of her sisters in community, especially the sick and elderly. From 1595 to 1598 she was given charge of the junior professed. In 1598 she became the novice mistress and in 1604 the subprioress. That same year, the ecstasies finally came to an end with the onset of her final illness, which brought intense physical suffering. She died peacefully on May 25, 1607, with the final words *"Benedictus Deus*—Blessed by God!" She was beatified in 1626 and canonized in 1669. Her feast day is celebrated on May 25.

An unusual feature of Mary Magdalen de' Pazzi's "works" is that, for the most part, they were not written by the saint herself. Rather, sisters in the community, present during her ecstasies, would describe her actions and record the words she uttered. Sometimes she would assume the voice of God the Father, or of Christ. Sometimes in her trances she would move about the monastery in a kind of pantomime of what she was experiencing (acting out scenes related to the Passion, etc.). Often the words and actions involved elaborate symbolism, and we cannot be sure that the sister-scribes always fully understood what they were witnessing. As a result, the "works" of Mary Magdalen de' Pazzi are somewhat difficult for contemporary readers to appreciate and understand. She left behind no systematic teaching on prayer and spirituality. Yet her ecstasies typically focused on the mysteries of the Christian faith: the Trinity, Jesus Christ as beloved Savior and spouse of the soul, the saving value of Christ's blood, the role of the Holy Spirit, the place of Mary, Scripture as God's inspired word, the meaning of religious life and the vows, and the centrality of love of God and neighbor. But above all, as Benedict XVI recently wrote in a letter marking the fourth centenary of her death, Mary Magdalen de' Pazzi represents a "living love that recalls the essential mystical dimension of every Christian life" and "manifests to all the dignity and beauty of the Christian vocation." The pope ends his letter with the prayer that this saint may "still make her voice heard in all the church, spreading to every human creature the proclamation to love God."[1]

From *The Forty Days*

FIRST. (May 27, 1584). During the morning of the feast of the Most Holy Trinity [i.e., Trinity Sunday], after I had made my profession, I felt myself altogether abstracted from corporal feelings and drawn to know and penetrate the bond and union that I had made with God. And I seemed to see that I was bound to the Most Holy Trinity by three chains, or bonds, which were the three vows that I had promised in my profession.

The first bond was the vow of chastity, by which I was bound and joined to the Eternal Father, Who is Purity Itself. I saw that this purity was one of the closest bonds and unions that the soul could have with God, through that conformity that the soul has with God by being pure. And I seemed to be united to God in such a way and so closely bound to Him that it did not seem possible for me to be ever, ever separated from God, if only I would not fall into a sin of the flesh. . . . And I saw that this bond was so precious that neither its grandeur nor the union that the soul has with God could ever be expressed by human tongue.

Then I saw myself bound and joined to my Spouse Jesus by the vow of obedience; and this also seemed to me to be a bond so great that it could never be comprehended. And as I saw the great worth and the grandeur and the utility of this virtue, I was quite grieved by the little knowledge that I had of the usefulness of this holy virtue that makes the soul conformed to Jesus, Who was so very obedient. And I saw that if creatures could know the greatness and usefulness that this virtue brings to the soul, they would subject themselves to every creature, even the least. . . .

Then I was bound to the Holy Spirit by the vow of poverty. Not that the soul becomes conformed to the Holy Spirit (by poverty), since the Holy Spirit is full of all heavenly treasures and riches; but I understood this bond to unite in the way that Jesus spoke of in the Gospel: "Blessed are the poor in spirit!" (Mt 5:3). And blessed are those souls that recognize and know how to receive and to preserve in themselves the riches and the treasures of that Spirit!

Afterwards, since I had offered my heart to Jesus on the vigil of the Most Holy Trinity, I knew through the following experience that He had accepted it; for during this morning of the Trinity I saw Jesus, Who returned it to me and, together with it, gave me the purity of the Virgin Mary, which purity I saw to be so grand that I could never explain it. And after this, Jesus, caressing me sweetly, as if I were a new bride, united me entirely to Himself and locked me in His side, wherein I found a most pleasant repose.

Then it seemed to me that the Lord took away my will and all my desires, so that I cannot will or desire anything, save that which the Lord wills; and I saw my will so conformed and united to the will of God that of myself I cannot will anything. . . .

SECOND. (May 28, 1584). On Monday morning, after I had taken Communion and while I was considering those words of Jesus, "No man cometh to the Father, but by Me" (Jn 14:16), I seemed to see Jesus in the manner of a bridge (I do not know what other comparison to give Him) and to understand that no one could save himself except by passing over that bridge, that is, except by the way of His commandments and of His life and passion. Then I seemed to see the Most Holy Trinity all filled with love for creatures; but I also saw that creatures did not recognize this love and did not put all their effort into loving God purely. And I saw that God has created the soul of an unfaithful person with the very same love with which He created the soul of His most holy Mother; but, whereas the Virgin cooperated with that grace and always continued to augment it and increase it in herself, the unfaithful make themselves unworthy. And I saw that that love was so great and unlimited that never, never could any creature comprehend it. Indeed, it seems to me that no one who does not experience it could understand it even a little.

And as I saw such great love, I was forced to cry, "Love, Love!" with such impetus and vehemence that I even said the words exteriorly with my mouth; and if I had been able, I would have gone running through the world shouting: "Love, Love!" But as I looked around and saw that creatures paid so little attention to this love, I could not help but feel the greatest sorrow, so that I wept even corporally, and I was very sad.[2]

From *Revelations and Enlightenments* (also known as *The Eight Days of the Holy Spirit*)

Here follows the Third Book of the Revelations and Enlightenments received by the beloved soul and spouse of Jesus Christ, Sister Mary Magdalen—the daughter of Sire Camillus Pazzi, and a nun of our monastery of Saint Mary of the Angels on St. Fredian street—on the solemn feast of the Holy Spirit in the year 1585 and throughout the octave, until the morning of the Most Holy Trinity.[3]

During all this time she remained rapt in an excess of mind both day and night, except for a period of about two hours [each day] that was granted to her to recite the Office and to take some little bit of food and a bit of repose.

Seven times she received the Holy Spirit in different forms, each morning at about the hour of Tierce [about 9 o'clock]: once as fire, once as a dove, once as a column, and so forth—as one will see, step by step, in these raptures, which we shall go on describing as well as we know how and can.

However, we could never, with tongue or pen, make one who has not seen her, capable [of understanding these things]. Neither [could we portray] her ways, her gestures and her words, spoken with so much grace, so much majesty and so much charm. Yet we shall try, assisted by the grace of the Lord, to write everything correctly, and with all sincerity and care, simply as we have had it from her own mouth while she spoke in these raptures. For, as has been said several times in the previously written Book of Colloquies, she is accustomed to speak at all times, sometimes in the role of the Eternal Father, sometimes in that of her Spouse, the Word, sometimes as herself. [And] after she has been silent for a good while—longer or shorter, according to how the Lord guides her—the Eternal Father speaks to her always, ordinarily, in the enlightenments of great importance; yet most of the time she speaks as herself.

FIRST NIGHT. A rapture of enlightenment regarding the Holy Spirit, and what one must do to receive Him worthily. . . .

Because of your restlessness, O Holy Spirit, You do not remain in the immovable Father; for since He is so powerful and wise, and since You likewise are powerful and wise, if You were to remain in the Father, You would not be able to communicate Yourself to creatures, who have so much need of You. So too, if You were to remain in the Incarnate Word, You could not be with creatures; for You know that the Word is of such immense purity, of such eternal truth, of such unequalled unity that You could not remain in a thing so impure as a creature is. And yet You are always in the Father, in the Word, in Yourself, and in all the blessed spirits and in creatures. . . .

You do no repose in creatures as creatures, of themselves inclined to sin; but You repose in them by communication, by operation, by wisdom, by power, by liberality, by benignity, by charity, by love, by purity, and in, fine, by Your own goodness, because, by infusing these graces into your creatures, You make them apt to receive You. . . .

You have honored Your Holy Spirit, O Eternal, Only-begotten, Incarnate Word Made Man! "He has exalted the horn of your Christ!" . . . And that Holy Spirit has then exalted You! You have exalted Him, and He has exalted You! . . .

And how has He exalted You? . . . By pouring Himself into Your elect, because in pouring Himself into them the Spirit makes them do Your works, O Word! And so You are as much exalted in them as You can be exalted by Yourself, inasmuch as they have become another You, by union and participation, through the infusion of that Spirit. But then, by the communication of Your christs and your gods, You are exalted in as many as {are those in whom} this Spirit infuses Himself; for You make all of them christs, gods, and words in You. "I have said: You are gods, and all of you the sons of the Most High" (Ps 81:6). There is no longer one God, but a thousand, thousand gods; one God in essence and in Three Persons, but a thousand, thousand gods by participation, communion and union. . . .

Please, O Word, I beseech You, do not take away from me the power of Your divinity! But keep me, O Lord, in that innocence that You gave me from the beginning! Keep the pact that You made with Yourself for me! Keep me, I beseech you, so that I can pour You into my neighbor, I mean, Your love, Your light, into the creatures that You love! Keep Yourself in me; and keep also all those who in labor and fatigue are walking along Your ways! Keep Your Holy Spirit in me; and confirm Your bride in Your grace, so that she can crown it with the regeneration accomplished in all Your creatures, in order to lead them to You![4]

John of St. Samson (1571–1636)

By the end of the sixteenth century, the Carmelite reform begun by Teresa of Avila had become juridically independent (as the Order of Discalced Carmelites), but in the following century, in France, a new renewal movement flowered on the ancient stock of Carmel, this time destined to remain within the original Order. Known as the reform of Touraine, this movement likewise stressed prayer, silence, and solitude, but also included a profound appreciation of the value of beautiful and well-celebrated liturgy.

The great spiritual master of the Touraine reform was the blind lay brother John of St. Samson. Jean de Moulin was born into a relatively prosperous family in Sens, but contracted smallpox at the age of three and lost his eyesight due to poor medical treatment. After the death of his parents, he went to live with an uncle, and developed a passion for poetry and music, becoming skilled in a variety of instruments, especially the organ. At the same time, he began exploring mystical authors and devoting himself to prayer. Later he moved to Paris, where he fell into near destitution. Providentially, he came into contact with the Carmelites at Place de Maubert, where he attended daily Mass and spent long hours in prayer. There he joined a group of Carmelite friars and laity who met regularly to read and discuss spiritual texts.

Eventually, John asked to be admitted to the Carmelite Order, and was sent for his novitiate to Dol, where he professed his religious vows in 1607, taking the name John of St. Samson. When the Dol monastery was evacuated during an outbreak of the plague, John chose to stay behind and tend the sick, and began an involvement in the ministry of healing. In 1612 John transferred to the community in Rennes, which had embraced the Touraine reform. Here he remained for the rest of his life, helping to form young friars in the spirit of the reform, providing spiritual guidance to all who came seeking his counsel, and dictating thousands of pages on contemplative prayer and spirituality.

Perhaps because of his blindness, John of St. Samson's works lack the colorful expressions and vivid images of an author like Teresa of Avila, which may explain why his texts have never been as popular as those of other Carmelite authors. Nevertheless, he is esteemed as one of Carmel's greatest mystics. Overall, his spirituality shows the strong influence of Ruusbroec, Herp, and others of the Rheno-Flemish "school" whose writings John had studied. Among his themes are the importance of *vacare Deo* (absolute availability to God), conformity to Christ and his cross, union with God in the deepest center of the soul, and the practice of what John calls "aspiring" or aspirative prayer, which he understands as "a loving and inflamed thrust of the heart and of the spirit, by which the soul surpasses itself and all created things and unites itself intimately with God."[1] In the passage selected here, John describes this form of prayer in greater detail.

Among John's immediate disciples were a number of significant Carmelite spiritual writers of the reform of Touraine, such as Dominic of St. Albert (1596–1634), who wrote treatises on prayer and mystical theology; Maur of the Child Jesus (d. 1690), who, as his name suggests, promoted devotion to the infant Christ; and Mark of the Nativity of the Blessed Virgin (1617–1696), who compiled and gave definitive shape to the spiritual directory of the Touraine reform. John himself has been called "the most profound of the French mystics" and the French John of the Cross. The projected ten-volume critical edition of his works, now under way, should make this important figure in the history of Carmelite spirituality accessible once more to contemporary readers.

From *The Goad, the Flames, the Arrows, and the Mirror of the Love of God, Designed to Impassion the Soul with the Love of God in Himself*

(This text was written by John of St. Samson for the bishop of Dol, Antoine Revol.)

Chapter Seven

On the Nature and Practice of Aspiring

Now we should reduce the exercise and practice of the mystical way to its purest and simplest terms. To prepare for this, we must first provide an accurate definition of the activity of aspiring [i.e., aspirative prayer].

Aspiring is, therefore, not merely an affectionate conversation, a good exercise in itself, from which aspiring is born and proceeds. Aspiring then is an expression of love: a love so purely and radically expressed that it transcends all loves that are comprehensible by the senses, the reason, or the intellect. By the impetuosity and force of the Spirit of God, it arrives at union with God, not by chance but by a sudden transformation of the spirit in God. In this, I say, the human spirit goes beyond all the love that can be understood and comprehended in the abundant and ineffable sweetness of God Himself, in Whom it is amorously immersed. Behold aspiring in its essence, its cause, and its effect.

The way of aspiring is mostly exercised by familiar, respectful, affectionate, and relaxed conversation. By it the lover is closely elevated to God by varying degrees. And this way is so excellent that by its exercise, you will soon arrive at the peak of all perfection, becoming in love with love.

It is normal for the habitual exercise and practice of aspiring to come after the affective and relaxed prayer of meditation. I say affective and relaxed to make it obvious that there is no question of laboring to satisfy the curiosity of the intellect. Rather the person must imagine the divine works that he desires to know. Having pictured them to himself in a way that makes them sufficiently envisioned and known, he should turn them over to the will so that it may be ignited and nourished by them, as by its proper prey in a hunt. One uses the dog to chase the hare in order to catch it. But when the quarry is caught, it is not fed to the dogs but is immediately taken from them to provide food for men. In a similar way, the understanding, like a good hunting dog, should not have a greater or different pleasure than its nature deserves. It ought to flush out light and truth to expand and extend itself to the fullness of its power. But having penetrated it completely, the will should take it as its own suitable supernatural nourishment, being excited and ignited by its power.

. . . The mystics have written enough about the primary methods and principles of this divine science. . . . Here I will merely say that the will is everything, so to speak. Of course, it is normal for a long period of meditative reasoning to precede aspiring. Thus, affection needs as a prelude the luminous representations of the understanding. Excited and afire with this knowledge, the affection instantly embraces it.

Finally, those who make great progress in this divine science are soon perfectly fit for this exercise of aspiring, especially if they are of a sensitive nature. On the other hand, others are never ready for it. They are too occupied with the simple and loving gaze with and in God—which, however, is still a very good form of mysticism. . . . Of the way of aspiring and its effects, the mystics have written excellent treatises. But I have shown their essence in the preceding chapters when I said that it did not involve deliberate exertion but instead the operation of the heart, the reason, and the spirit. Most important, you cannot begin this exercise too soon; you may start even sooner than I said, provided you have understood the full meaning of my words. But if someone consciously desires to make himself the prey of love, he will soon find himself so well instructed in this divine science that he can deal with love itself in all its successive steps.

Love is the means to love, the less excellent love is the means to the more excellent love, and the more excellent love is the means to the highest love and to the ultimate and supreme exercise of active love. All these modes and stages have their own theory and practice. They all lead to simple and eminent contemplation within their object, love itself: contemplation that is ethereal, subtle, lofty, profound, extensive and unique. By such contemplation one is always—in a manner of speaking—powerfully acted upon and intensely ravished.

Entering this way is easy for sensitive souls but difficult for less sensitive ones. Thus, the former are very easily ravished by the Beauty of their love's Object; but the latter, it seems, are ravished in the same love, which does not stop in the understanding. As a result, the object that overpowers them carries away their will along with their understanding. Indeed this love is so overpowering that the will alone enters the amorous bosom of love, where it savors an unutterable love beyond all understanding and all expression. All the while, the dumbfounded intellect remains paralyzed at the gate.

Such is the effect of love's flood rushing into its lovers. It sweeps them away, ravishes them, and swamps them in its waves. These people become love itself—its spirit, its divinity—insofar as it is possible for any creature in this life. Nothing is past, future, or even eternal; all is present in this deliriously wonderful sea. When one returns to and in himself, he sees and feels himself to be less than the tiniest jot. Thereupon, one reanimates his flight, but not for himself. Instead, he moves in God, desiring to be engulfed in His infinite expanse, in order to continue his own life in that infinite life.

Thus, the action of this love is so supernatural and so divine in God that it becomes both the means and the end. It is the means because the creature lovingly joins his own love to it. It is the end because the creature abides in it with ineffable love, joy, and delight. The sight of the intuitive and ravishing Beauty of God holds her as if asleep in its delectable bosom. This state surpasses all human definition and comparison.

What must be avoided, especially at the beginning of the exercise, is too much exertion of either head or heart. Such an effort might interfere and render the soul incapable of this exercise. This most excellent and noble exercise must be perfectly received by the soul. Thus acquired, it can easily, powerfully, and sublimely create the union beyond union—if I may say so—of the loving creature in God, its blessed lover. It is most important to avoid setting up any obstacle, and one must be vigilant about immoderate exertion, especially for one's own enjoyment. Such selfishness would be an iniquitous and perverted act, completely unworthy of true love. Whatever good of His may be in the creature and whatever the creature's good in Him, His Majesty still wills that he conserve enough energy for the functions and activities of human life, especially the duties of his vocation and station.

The proper thing to do in this divine way is to try to begin at a distance with loving conversations. Then you must motivate yourself to love love itself in itself by considering all the emanations and creations of His love, not only in grace and nature but also in glory. Think of how men converse with incomparable admiration, astonishment and wonder about the prodigious deeds of goodness and love by a human king. For an infinitely greater cause, all men— especially you—have a limitless subject of eternal wonder and delight. I mean the infinite prodigies that they see and should see of our good God: His ecstatic love in itself that is emitted to us men— so poor, weak, and miserable in countless ways both natural and supernatural—for His infinite glory and our infinite good.

Just as in Him we live, move, and have our being [see Acts 17:28], it is in Him that we must flow back with a most active and unflagging current. We must not only always know and perform supernatural works. We must also know Him with excellence and love Him with constant ardor. And this we must enjoy most wonderfully, fully, and eternally with our whole being. Meanwhile, after this life we look forward to our full and consummated beatific pleasure in the immensity of His totality, in the infinite expanse of His amorous furnace, aglow with His infinite fire. In such a life, those who live in holiness and love realize by felt experience their status as pilgrims on earth. Thus, they feel that there are no more miserable people in this world than they. I should add that, for countless reasons, the humiliations of the perfect are far from and most unlike those of the imperfect.

Until now I have shown you in copious detail the excellence of the true mystics in their own mystical way. I also have shown you—at least in outline—the means of embarking on it usefully and fruitfully as well as of persevering on it to the end of the journey. In addition, I have shown you how to avoid danger or harm. Therefore, it is here appropriate for me to compose a concrete act of aspiring. It will lead you, as by the hand, joyfully along this holy and loving trail. This path is so delightful and delectable that anyone who knows it will lovingly travel it at his own cost and expense. Such happiness is beyond words.

An Act of Aspiring

Why did you bother, Lord my God, to create a universe that could add nothing to your happiness? Did You not have within Your own Being the source of infinite beatitude? Why did You share this being by creating so many varied creatures that could add nothing to You in return?

O Goodness! O immense Love! Your will attracts these creatures so that they can witness Your divine and eternal thoughts. So that they can know and love you and always act attuned to your glorious love. So that they can know and love only You in every other being. So that they will always remain adorned with Your divine image, their beauty and their supernatural crown.

Of what do I speak, O lover of men and angels? How great is the distance from being to non-being? From being to nothingness? From nothing, the universe in all its greatness and excellence has been created. The angels are right to marvel at the boundless infinity of Your Majesty. At Your love and limitless goodness. How much more, then, should they astound us men—who are as nothing compared to them?

But let us go on rejoicing. We are the most excellent creations of You, Who are the ecstasy of love and create the ecstasy of love. The holy angels and holy men are creations so powerful that they reduce lesser men to nothing. The latter receive God's gifts and spoil them all, using them in ways that are as evil as themselves. They are content to exist in a state of natural well-being, without any consideration of the One Who is their very existence and all their good.

Think about these things in any way you like, for all such reflection is good. But you, what do you think of yourself? And what could you say to God about yourself, except something like this: Who am I, Lord? Who am I? Whence have You drawn me by creation—by a second creation—except from the mud of all corruption? From the dirt, where I was truly poorer than poverty itself? You raised me up to understand truly, to act honestly, and to love sincerely. You called me forth to speak with me and seat me with the princes of your elect and chosen people.

O love! O Goodness! O immense Mercy! O all-filling Majesty! You sanctify [everyone] who comes into the world—except those who love nothing but the world. Who can place limits and restraints on what is done in me by You and on what I am in You? No one, Lord. No one could do it. Now I feel myself totally obliged to Your infinite Majesty: both for what Your Majesty is in itself and for all the blessings it has bestowed on my entire being throughout my life—blessings of nature and of grace.

But if I present your Majesty with an accounting of the blessings received by nature, how many magnificent realities must I neglect to mention? And if I add to them an accounting of the blessings received by grace, how can I ever finish? I speak here of the gifts that go above and beyond the ordinary graces You bestow on all Your chosen ones: new creation, baptism, conservation, election. These are things of which I am scarcely deserving, except for Your love and its special grace.

No, my love and my life. I am dumbfounded, for of myself I have nothing. If I know anything of myself, it is that I am so wretched and corruptible that of myself I would go off and drown myself in sin, the abyss of all corruption.

O my dear Life! O my dear Love! You have given me my very self when you gave me free will. By it I return myself to You as a pure and eternal holocaust, to the full extent of my power. I am infinitely unworthy, for so late have I known You and so late have I loved You.

O truth eternal! O truth ever-new! How often, in the fullness of their life, have creatures called out to me: Where is your God? And how inadequate were my answers? For all along were You within me, as if in Your own kingdom. Yet not always did I feel the presence of Your love. Thus, I compelled myself to search everywhere for You. I sought to know You, to feel You, and to love You. I wanted to be

Your royal abode, whose sanctification You eternally desired. Seeking what I already possessed, dear Love, brought me endless regret.

Ah! What greater misery can be imagined than to live only by and for oneself, not experiencing the wonderful operation of God's perfecting love within oneself? What can this be, O my dear Life? You have commanded me to be perfect as You are perfect and to be holy as You are holy. Yet I completely fail to apply myself to such an effort, as if I had never heard You.

But now, my dear Love and my dear Life, I rue my loss—not by myself but by You within me. I will not spare myself as I vigorously put my hand to the plow with no thought of rest. No matter what the cost, I will turn all the activity of my inner powers and my heart back to You in order to love You eternally. Alas! Alas! My dear Love! In the past my heart was ever turbulent, like the sea agitated by furious tempests. Thus, I lived with an unsteady and restless heart, not even guessing the cause of my misery.

Ah! My dear Love! My dear Life! What is a heart not dedicated to loving You except a den for all sorts of thieves, each one of whom tears away at it, greedy for his share? Thus is a man horribly violated by his own invited guests. He is a wretched captive, and each captor does his larceny, lest he lose his share. O how the misery of men is unfathomably beyond comprehension! And how much greater their misery because they enjoy their servitude, lusting ever more for subjection to the masters of their misery.

Yet go on, go on once more, my Love and my Life! By Your mercy the snare has been broken, and I have been freed from those who would carry me off with them to perdition. It is You who have done it; it is You whom I want to love with a love that is perfecting and sovereign. With a love that is sublime, a love that is strong. For this, I confide myself totally to Your Goodness because I know I cannot trust myself.

Conclusion

From this you can see the fullness of love, which grows not only larger but also denser by the living flame of aspiring. Yet for love all things are good. Love does not need academic research to flash the abundant simple flames of its heart with endless ardor. The heart knows neither discretion, nor moderation, nor measure; for its Beloved ravishes it with His sweet impulse and adorable beauty. Thus, with no other hope it desires to lose itself deeper and deeper in the Beloved.[2]

Lawrence of the Resurrection (1614–1691)

Few Carmelite authors have touched as many hearts as Br. Lawrence of the Resurrection. Yet, paradoxically, the impact of his simple but inspiring call to "practice the presence of God" has been far greater beyond rather than within his own homeland, religious order, and denomination.

Biographical details are sketchy. In 1614 Nicolas Herman was born in the small village of Hériménil, in the region of Lorraine (now part of France). His parents, Dominic and Louise, were apparently devout but poor, and he seems to have received little formal education, though he learned to read and write.

When he was eighteen years old, Nicolas experienced a profound "conversion" at the sight of a barren tree in winter, recognizing how God's providence would soon bring it to life again. But before turning to religious life, he entered the military on the side of his native Lorraine in the bloody Thirty Years' War. At one point he was taken prisoner and nearly executed as a spy before convincing his captors of his innocence. After being released and rejoining his regiment, he was seriously wounded in 1635 and returned home to recuperate. Like Ignatius of Loyola and many others, the young Nicolas began to ponder the "disorders of his youth" (Eulogy, 12) during his convalescence.[1] We are told that he "often relived the perils of his military service, the vanity and corruption of the times, the instability of other people, the treason of an enemy, and the infidelity of his friends," finally resolving "to undertake a holier profession and fight under the standard of Jesus Christ" (Eulogy, 10–11).

But there were several false starts. At first he tried living as a hermit. He quickly discovered, however, that he lacked the mature emotional stability needed for this way of life. Next he tried his luck as the valet of the treasurer of the savings bank, but proved to be, as he admits, "a clumsy oaf who broke everything." Finally, at twenty-six, he applied to the Order of Discalced Carmelites on the rue de Vaugirard in Paris, where he was accepted as a lay brother and given the religious name "Lawrence of the Resurrection."

By his own account, Lawrence fully expected to be "skinned alive" for his shortcomings, but was surprised to find religious life very much to his liking. However, in his early years as a Carmelite he underwent a kind of "dark night," fearing that he might be damned for having responded so poorly to God's many graces, and unable to find any help in the complicated prayer manuals of his day. But he resolved to continue acting purely for the love of God, regardless of his ultimate fate. "When I accepted the fact that I might spend my life suffering these troubles and anxieties . . . I found myself changed all at once," he recounts. "And my soul, until that time always in turmoil, experienced a deep inner peace as if it had found its center and place of rest" (Letter 2). From that point on, Lawrence set aside all other devotions and methods not required by his Order and dedicated himself to the continual "practice of the presence of God," in which he finally found deep peace and satisfaction.

After religious profession, he was assigned to the monastery kitchen, "to which he had the strongest natural aversion." He was responsible for feeding a growing community, which eventually reached about one hundred friars, many of whom were young candidates studying for the priesthood. In addition, at a time when lay brothers were assigned most of the manual work, Br. Lawrence's duties included answering the door and welcoming visitors, directing the day laborers coming from outside, assisting the poor who came for help, and running errands. Moreover, as the city grew, the area around the monastery quickly developed and there was often construction going on in the neighborhood. But "he got used to doing everything for the love of God, asking him at every opportunity for the grace to do his work," and so "was able to carry it out with great ease" (*Conversations*, 18). Thus Lawrence found his path to inner peace not in the withdrawn life of a hermit but amid the bustle of everyday life. Then, over time, Lawrence developed a worsening limp (perhaps due to the old war wound), and after fifteen years in the kitchen, he was shifted to the job of community sandal maker, which he could carry out while seated. After three serious illnesses in his later years, he passed away peacefully on February 12, 1691, at the age of seventy-seven, joking to his confreres that his only suffering was that he had not suffered enough for love of God.

For Lawrence, "the practice of the presence of God" means "to take delight in and become accustomed to his divine company, speaking humbly and conversing lovingly with him all the time, at every moment, without rule or measure, especially in time of temptation, suffering, aridity, weariness, and even infidelity and sin" (Maxims, 6). Though simple, he admits this approach is not always easy, especially at the outset if the mind and imagination are inclined to wander. It takes great faith, he says, to persevere until the practice becomes habitual and one begins to feel its beneficial effects. Lawrence advises beginners to use short interior aspirations such as "My God, I am completely yours" (Maxims, 30) as a way of curbing distractions and bringing the attention back to God. It is also crucial, he notes, to be striving for virtue, and this practice will assist us in becoming more like the One we love and in whose divine presence we constantly live.

We are told that, despite his "rough exterior" and blunt manner by cultured Parisian standards of that time, "his heart was open, eliciting confidence, letting you feel you could tell him anything, and that you had found a friend" (Ways, 3). In later years, as his reputation spread, he received a steady stream of visitors from all walks of life coming for spiritual advice. Among these was Joseph de Beaufort, vicar general to Louis-Antoine de Noailles who subsequently became cardinal-archbishop of Paris. It was de Beaufort who, after Lawrence's death, gathered what writings he could find and published them, along with his own recollections of the saintly friar, in two small volumes (the second prefaced by de Noailles's approbation of Lawrence's life and teachings), later combined into the single work known today as *The Practice of the Presence of God*.

A more prominent, if less frequent, visitor was Archbishop François de Fénelon, already well known for his progressive views on politics and women's education. In 1697 Fénelon published his *Explication des maximes des saints*, in part to support the teaching of his friend Madame Guyon that "pure love" of God required moving beyond a merely "mercenary love" concerned about one's own salvation. When critics insisted that such a doctrine was contrary to Scripture and an invitation to moral indifference, Fénelon pointed to the example of devout predecessors such as Br. Lawrence, who had overcome his fear of damnation by resolving to love God "purely," and whose book had been recommended by no less than the archbishop of Paris himself! Thus when twenty-three propositions from Fénelon's book were later condemned in 1699, the taint of suspicion also fell on authors he had invoked, and the Catholic faithful for the most part neglected Br. Lawrence (and mystical spirituality in general) for generations. However, the condemnations only piqued Protestant interest, especially among those of the Pietist Movement, and soon

Br. Lawrence's texts were appearing in numerous Protestant editions, especially in German and English. John Wesley, for example, included Br. Lawrence in his "Christian library" and recommended him to his followers. More recently, Lawrence has become a favorite spiritual guide even to many of other faiths.

Not surprisingly, contemporary editions of *The Practice of the Presence of God* hoping to attract the broadest readership often say little about Lawrence's Catholic and Carmelite roots, and until recently he was often overlooked in surveys of Carmelite spirituality. Still, perceptive readers will find in him many echoes of Teresa and John of the Cross, whose teachings he would have studied as a young religious. And long before Thérèse of Lisieux, Lawrence "threw himself headlong into the arms of infinite mercy" (Eulogy, 44) and spoke of serving God in the littlest things, even to "picking up a straw" out of pure love for God. One can argue that Br. Lawrence took the high spiritual doctrine of the Carmelite tradition and made it simple and accessible to everyone. It has become increasingly clear that this humble lay brother deserves a place of honor among Carmel's great spiritual teachers.

From "Conversations" recorded by Joseph de Beaufort[2]

First Conversation (August 3, 1666)

1. I saw Brother Lawrence for the first time, and he told me that God had granted him a special grace of conversion at the age of eighteen when he was still in the world. One day in winter while he was looking at a tree stripped of its leaves, and he realized that in a little while its leaves would reappear, followed by its flowers and fruit, he received a profound insight into God's providence that has never been erased from his soul. This insight completely freed him from the world, and gave him such a love for God that he could not say it had increased during the more than forty years that had passed.

2. He had been the valet of Monsieur de Fieubet, the treasurer of the Savings Bank, and was a clumsy oaf who broke everything.

3. He had asked to be admitted to religious life, thinking he would be skinned alive for his awkwardness and imperfections, and thereby would offer God his life and all its pleasures. But God had fooled him, for he experienced only satisfaction. This led him to tell God frequently: "You have tricked me."

4. [He said] that we must establish ourselves in God's presence by continually conversing with him, and that it was shameful to give up conversation with him to turn to foolishness. We must nourish our souls with an exalted idea of God, and thereby we will draw great joy from being with him. We must enliven our faith, for it is a shame that we have so little. Instead of taking faith as our rule and guide, we amuse ourselves with insignificant, constantly changing devotions! This way of faith is the mind of the church, and is all we need to reach perfection.

5. We must give ourselves to God entirely and in complete abandonment in the temporal and spiritual realms, finding joy in carrying out his will whether he leads us by the way of suffering or consolation, for it is all the same to one who is completely abandoned. We must remain faithful even in times of aridity when God is testing our love for him. This is when we make suitable acts of resignation and abandonment, a single one of which will result in great progress.

6. [He recounted] how he was not astonished on hearing every day about miseries and sins; on the contrary, he was surprised there were not more, considering the evil of which the sinner is capable. He did pray for sinners, but knowing that God could set them straight when he wanted, he worried no more about it.

7. [He said] that in order to arrive at self-abandonment to God to the extent that he willed, we must watch over all the movements of the soul, since it can become entangled in spiritual things as well as in the most base. God gives the necessary light to those who have the true desire to be with him, and that if I had this intention I could ask to see him whenever I wanted without fear of bothering him, and if not, I ought not come to see him at all.

From "Letters" of Br. Lawrence

Letter 2: To a Spiritual Director (1682–1683)

Dear Reverend Father,

Since I am not able to find my way of life described in books—although this does not really disturb me—I would, nonetheless, like to have the reassurance of knowing your thoughts on my present state.

Several days ago during a discussion with a pious person, I was told the spiritual life was a life of grace that begins with servile fear, that intensifies with the hope of eternal life, and that finds its consummation in pure love; and that there are various ways of ultimately arriving at this blessed consummation.

I haven't followed these methods at all; on the contrary, I don't know why they provoked such fear in me in the beginning. But for this reason, on my entrance into religious life I made the resolution to give myself entirely to God in atonement for my sins, and to renounce everything else for the sake of his love.

During the first years I ordinarily thought about death, judgment, hell, paradise, and my sins when I prayed. I continued in this fashion for a few years, carefully applying myself the rest of the day—even during my work—to the practice of the presence of God who was always near me, often in the very depths of my heart. This gave me a great reverence for God, and in this matter faith alone was my reassurance.

I gradually did the same thing during mental prayer, and this gave me great joy and consolation. This is how I began. I will admit that during the first ten years I suffered a great deal. The apprehension that I did not belong to God as I wished, my past sins always before my eyes, and the lavish graces God gave me, were the sum and substance of all my woes. During this period I fell often, but I got back up just as quickly. It seemed to me that all creatures, reason, and God himself were against me, and that faith alone was on my side. I was sometimes troubled by thoughts that this was the result of my presumption, in that I pretended to be all at once where others were able to arrive only with difficulty. Other times I thought I was willingly damning myself, that there was no salvation for me.

When I accepted the fact that I might spend my life suffering from these troubles and anxieties—which in no way diminished the trust I had in God and served only to increase my faith—I found myself changed all at once. And my soul, until that time always in turmoil, experienced a deep inner peace as if it had found its center and place of rest.

Since that time I do my work in simple faith before God, humbly and lovingly, and I carefully apply myself to avoid doing, saying, or thinking anything that might displease him. I hope that, having done all that I can, he will do with me as he pleases.

I cannot express to you what is taking place in me at present. I feel neither concern nor doubt about my state since I have no will other than the will of God, which I try to carry out in all things and to which I am so surrendered that I would not so much as pick up a straw from the ground against his order, nor for any other reason than pure love.

I gave up all devotions and prayers that were not required and I devote myself exclusively to remaining always in his holy presence. I keep myself in his presence by simple attentiveness and a general loving awareness of God that I call "actual presence of God" or better, a quiet and secret conversation of the soul with God that is lasting. This sometimes results in interior, and often exterior, contentment and joys so great that I have to perform childish acts, appearing more like folly than devotion, to control them and keep them from showing outwardly.

Therefore, Reverend Father, I cannot doubt at all that my soul has been with God for more than thirty years. I will omit a number of things so as not to bore you. I think, however, it would be appropriate to indicate the manner in which I see myself before God, whom I consider as my King. . . .

My most typical approach is this simple attentiveness and general loving awareness of God, from which I derive greater sweetness and satisfaction than an infant receives from his mother's breast. Therefore, if I may dare use the expression, I would gladly call this state the "breasts of God," because of the indescribable sweetness I taste and experience there.

If on occasion I turn away either because of necessity or weakness, inner movements so charming and delightful that I am embarrassed to talk about them, call me immediately back to him. I beg you, Reverend Father, to think about my great weaknesses, of which you are fully aware, rather than these great graces with which God favors my soul, unworthy and ignorant as I am.

Regarding the prescribed hours of prayer, they are nothing more than a continuation of this same exercise. Sometimes I think of myself as a piece of stone before a sculptor who desires to carve a statue; presenting myself in this way before God I ask him to fashion his perfect image in my soul, making me entirely like himself.

At other times, as soon as I apply myself I feel my whole mind and soul raised without trouble or effort, and it remains suspended and permanently rooted in God as in its center and place of rest.

I know that some would call this state idleness, self-deception, and self-love. I maintain that it is a holy idleness and a blessed self-love, should the soul in this state be capable of it. In fact, when the soul is in this state of rest its former acts do not trouble it; these acts were formerly its support but now they would do more harm than good.

I cannot agree to calling this self-deception, since the soul in this state desires God exclusively. If this is self-deception then it is

Lawrence of the Resurrection (1614–1691) 93

up to God to correct it; may he do with me as he pleases, for I seek him alone and want to be entirely his. I would appreciate it if you would let me know your impressions of this. It would mean a great deal to me for I have a special regard for you, Reverend Father, and am, in Our Lord,

Yours,

From "Spiritual Maxims" of Br. Lawrence

Chapter Two: *Practices Necessary to Attain the Spiritual Life*

6. The holiest, most ordinary, and most necessary practice of the spiritual life is that of the presence of God. It is to take delight in and become accustomed to his divine company, speaking humbly and conversing lovingly with him all the time, at every moment, without rule or measure, especially in times of temptation, suffering, aridity, weariness, even infidelity and sin.

7. We must continually apply ourselves so that all our actions, without exception, become a kind of brief conversation with God, not in a contrived manner but coming from the purity and simplicity of our hearts.

8. We must perform all our actions carefully and deliberately, not impulsively or hurriedly, for such would characterize a distracted mind. We must work gently and lovingly with God, asking him to accept our work, and by this continual attention to God we will crush the head of the devil and force the weapons from his hands.

9. During our work and other activities, even during our reading and writing, no matter how spiritual—and, I emphasize, even during our religious exercises and vocal prayers—we must stop for a moment, as often as possible, to adore God in the depths of our hearts, to savor him, even though in passing and stealthily. Since you are aware that God is present to you during your actions, that he is in the depths and center of your heart, stop your activities and even your vocal prayers, at least from time to time, to adore him within, to praise him, to ask his help, to offer him your heart, and to thank him. Nothing is more pleasing to God than to turn away from all creatures many times throughout the day to withdraw and adore him present within. Moreover, this turning inward imperceptibly destroys the self-love found only among creatures. In the end, we can offer God no greater evidence of our fidelity than by frequently

renouncing and scorning creatures in order to enjoy their Creator for a moment. I do not mean by this that you must withdraw forever from your duties, for that would be impossible; prudence, the mother of all virtues, must be your guide. I do say, nonetheless, that it is a typical error among the spiritually minded not to withdraw from what is external from time to time to adore God within themselves and enjoy his divine presence in peace for a few moments. This digression was long but I thought the matter called for some explanation. Let's get back to our exercises.

10. All these adorations must be made by faith, believing that God is truly in our hearts, that we must adore, love, and serve him in spirit and in truth, that he sees everything that happens and will happen in us and in all creatures; that he is independent of everything and the one on whom all creatures depend, infinite in every kind of perfection. He is the one who, by virtue of his infinite excellence and sovereign domain, deserves all that we are as well as everything in heaven and on earth, of which he can dispose as he wishes in time and in eternity. All our thoughts, words and actions belong by right to him. Let's put this into practice.

11. We must carefully examine which virtues are the most essential, which are the most difficult to acquire, which sins we commit most often, and which are the most frequent and inevitable of our falls. We must have recourse to God with complete confidence at the moment of combat, remain firm in the presence of his divine majesty, adore him humbly, bring him our miseries and weaknesses, and lovingly ask him for the help of his grace. In this way we will find every virtue in him without our having any of our own.

Chapter Six: *Means to Acquire the Presence of God*

27. The first means is great purity of life.

28. The second is great fidelity to the practice of this presence and to the fostering of this awareness of God within, which must always be performed gently, humbly, and lovingly, without giving in to disturbance or anxiety.

29. We must take special care that this inner awareness, no matter how brief it may be, precedes our activities, that it accompanies them from time to time, and that we complete all of them in the same way. Since much time and effort are required to acquire this

practice, we must not get discouraged when we fail, for the habit is only formed with effort, yet once it is formed we will find contentment in everything. . . .

30. It would be appropriate for beginners to formulate a few words interiorly, such as: "My God, I am completely yours," or "God of love, I love you with all my heart," or "Lord, fashion me according to your heart," or any other words love spontaneously produces. But they must take care that their minds do not wander or return to creatures. The mind must be kept fixed on God alone, so that seeing itself so moved and led by the will, it will be obliged to remain with God.

31. This [practice of the] presence of God, somewhat difficult in the beginning, secretly accomplishes marvelous effects in the soul, draws abundant graces from the Lord, and, when practiced faithfully, imperceptibly leads it to this simple awareness, to this loving view of God present everywhere, which is the holiest, the surest, the easiest, and the most efficacious form of prayer.

32. Please note that to arrive at this state, mortification of the senses is presupposed. . . .

Chapter Seven: *Benefits of the Presence of God*

33. The first benefit that the soul receives from the [practice of the] presence of God is that its faith becomes more intense and efficacious in all life's situations, and especially in times of need, since it easily obtains graces in moments of temptation and in the inevitable dealings with creatures. For the soul, accustomed to the practice of faith by this exercise, sees and senses God present by a simple remembrance. It calls out to him easily and effectively, thus obtaining what it needs. It can be said that it possesses here something resembling the state of the blessed, for the more it advances, the more intense its faith grows, becoming so penetrating in the end that you could almost say: I no longer believe, for I see and experience.

34. The practice of the presence of God strengthens us in hope. Our hope increases in proportion to our knowledge. It grows and is strengthened to the extent that our faith penetrates the secrets of the divinity by this holy exercise, to the extent that it discovers in God a beauty infinitely surpassing not only that of the bodies we see on earth but even that of the most perfect souls and of the angels.

The grandeur of the blessing that it desires to enjoy, and in some manner already tastes, satisfies and sustains it.

35. This practice inspires the will with a scorn for creatures, and inflames it with a sacred fire of love. Since the will is always with God who is a consuming fire, this fire reduces to ashes all that is opposed to it. The soul thus inflamed can live only in the presence of its God, a presence that produces in its heart a holy ardor, a sacred zeal and a strong desire to see this God loved, known, served, and adored by all creatures.

36. By turning inward and practicing the presence of God, the soul becomes so intimate with God that it spends practically all its life in continual acts of love, adoration, contrition, trust, thanksgiving, oblation, petition, and all the most excellent virtues. Sometimes it even becomes one continuous act, because the soul constantly practices this exercise of his divine presence.

37. I know that few persons reach this advanced state. It is a grace God bestows only on a few chosen souls, since this simple awareness remains ultimately a gift from his kind hand. But let me say, for the consolation of those who desire to embrace this holy practice, that he ordinarily gives it to souls who are disposed to receive it. If he does not give it, we can at least acquire, with the help of ordinary grace, a manner and state of prayer that greatly resembles this simple awareness, by means of this practice of the presence of God.

Michael of St. Augustine (1621–1684)
and Maria Petyt (1623–1677)

As the reform of Touraine began to spread, it produced a number of important spiritual writers. Michael of St. Augustine was a member of the "stricter observance" in the Flemish Province. Born in Brussels into a fervently Catholic family, he entered the Carmelites in 1639 and spent most of his religious life in Mechelen, serving many years as prior of the community and several terms as provincial. He was a tireless writer on many themes, but is best remembered today for his treatise *The Mariform Life*, which presents the Christian goal of union with God and conformity to Christ from a thoroughly Marian perspective.

Two years his junior, Maria Petyt was born into a wealthy merchant family from Hazebrouck. She tried to join the Canonesses of St. Augustine but was refused for health reasons, after which she joined a group of beguines in Ghent. Here she came under the spiritual care of Michael of St. Augustine, who guided her into the paths of mystical prayer. Later she moved next to the Carmelite church in Mechelen, where she lived for many years as a lay anchorite and Carmelite "tertiary." With the encouragement of her director, she began writing down her spiritual experiences, which Michael eventually published in a four-volume edition. Maria Petyt's writing style is simple, direct, vivid, and even humorous at times. Most striking is her profound experience of the presence and role of Mary even in the highest states of mystical union.

Carmel has always associated itself with Mary, and Michael of St. Augustine and Maria Petyt are included here because they represent the culmination of a certain strand of Marian spirituality, one that foreshadows that of Louis Grignion de Montfort. The writings of Michael and Maria complement each other; he presents in theological terms what she describes from her own religious experience. Though some expressions used may sound extreme and not to everyone's taste, as Michael acknowledges, these Carmelites are careful never to separate Mary from her divine Son.

They clearly recognize that, however exalted Mary's status and privileges may be, these are entirely the work of grace in her, a grace won by her Son's death and resurrection, and a work accomplished by the God who "lifts up the lowly." There is no fundamental competition between love of God and love of Mary, Michael argues, since both loves were united in the heart of Jesus, and the same spirit within us that cries "Abba, Father" also cries out "Ave, Mater" (Hail, Mother). For both Michael of St. Augustine and Maria Petyt, the Mother of Jesus continues the role she played at Cana: to bring us to Christ and say, "Do whatever he tells you."

From *Union with Our Lady: Marian Writings of the Venerable Mary Petyt of St. Teresa, T. O. Carm.*[1]

5. How she honors and prays to the Blessed Virgin, in God

As for my love, my knowledge of divine things, the lights which I receive concerning revealed truths, my supernatural attractions—all this, it seems to me, is drawn from its source, which is the Unity of the Divine Being, although it sometimes flows superabundantly into my soul. Yet such a superabundant flood does not distract the soul from this Unity, for in all things the soul sees, recognizes, and tastes the one Divine Unity, in a mysterious and wonderful manner. The strength and the light of God alone aid the soul and raise it up to this level.

In like manner, it is in the Divine Being as in a mirror that I behold, honor, and love our all-lovable Mother, and that I pray to Her. I behold Her as making but one with this Divine Mirror, with this ineffable Being. And so when I kneel before one of Her statues and implore Her help for some intention towards which I feel an inner attraction—for the welfare of souls, the needs of my country, or something similar—soon Her image becomes present in this interior mirror, where She is contained together with all other creatures. At other times I seem able, in some manner, to penetrate beneath the exterior image, noticing nothing corporal, and I behold her totally contained in the hidden depth of my spirit.

6. A tender love impels her towards Jesus and Mary. . . .

It is an extremely tender love which I feel for Jesus and for His dear Mother, who is my Mother also. And this kind of love gives me great familiarity with Jesus, great ease in His company. With Him I am like a spouse, full of tenderness and affection. And the feeling He evidences for me in return also appears to be full of affection. The same is true of my dear Mother. She seems to have adopted me as Her child; She instructs me in perfection and purity of spirit, so that I may become more pleasing to Jesus. She leads me to the love of Jesus and to loving commerce with Him. . . .

12. . . . She is shown how to love Jesus, Mary and Joseph, and how to converse in spirit with them.

. . . I contemplate Jesus, Mary, and Joseph and enjoy their presence in the depth of my soul, seeing them as united for all eternity to the Divine Being with whom they are totally permeated.

At present, these Three show themselves to me all together, without there being introduced the least intermediary in my contemplation of the Divine Being. For he, as it were, overshadows them and fills them. They seem, in some way, to be absorbed in him, and it is thus they present themselves. So true is this, that it is impossible for me to lose the presence of God, even for an instant, when I consider them or raise up my love to them. In them, I see and love nothing except God alone and that which is divine. The remembrance of them in no way prevents me from remaining in God. It in no way detracts from my simplicity of spirit.

Thus I have come to understand how the blessed in heaven can see and love each other in God without impeding their beatific vision, their joy and their love. I have learned by experience that it is the same here.

18. . . . She sees Mary present in choir during the chanting of the Salve Regina. She asks Her blessing and rejoices in the fact that she belongs to the Order.

. . . On the eleventh of August, 1668, while the [Carmelite] religious were chanting the Hail, Holy Queen and the Litany, I experienced a particular joy and contentment of heart because I seemed to see our most tender Mother there among Her dear Brothers. She was greatly pleased, and the praise, gratitude, and respectful devotion paid to Her seemed to delight Her immensely. . . .

Full of gratitude, I rejoiced that this lovable Mother had called me to be a part of such an Order. [She was living as a "third order" Carmelite in a small house attached to the Carmelite church in Maline, Belgium. —Ed.] I saw well with what a special love She cherished this Order, because it is so dedicated to Her veneration and Her love, because it celebrates Her feasts with such devotion and respectful familiarity, such as befit Her true children and Brothers. For this reason did I feel so happy at being able, like the others, to take refuge under Her maternal protection; at being a member, no matter how insignificant, of the Order; at being a small shoot of this Vine of Carmel, in which I should love to bring forth fruits in superabundance for the pleasure of my Beloved and His lovable Mother.

22. The Blessed Virgin commands her to explain in what the "Marian Life" consists. . . .

I believe that my dearest Mother is commanding me to explain at some greater length what it has often been freely given me to experience of this life in Mary, or "Marian Life." . . .

Without a doubt it is true that, according to the usual manner of expressing it, God is our sole and final end. In obtaining this end, in contemplating and enjoying this Supreme Good, there is contained the soul's complete happiness, whether in this life or in the next. In this sense, the soul can neither aspire nor attain to anything higher.

But in another sense the soul can aspire to something more, can tend to something higher, and this in a manner which bears some analogy to the condition of the blessed in heaven. The Saints possess, each of them, one glory, one happiness, one satisfaction which comes to them from the contemplation, love, and fruition of the Divine Face and the Divine Being. . . . Yet certain Saints and Blessed, it is commonly known, receive a glory and happiness over and above that described already, a glory and happiness that is to a certain extent supplementary, each one according to his merits or according to the providence of God.

A similar situation comes to pass in this life, when certain souls are favored with supplementary gifts, graces, and favors, through which, if I may so speak, they become like the Saints and arrive at a more lofty manner of life in union with God. In this sense, such a situation constitutes a higher degree of spiritual life than the degree of simple mystical union, and hence one may truly speak of a more eminent degree. That which I experience of this life in Mary, or Marian life, seems to be a twofold life . . .

From Michael of St. Augustine, *Life with Mary: A Treatise on the Marian Life*[2]

Chapter One: Just as we can live a deiform and divine life, so we can live a mariform and marian life, that is, a life in conformity with Mary's good pleasure and in her spirit.

. . . We have said elsewhere that we must live deiformly, that is, conformably to God's good pleasure and according to the demands of the divine will. In like manner, it is fitting for us to live mariformly, that is, conformably to the good pleasure of Mary, the Mother of God. This is the reason why those who profess to be Mary's most dear children use one and the same eye of discretion to judge whether all that they do and omit be according to the good pleasure of God and their lovable Mother. . . .

Chapter Five: Life and death for Mary must be directed, further, to God, just as in the veneration of other saints.

Here it must be noted that life for Mary must be directed and ordered also to God. (This is true, in the same way, of love and veneration of other saints.) Mary herself is totally devoted to God's good pleasure, and she lives for God eternally, according to his will, his love, and his glory. Hence all life for Mary must be further directed to God, so that we do not live and die for Mary as for our ultimate end, with inordinate self-seeking and attachment to [anything] which is not God. This should be our aim: through life and death in and for Mary to live and die more perfectly in and for God, for the love of God and according to his good pleasure and to establish the kingdom of Mary within us, together with the reign of Jesus. For the kingdom of Mary is not opposed to the kingdom of Jesus; it is, rather, completely directed to the kingdom of Jesus.

Therefore, the soul which loves God and which professes to be a true child of this lovable Mother should watch carefully, so that in all its works it allow its love of God (which is poured forth in its heart by the Holy Ghost who is given to it) to extend to Mary. Such a soul must lovingly have recourse to her, keep itself reverently turned towards her by the constant filial remembrance of her presence. Yet the soul must see to it that this extension of the divine love to Mary return again to God, to terminate ultimately in him. For the love of Mary is not permitted, nor is it to be exercised, for any reason other than God's sake.

When the soul is led and directed in its marian life by the Spirit of God, inwardly and almost spontaneously, then there is no problem in this regard. For then the soul learns by experience that this life for Mary is in no way a hindrance to life for God, but rather a help and a stimulus. It finds that its love reaches God with and through Mary, that it rests simultaneously in Mary and in God, though ultimately, of course, in God as in its final end.

Chapter Six: The marian life is, in a certain sense, more perfect than a life of simple union. We find an illustration of this in the life of the blessed in heaven.

. . . The blessed in heaven all enjoy perfect glory and joy in the face-to-face contemplation of God. They are filled with the light of glory and their souls are flooded with beatific love, and in this consist their supreme joy and happiness. Yet, as everyone admits, the blessed possess, besides this essential beatitude and glory, other accidental joys, each one according to the measure of his merits and according to the disposition of God, the Rewarder. Such accidental joys are found, for example, in the contemplation of the most sacred humanity of Christ, of his holy wounds, of the holy cross as the instrumental cause of the soul's beatitude; in the delights of intimacy with the most glorious Mother of God, with the blessed Joseph, or other of the saints; in an especially clear and profound knowledge of some of God's mysteries. There are many like joys, in which one of the blessed shares more, another less. Thus is one saint more sublime in glory than another, because the beatific love in one is more intense and also extends to more delightful objects than in another. . . .

It is in this sense that the marian life joined to the divine life is more perfect, is one grade higher than the ordinary contemplative and unitive life, since the marian life is twofold: divine-marian, life in God and in Mary, through the simple contemplation, love and enjoyment of God in Mary and of Mary in God. . . .

Chapter Eight: The marian life in no way hinders the simple contemplative life. . . .

. . . True, some souls are found, even among those who tend towards the summit of perfection, to whom this marian life is foreign and seems senseless. To such souls this life seems not a little opposed to detachment from all creatures, and hence alien to true perfection. But they must beware of despising this life or of judging it proper to imperfect spirits, beginners, or proficients. Let them know that, as we have earlier explained, the marian life can easily accompany the divine life without in any way hindering it; in fact, it can serve as a help and a stimulus to the divine life, especially when it is caused in the soul by the direct action of God.

Yet our interior attraction must be followed. Thus, aside from the actual influence of the Holy Spirit, it is unwise to force the spirit or to urge it to act in the manner outlined above. It suffices to regard one's dear Mother with deep affection, to love her in what might be called a more mature manner, until she deigns to infuse this spirit of marian life into the soul. . . .

Chapter Thirteen: The Spirit of Jesus produces in the soul love for God the Father; it also produces love for Mary, the Mother of God, as it did in Jesus himself. . . .

"Because you are the sons of God, God hath sent the Spirit of his Son into your hearts, crying: Abba, Father," writes St. Paul [see Gal 4:6]. From this we learn that the Spirit of Jesus abides in the children of God, producing in them, according to their capacity, a tender love for God the Father. But just as this Spirit produced in Jesus a filial love for his Eternal Father, so it also produced in him a filial affection for his most dear Mother, and this it will continue to do for all eternity. Is it any wonder, therefore, if the Spirit of Jesus which, in the hearts of the children of God cries Abba, Father (that is, produces love for the Father of Jesus), also cries from those same hearts Ave, Mater [Hail, Mother] (that is, produces filial and reverential love and affection for Mary) even as happened in Jesus himself during his lifetime and happens now in heaven?

. . . For it is one and the same Spirit of Jesus which produces all in these souls; namely, both divine and marian love, without hindering either. Only think how this took place in Christ without prejudice to the highest perfection, and you will realize how it can take place in certain of Mary's chosen children without prejudice to the contemplative life of perfection.

. . . One and the same Spirit of Jesus, as we have said, accomplishes all this in the faithful soul, according to the capacity of each one and the desire of the Spirit. Hence, there should be, in the future, no cause for wonderment, since this union of marian and divine life is thus justified theoretically and, practically, is established as being realized in certain souls.

Martyrs of Compiègne (d. 1794)

After the official condemnations of Quietism and semi-Quietism in the late 1600s, though interest in mystical spirituality continued among groups such as the Protestant Pietists, Catholics increasingly turned toward the seemingly safer path of more "activist" spiritual practices. The mystical works of Teresa, John of the Cross, and others tended to be relegated to the shelves of monastic libraries. Popular devotions (like those associated with the brown scapular of Carmel and Carmelite devotion to the Infant of Prague) abounded. Mental prayer came to be understood largely in terms of highly structured meditations on set religious themes, leading to edifying resolutions. Carmelite scholars expended enormous intellectual energy trying to fit the teachings of John and Teresa into the categories of scholastic theology, and to identify a Teresian "method" of meditation that could stand alongside the Ignatian, Sulpician, and other "methods."

Given such trends, it is hardly surprising that Carmel in the eighteenth century produced no great spiritual classics. It did, however, offer the world inspiring witnesses of another sort. Chief among them were the sixteen Discalced Carmelite nuns of Compiègne who died at the guillotine during the Reign of Terror in 1794.

The monastery of Compiègne, about fifty miles north of Paris, was founded in 1641, and had long enjoyed friendly relations with the French royal family, who spent several weeks each year at a nearby chateau. In fact, the youngest daughter of Louis XV, Madame Louise Marie of France (1737–1787), had entered the Carmel of Saint-Denis (Paris) in 1770, and had played a role in the vocation of several Compiègne nuns. Among them was Marie Madeleine Claudine Lidoine, prioress at the time of the martyrdom, who took the same religious name as her royal benefactor, Teresa of St. Augustine. Nevertheless, the members of the Compiègne community represented a broad cross-section of French society, from descendants of military officers, government officials, and the nobility to the daughters of cobblers, saddlers, haberdashers, tax collectors, and ordinary laborers.

The causes and consequences of the French Revolution are still widely discussed and variously interpreted. Here it is sufficient to recall that what began as a movement promoting certain urgent but somewhat limited political and social reforms gradually took a more radical and violent turn, and became increasingly hostile toward the institutional Catholic Church, which was viewed as too closely tied to the *Ancien Régime.* Religious orders were targeted for extinction, since their vows seemed to run contrary to the Enlightenment ideals of freedom and the ultimate authority of human reason. Contemplative religious in particular were seen as social parasites who contributed nothing useful to the welfare of society.

In 1790 the National Constituent Assembly canceled the previous privileges of the clergy, confiscated church property in the name of the state, and declared the permanent suspension of all religious vows. Wearing religious habits in public was forbidden, and thousands of French religious returned to secular life, went into hiding, or fled into exile. Though the Compiègne nuns unanimously assured the authorities that they wanted only "to live and die" as Carmelites, they were expelled from their convent on September 14, 1792, the feast of the Triumph of the Holy Cross. Nevertheless, they found lodgings in four small apartments nearby, and remained in continual contact with one another under the leadership of the prioress, Mother Teresa of St. Augustine (Madame Lidoine), following their previous way of life as best they could.

Even before their expulsion, Madame Lidoine had discovered in the community archives a brief account of a "mystic dream" experienced by one of their aspirants in the previous century. In the dream, this young lodger who would later enter the Carmel seemed to see the Compiègne community—with the exception of a few members—appearing in glory "following the Lamb," who had earlier appeared as the suffering Christ. Sensing that this might be a premonition of their own fate, Mother Teresa of St. Augustine proposed to her Carmelite sisters that they make an act of consecration as a community, offering themselves as a holocaust "to restore peace to France and to the church." After some initial hesitation, the nuns all agreed and began renewing this act of consecration each day for nearly two years.

On June 22, 1794, the community was finally arrested and imprisoned at the former Visitation convent of Compiègne. (Three of the sisters were away at the time and thus escaped arrest, including Sr. Marie of the Incarnation, who was in Paris and fled to safety with the prioress's mother; in her later years she would write an account of the martyrdom of her former community.) After about three weeks, just as they had been given permission to wash their secular clothing, word came that the Compiègne nuns were to be transported to Paris for trial. Accordingly, contrary to usual protocol, they were taken to the capital in the only dry clothing they had, their religious habits (with small caps substituting for the traditional veils).

At a brief show trial on July 16 (solemnity of Our Lady of Mount Carmel, patron of the Order), the nuns were accused of conspiring against the Republic, and the judge described them as "fanatics" for clinging to their "religion." In fact, these Carmelites were not recklessly seeking their own destruction; Madame Lidoine attempted to refute the accusations and argued that if any wrong had been done, she alone was responsible and the others should be spared. In the end, however, all sixteen community members present received the death sentence.

The following day they were taken to the Place du Trône (now the Place de la Nation) for execution. Eyewitnesses report that the usually bloodthirsty mob fell strangely silent at the appearance of the tumbrels full of nuns in their Carmelite habits, chanting the *Salve Regina*, the *Miserere*, the *Veni Creator Spiritus*, and other ancient hymns as they approached their deaths. It was a sobering reminder to many of how monstrous the Reign of Terror had become.

At the foot of the scaffold the nuns renewed their vows and kissed the small image of the Madonna and child held in the palm of Mother Teresa of St. Augustine. Thus the youngest member, Sr. Constance, who had remained a novice for six years due to the civil laws against the taking of religious vows, was finally able to make her religious profession before ascending to the guillotine. Madame Lidoine herself was the last to be executed, after assisting the others. The bodies of the nuns were deposited in a mass grave in the nearby Picpus cemetery. Only ten days later, Robespierre was executed at the same guillotine, and the Reign of Terror effectively ended, a sign to many that the Compiègne nuns' generous act of consecration had been accepted.

"Teresa of St. Augustine and Companions" were beatified on May 27, 1906. Their story attracted increasing attention in the twentieth century with the publication in 1931 of Gertrud von Le Fort's religious novella *Die Letzte am Schaffott* (The Last One at the Scaffold), later translated into English as *Song at the Scaffold*. Le Fort's narrative centers on the fictional Blanche de la Force, a fearful young woman from an aristocratic family who first seeks refuge in a Carmelite vocation at Compiègne, later fleeing the convent as the political situation becomes more threatening, and finally returning to join the nuns at the guillotine, thus becoming "the last one" executed. (Contrary to the historical record, in Le Fort's version it is Marie of the Incarnation, zealous for martyrdom, who pushes for the "act of consecration" despite the reservations of her superior, Madame Lidoine, yet is ultimately frustrated in her desire for courageous self-sacrifice.) The Dominican R. L. Bruckberger acquired screen rights to the story and arranged for George Bernanos, then dying of cancer, to write the dialogues. Bernanos's text was later used by composer Francis Poulenc in his *Dialogues of the Carmelites*, one of the most acclaimed of modern operas. Gertrud von Le Fort had reshaped the story to grapple artistically with her own fears in the face of Nazism's rising tide, while Bernanos's version served as a kind of "final testament" as he faced his own approaching death. Yet despite liberties taken with the historical record, both fictional versions remain true to a central lesson from the witness of the Compiègne nuns, namely, that Christian martyrdom is not the product of merely human courage but a manifestation of the grace of God, "who chooses the weak and makes them strong."

Christmas Hymn by Teresa of St. Augustine (Madame Lidoine)

("To Be Sung at the Crèche"; composed some time after the community's expulsion from their convent)

Heavenly Child, I long for you,
Nothing else satisfies my heart;
Therefore I'm under your sway.
I feel the intensity of your love.
Heal this guilty, sinful heart,
Let it be wounded with sorrow and love!
Heavenly wounds, O wounds so welcome!
Break this heart, that it may ache night and day!

Divine love, with my whole being
I come to your cradle to bring a gift:
My soul surrenders itself to your judgments,
And my mind submits to them forever. . . .
I want nothing; your heart is all things;
Here I sacrifice my own views and desires.
In your heart, I want to be enclosed.

For your love's sake, I accept martyrdom. . . .

Ah! my hopes are founded on death
For I die of being unable to die.
And hasten, Lord, hasten my deliverance!
Break these bonds, fulfill my longing!
Immolate your victim as you will!
Your divine blows are sacred to me!
If I die beneath your hand, it is my happiness.
To my heart, your demands are but an attraction!

Divine Shepherd, I place beneath your staff
This little flock entrusted to my care.
Loving Child, alongside your crib
I surrender to you mother and children.
O Mother of love, O august Sovereign,
Deign, oh! deign to place us in your bosom.
In your help, O powerful Queen,
Your dear children have every right to hope.[1]

Song Composed in Prison by Julie-Louise of Jesus

(to the tune of *La Marseillaise*)

Let our hearts be joyful
The day of glory is here!
Far from us every weakness
Seeing the banner come,
Seeing the banner come!
Let us prepare ourselves for victory,
Let us all march like true conquerors
Beneath the flags of a crucified God!
Let us run, let us fly to glory;
Let us revive our ardor!
Our bodies belong to the Lord:
Let us climb, let us climb the scaffold
And make him victorious!

O ever-desirable happiness
For the Catholics of France:
To follow the admirable road,
So often traveled before
So often traveled before

By the martyrs, toward execution
Following Jesus, with the King!
Christians, let us proclaim our faith;
Let us adore the justice of God;
May the fervent priest,
The faithful believer,
Seal, seal with every drop of their blood,
Faith in a crucified God!

Great God, you see my weakness,
I long for it—yet I'm still afraid.
Confidently my ardor impels me,
But give me your help.
But give me your help.
I cannot hide my fear from you
When I think of paying the price of death;
But you will be my comfort.
No, I say, no more hesitation.
Hasten the moment!
I await my transformation.
Lord, Lord, without delay
Make my heart content!

Holy Virgin, our model,
August Queen of martyrs,
Deign to support our zeal
By purifying our intentions.
By purifying our intentions.
Protect France still;
Help us from heaven's height.
Make us feel, even here,
The effects of your power.
Sustain your children,
Submissive, obedient.
Let us die, let us die with Jesus
And our faithful King!

See, O divine Mary,
The holy rapture of your children.
If our life comes from God,
For his sake, we accept death.
For his sake, we accept death.
Show yourself our tender Mother;

Present us to Christ Jesus,
And, enlivened by his Spirit,
On fire with his holy love,
May we, in leaving this earth
For our heavenly abode,
Sing, sing with the saints
His goodness forever![2]

From *To Quell the Terror* by William Bush (chap. 10)

The journey to the scaffold had begun. Escorted by mounted guards and foot soldiers on that hot late afternoon in July, the tumbrels bearing the 40 condemned bumped slowly over the paving stones of the Conciergerie courtyard before emerging from the gates of the Palace of Justice. As the procession of guards, horses, foot-soldiers and jolting, springless tumbrels advanced along the uneven stone streets, accompanied by a highly eclectic escort of vociferous regulars, curious street rabble, and a few sympathizers, the *Miserere* arose from the tumbrels. . . .

The universal silence greeting the procession has been attested to by all witnesses. On that evening those passionate voices which daily railed against the condemned were struck dumb, even to the "furies of the guillotine" at the place of execution. All watched silently, waiting in a sort of eerie, hushed expectancy. . . .

Was it the nuns' serene expressions, their white cloaks, or their singing that produced the strange, embarrassed silence along the route? . . . They projected no hint of tragedy, no reason for regret. A rare glory of being seemed to demonstrate that death by the guillotine was for them the crowning of their lives. Had they not, just the night before, sung of this as their own "day of glory"?

. . . Also sung en route to the guillotine were the words of tender, helpless abandon of the *Salve Regina*. Never for these Christian women consecrated to Our Lady of Mount Carmel had they seemed more appropriate. . . .

The 24 other prisoners could not but be engulfed by the strange hush as the procession advanced. . . .

The comments of one Parisian working-class woman that evening as she watched the Carmelites pass by have been preserved for us. . . . They could have come only from an eyewitness who heard this simple woman observe to all and sundry, as the people of Paris have ever been wont to do at public events: "What good souls! Just look at them! Tell me if you don't think they look just like angels! I tell you, if those women don't go straight to Paradise then we'll just have to believe it doesn't exist!". . .

Between the time the sentence was passed in the late afternoon and the arrival at the Place du Trône, three hours would probably have elapsed. The hot evening was thus well advanced before the bumping tumbrels finally reached the vast site. Even at an hour nearing eight o'clock, however, the light would still have been intense, as it is at the end of long, clear Parisian midsummer days, when an intense twilight's bright, hot light tenaciously holds night at bay. . . .

Mounted on its high scaffold, stark against the still bright midsummer evening sky, the realism of the naked blade defied the courage of the would-be martyrs. The resourceful prioress allowed no time, however, for inner battles with fear. As we have seen, she was prepared for this fateful moment and greeted the scaffold's uncompromising reality with the equally uncompromising theological affirmations of the *Te Deum*. . . .

After the singing of the *Te Deum*, the devotions led by Madame Lidoine were those normal for a dying Carmelite. If possible, the dying nun, after the Holy Spirit had been invoked, renews her monastic vows of poverty, chastity, and obedience, her hands between those of the prioress. Thus is explained the hymn next sung before the guillotine: the *Veni Creator Spiritus*, invoking the Holy Spirit to quicken and enflame the nuns with the Holy Spirit as their consecration to him was renewed. . . .

Monseigneur Jauffret specifies that this hymn of invocation completed, the nuns renewed their vows in "loud and intelligible voices," led by the prioress. . . .

Certainly the Carmelites' sacrifice on July 17, followed by Robespierre's fall one republican *décade* later on July 27, has caused many to believe that their sacrifice was efficacious. What is sure is that with the Great Terror ended, a less ominous fate awaited prisoners such as the English Benedictines. . . .

The 41-year-old Madame Lidoine moves up to the foot of the scaffold, the worn little clay image of the Virgin and child clutched tightly in her palm, a last, pathetic relic of all that had once been the royally favored Carmel of Compiègne. . . .

Sister Henriette of the Divine Providence, Madame Pelras, the community's young infirmarian, now offers to stand by Mother Lidoine and assist the others up the steps. . . .

. . . Sister Constance, the [community's] youngest member at age 29, had been the last to join the community. For five long years she had been forbidden by law to make her final vows. Now, just moments before, as the others renewed their vows, she, joining in, had at last also pronounced hers. Let her then, the last, be the first to enter into the bridal chamber. . . .

Madame Lidoine is ready. Sister Constance, in a panic so shortly before for not having finished her office, is summoned by the prioress and confidently approaches. Reports are that all panic was suddenly gone. Fully conscious that her vows had at last been pronounced and that she was indeed dying as a professed Carmelite, she seemed transfigured by the life-giving Spirit just invoked. She kneels at her prioress's feet, her first and last act of submission as a professed Carmelite. A final maternal blessing is given and the tiny clay image of the Virgin and Child, cupped in the prioress's palm, is proffered to this youngest daughter for a last kiss.

Head humbly bowed, Sister Constance, asks in a clear, young voice: "Permission to die, Mother?" "Go, my daughter!" It is reported that it was after rising from her knees to face the machine, and as she started up the steps of the scaffold, that Sister Constance intoned the first line of the psalm, *Laudate Dominum omnes gentes*. It was the psalm sung by Saint Teresa of Avila at the foundation of a new Carmel. In 1604 Mother Anne of Jesus, just arrived from Spain under the escort of Cardinal de Bérulle, had introduced this Teresian custom into France when she walked into the church of the first Carmel in Paris. At that historic moment the great Spanish nun is reported to have startled her sisters by this sudden outburst of praise . . .

Now, 190 years later, in that same city where Christian civilization seemed to be in its death throes as the old order collapsed, the familiar verses, spontaneously begun by Sister Constance at the foot of the guillotine, were again taken up by the surprised nuns "with greater fervor than harmony." They would continue throughout the community's immolation, punctuated by the recurring fatal thud cutting short voice after voice. . . .

Said to have been as radiant as "a queen going to receive her diadem" as she mounted the steps singing, Sister Constance is also reported to have waved aside the executioner and his two valets upon reaching the top of the steps. She thus approached the vertical balance plank unaided, chanting that God's mercy was confirmed upon her. . . .

Professionals hardened to the most violent of human emotions, ever confident in their professional ability to assure death, whatever might be the resistance of the condemned, [the executioners] Sanson and his valets had guillotined nuns on several occasions. The blood of Madame Lidoine's friend, Madame Chamboran of the Carmel of Saint-Denis, had been poured out on this same scaffold in March. Still the execution of a whole community of 16, determined to offer themselves in what appeared to be a ritual sacrifice, was unprecedented. The women's implacable acceptance of everything happening to them, their simple joy as they sang, awaiting certain death, pointed towards a dimension beyond their expertise. Normally masters on their own scaffold, this evening the executioners found themselves minor players in an unfamiliar drama where death had lost its dread. The crowd of regulars gathered around the scaffold this evening had mysteriously sensed this. All watched in an unprecedented silence.

Apart from Sister Constance's being the first to die, and Madame Pelras dying just before Madame Lidoine at the end, we know nothing of the order in which the martyrdom proceeded. . . .

Fourteen times the implacable three sounds have been heard. Fourteen times a headless body has been tossed into the cart. Now Madame Pelras' turn has come. She kneels before the prioress, is blessed, and gives her last kiss to the little image cupped in Madame Lidoine's palm. "Permission to die, Mother?" "Go, my daughter!"

The 34-year-old Sister Marie Henriette of the Divine Providence, reported to have been of great natural beauty, remains unshaken either by the spectacle in the red cart below, or the blood on the scaffold, or even by the splattered executioners as she climbs up to face them. As the chanting fades the appearance, up on the scaffold, of this young nun who had proven of such *sang-froid* in helping all the others, could not but make a profound impact upon the still silent crowd. . . .

From the foot of the scaffold, . . . Mother Teresa of Saint Augustine watches. Her gratitude is great as she beholds this last, so touchingly faithful daughter strapped to the vertical plank, her arms bound behind her. It is now all almost over. By His mercy it had been given her to escort all 15 of them to the threshold of His bridal chamber. Now she must make haste. She too was invited to the feast. . . .

Climbing the steps, Mother Lidoine is transfigured. Briefly freed in these fleeting seconds from all worldly responsibilities to others, she savors a bride's joyous assurance of belonging only to the Bridegroom in the hour of her nuptials.

. . . Below in the crowd all eyes are fixed upon the yet unsullied white mantle of the 41-year-old prioress. The blood-spattered executioners bind her hands and strap her to the balance plank. Like a sheep before its shearers, like a lamb led to the slaughter, she, like her Master, opens not her mouth (Is 53:7). For a few shining seconds she grasps that it is being given, even to her, to enter into the fullness of the most ineffable divine mystery known to the race, a mystery older than the world itself: the mystery of the Lamb, slain from the foundation of the world (Rev 13:8).

The balance plank swings forward. It is finished. . . .

Because it thus bears all the marks of Christian martyrdom according to the great unbroken Christian tradition of both Eastern and Western Churches, the execution of the 16 Carmelites should never be dismissed as a mere manifestation of the martyrs themselves, or even of the powerful personality of their prioress. Rather must it be viewed, as martyrdom should always be viewed, as an exceptional but very great mystical manifestation of God at work, making of the martyrs "bearers of God" through their oblation. For through the inexplicable, self-imposed, and unprecedented silence that accompanied their long procession and continued throughout their ceremonial sacrifice, it was *he*, through them, who was revealing something of his presence and power in the world at that hour. . . .

The glory of Jesus Christ the world can never contain, for it is not of this world. Yet, even so, in the Father's great mercy to our fallen race through the Holy Spirit, the glory of the only-begotten Son can be seen and experienced in this world. The records show it was indeed seen and experienced by those who, in self-imposed silence, participated in the theophany that constituted the martyrdom of the 16 Carmelites of Compiègne.[3]

Thérèse of Lisieux (1873–1897)

On September 30, 1897, after a long and agonizing struggle with tuberculosis, Thérèse Martin died at the age of twenty-four in the Carmel of Lisieux, all but unknown outside her religious community and immediate family circle. Few imagined that during her last eighteen months Thérèse had been struggling with a profound "trial of faith," assailed by terrible doubts about the reality of heaven—a trial she nevertheless chose to embrace, for as long as God wished, in solidarity with sinners and those without faith. Even some of her community members wondered what could possibly be said of this "sweet and simple" young nun after her death. Yet within a few years she had become not only Carmel's best known modern figure but one of the most popular saints of all time.

The basic facts of Thérèse's life are well known and often recounted. Marie-Françoise-Thérèse Martin was born in Alençon in Normandy, France, on January 2, 1873. She was the last of Louis and Zélie Martin's nine children, among whom only five daughters—Marie, Pauline, Léonie, Céline, and Thérèse herself—survived into adulthood. As an infant she was separated for a year from her family in order to be cared for by a wet nurse. Then at the age of four she lost her mother to breast cancer, and immediately chose her older sister Pauline as "second mother." Some years later, further traumatized by the shock of her beloved Pauline leaving home for the Carmelite convent, Thérèse lapsed into a "strange sickness" in which she "appeared to be almost always delirious." After two months, she suddenly recovered upon seeing the "ravishing smile" of the statue of Mary at her bedside. She had finally found a maternal figure from whom she could never be separated.

Nevertheless, for some years Thérèse remained a nervous and emotionally high-strung child, until she experienced a kind of "conversion" following Christmas Midnight Mass in 1886, mastering her emotions after an uncharacteristically sharp remark from her father that previously would have reduced her to tears. "I felt charity enter into my soul," she later wrote, "and the need to forget myself and to please others; since then I've been happy!" Soon after she began to feel a powerful urge to save souls, especially those of great sinners, such as the notorious murderer Henri Pranzini, whose apparent final repentance she believed her prayers had helped to bring about. Deciding that she, too, was called to Carmel, where Pauline and Marie had now preceded her, she began her efforts to enter the convent before the usual age. During a pilgrimage to Rome, she even broke normal Vatican protocol by appealing directly to Leo XIII during a papal audience. He reassured the young woman that she would indeed enter "if God wills it."

Finally obtaining the necessary permissions, Thérèse entered the Carmel of Lisieux in April 1888 at the age of fifteen and quickly adapted herself to the convent regimen. Gradually she was given a number of responsibilities, such as helping with the formation of novices, among whom later was her own sister Céline. During her nine years in Carmel, she was known for her generosity and fidelity, her joyful yet mature spirit, her kindness even to the most difficult members, and her notable avoidance of favoritism toward relatives.

Yet she also felt keenly the disparity between her childhood aspirations to heroic sanctity and the reality of her own weaknesses. She began searching for a "new way." Refusing to become discouraged, she concluded that God would not have inspired such aspirations without intending to fulfill them, and decided that what was required was to entrust herself entirely to God's merciful love with childlike confidence. Thus she "discovered," or rediscovered, what she called her "little way," later characterized by others as the "little way of spiritual childhood."

This "little way" found further expression in her famous "Oblation to Merciful Love." Impressed but not attracted by the accounts of heroic nuns who had offered themselves as "victims" of God's justice (to take upon themselves the penalty of others' sins), Thérèse offered herself instead to merciful love, reasoning that God wished all the more to find souls willing to receive the infinite divine love.

Like her spiritual mother Teresa of Avila, Thérèse was keenly aware of the apostolic significance of her contemplative Carmelite vocation, and took to heart the needs of the church and world. She was assigned to pray for, and correspond with, two "missionary brothers" (Maurice Bellière and Adolphe Roulland), which further inflamed her zeal for the missions. She even dreamed of one day being assigned to a Carmel in the missions herself.

Toward the end of Thérèse's brief life, her older sister Pauline (Mother Agnes) directed her to transcribe her childhood memories. Later, at the request of her sister Marie, she wrote out an explanation of her "little way" and her vocation. Finally, as her tuberculosis began to take its toll and it was obvious she would not live much longer, Mother Agnes's successor, Mother Marie de Gonzague, told Thérèse to continue the story, adding details about her life in the convent.

After Thérèse's death, Pauline edited these three manuscripts (often referred to as A, B, and C) into a continuous text known as *Story of a Soul*, published a year after her death in place of the usual obituary letter. The book quickly became one of the best-selling religious texts of all time, translated into dozens of languages. Devotion to Thérèse also spread rapidly, as people everywhere felt their prayers were answered through the intercession of the "Little Flower" who had promised to send a "shower of roses" and to "spend her heaven doing good on earth." The speed with which she was beatified (1923) and canonized (1925) was unprecedented. In 1927, at the request of missionaries, she was named copatron of the missions alongside Francis Xavier, and in 1997 she became only the third woman to be named a doctor of the church. On October 19, 2008, her parents were beatified.

The selections that follow are from *Story of a Soul*. In the first, Thérèse briefly describes her discovery of the "little way." The second comes from the text written for her sister Marie (Manuscript B), mentioned above. Both contain much of Thérèse's teaching, and some of her most famous passages.

From *Story of a Soul*

Chapter 10

. . . I have always wanted to be a saint. Alas! I have always noticed that when I compared myself to the saints, there is between them and me the same difference that exists between a mountain whose summit is lost in the clouds and the obscure grain of sand trampled underfoot by passers-by. Instead of becoming discouraged, I said to myself: God cannot inspire unrealizable desires. I can, then, in spite of my littleness, aspire to holiness. It is impossible to me to grow up, and so I must bear with myself such as I am with all my imperfections. But I want to seek out a means of going to heaven by a little way, a way that is very straight, very short, and totally new.

We are living now in an age of inventions, and we no longer have to take the trouble of climbing stairs, for, in the homes of the rich, an elevator has replaced these very successfully. I wanted to find an elevator which would raise me to Jesus, for I am too small to climb the rough stairway of perfection. I searched, then, in the Scriptures for some sign of this elevator, the object of my desires, and I read these words coming from the mouth of Eternal Wisdom: *"Whoever is a LITTLE ONE, let him come to me"* [see Prov 9:4]. And so I succeeded. I felt I had found what I was looking for. But wanting to know, O God, what You would do to *the very little one* who answered Your call, I continued my search, and this is what I discovered: *"As one whom a mother caresses, so will I comfort you; you shall be carried at the breasts, and upon the knees they shall caress you"* [see Isa 66:12-13]. Ah! Never did words more tender and more melodious come to give joy to my soul. The elevator which must raise me to heaven is Your arms, O Jesus! And for this I had no need to grow up, but rather I had to remain *little* and become this more and more.[1]

Chapter 9

Do not believe I am swimming in consolations; oh, no, my consolation is to have none on earth. Without showing Himself, without making His voice heard, Jesus teaches me in secret; it is not by means of books, for I do not understand what I am reading. . . . I understand so well that it is only love that makes us acceptable to God, that this love is the only good I ambition. Jesus deigned to show me the road that leads to this Divine Furnace, and this road is the *surrender* of the little child who sleeps without fear in its Father's arms. "Whoever is a *little one*, let him come to me" [see Prov 9:4]. So speaks the Holy Spirit through the mouth of Solomon. This same Spirit of Love also says: *"For to him that is little, mercy will be shown"* [see Wis 6:7]. The Prophet Isaiah reveals in His name that on the last day: *"God shall feed his flock like a shepherd; he shall gather together the lambs with his arm, and shall take them up in his bosom"* [see Isa 40:11]. As though these promises were not sufficient, this same prophet whose gaze was already plunged into the eternal depths cried out in the Lord's name: *"As one whom a mother caresses, so will I comfort you; you shall be carried at the breasts and upon the knees they will caress you"* [see Isa 66:12-13].

After having listened to words such as these, dear godmother [i.e., her sister Marie, a nun in the same community], there is nothing to do but to be silent and to weep with gratitude and love. Ah! if all weak and imperfect souls felt what the least of souls feels, that is, the soul of your little Thérèse, not one would despair of reaching the summit of the mount of love. Jesus does not demand great actions from us but simply *surrender* and *gratitude*. . . .

See, then, all that Jesus lays claim to from us; He has no need of our works but only of our *love*, for the same God who declares He *has no need to tell us when He is hungry* did not fear *to beg* for a little water from the Samaritan woman. He was thirsty. But when He said: *"Give me to drink,"* it was the *love* of His poor creature the Creator of the universe was seeking. He was thirsty for love. Ah! I feel it more than ever before, Jesus is *parched*, for He meets only the ungrateful and indifferent among His disciples in the world, and among *His own disciples*, alas, He finds few hearts who surrender to Him without reservations, who understand the real tenderness of His infinite Love. . . .

You asked me, dear Sister, to write to you *my dream* and *"my little* doctrine" as you call it. I did this in these following pages, but so poorly it seems to me you will not understand it. Perhaps you will find my expressions exaggerated. Ah! pardon me, this will have to be put down to my poor style, for I assure you there is *no exaggeration* in my *little soul*. Within it all is calm and at rest.

When writing these words, I shall address them to Jesus since this makes it easier for me to express my thoughts, but it does not prevent them from being very poorly expressed!

J.M.J.T.
September 8, 1896

(To my dear Sister Marie of the Sacred Heart)

O Jesus, my Beloved, who could express the tenderness and sweetness with which You are guiding my soul! It pleases You to cause the rays of Your grace to shine through even in the midst of the darkest storm [i.e., her "trial of faith"]! . . .

At the first glimmerings of dawn I was (in a dream) in a kind of gallery and there were several other persons, but they were at a distance. Our Mother was alone near me. Suddenly, without seeing how they had entered, I saw three Carmelites dressed in their mantles and long veils. It appeared to me they were coming for our

Mother, but what I did understand clearly was that they came from heaven. In the depths of my heart I cried out: "Oh! how happy I would be if I could see the face of one of these Carmelites!" Then, as though my prayer were heard by her, the tallest of the saints advanced toward me; immediately I fell to my knees. Oh! what happiness! the Carmelite *raised her veil or rather she raised it and covered me with it.* Without the least hesitation, I recognized *Venerable Anne of Jesus*, Foundress of Carmel in France. Her face was beautiful but with an immaterial beauty. No ray escaped from it and still, in spite of the veil which covered us both, I saw this heavenly face suffused with an unspeakably gentle light, a light it didn't receive from without but was produced from within. . . .

Seeing myself so tenderly loved, I dared to pronounce these words: "O Mother! I beg you, tell me whether God will leave me for a long time on earth. Will He come soon to get me?" Smiling tenderly, the saint whispered: *"Yes, soon, soon, I promise you."* I added: "Mother, tell me further if God is not asking something more of me than my poor little actions and desires. Is He content with me?" The saint's face took on an expression *incomparably more tender* than the first time she spoke to me. Her look and her caresses were the sweetest of answers. However, she said to me: "God asks no other thing from you. He is content, very content!" After again embracing me with more love than the tenderest of mothers has ever given to her child, I saw her leave. My heart was filled with joy, and then I remembered my Sisters, and I wanted to ask her some favors for them, but alas, I awoke!

O Jesus, the storm was no longer raging, heaven was calm and serene. I *believed*, I *felt* there was a *heaven* and that this *heaven* is peopled with souls who actually love me, who consider me their child. This impression remains in my heart, and this all the more because I was, up until then, *absolutely indifferent to Venerable Mother Anne of Jesus.* I never invoked her in prayer and the thought of her never came to my mind except when I heard others speak of her, which was seldom. And when I understood to what a degree *she loved me*, how *indifferent* I had been toward her, my heart was filled with love and gratitude, not only for the Saint who had visited me but for all the blessed inhabitants of heaven.

O my Beloved! this grace was only the prelude to the greatest graces You wished to bestow upon me. Allow me, my only Love, to recall them to You today, *today* which is the sixth anniversary of *our union.* Ah! my Jesus, pardon me if I am unreasonable in wishing to express my desires and longings which reach even unto infinity.

Pardon me and heal my soul by giving her what she longs for so much!

To be Your *Spouse*, to be a *Carmelite*, and by my union with You to be the *Mother* of souls, should not this suffice me? And yet it is not so. No doubt, these three privileges sum up my true *vocation*: *Carmelite, Spouse, Mother*, and yet I feel within me other *vocations*. I feel the *vocation* of the WARRIOR, THE PRIEST, THE APOSTLE, THE DOCTOR, THE MARTYR. Finally, I feel the need and the desire of carrying out the most heroic deeds for *You, O Jesus*. I feel within my soul the courage of the *Crusader*, the *Papal Guard*, and I would want to die on the field of battle in defense of the Church.

I feel in me the *vocation of* the PRIEST. With what love, O Jesus, I would carry You in my hands when, at my voice, You would come down from heaven. And with what love would I give You to souls! But alas! while desiring to be a *Priest*, I admire and envy the humility of St. Francis of Assisi and I feel the *vocation* of imitating him in refusing the sublime dignity of the *Priesthood*.

O Jesus, my Love, my Life, how can I combine these contrasts? How can I realize the desires of my poor *little soul*?

Ah! in spite of my littleness, I would like to enlighten souls as did the *Prophets* and the *Doctors*. I have the *vocation of the Apostle*. I would like to travel over the whole earth to preach Your Name and to plant Your glorious Cross on infidel soil. But *O my Beloved*, one mission alone would not be sufficient for me, I would want to preach the Gospel on all the five continents simultaneously and even to the most remote isles. I would be a missionary, not for a few years only but from the beginning of creation until the consummation of the ages. But above all, O my Beloved Savior, I would shed my blood for You even to the very last drop.

Martyrdom was the dream of my youth and this dream has grown with me within Carmel's cloisters. But here again, I feel that my dream is a folly, for I cannot confine myself to desiring *one kind* of martyrdom. To satisfy me I need *all*. Like You, my Adorable Spouse, I would be scourged and crucified. I would die flayed like St. Bartholomew. I would be plunged into boiling oil like St. John; I would undergo all the tortures inflicted upon the martyrs. With St. Agnes and St. Cecilia, I would present my neck to the sword, and like Joan of Arc, my dear sister, I would whisper at the stake Your Name, O JESUS. When thinking of the torments which will be the lot of Christians at the time of Anti-Christ, I feel my heart leap with joy and I would that these torments be reserved for me. Jesus, Jesus, if I wanted to write all my desires, I would have to borrow Your *Book of Life*, for in it are reported all the actions of all the saints, and I would accomplish all of them for You.

O my Jesus! what is your answer to all my follies? Is there a soul more *little*, more powerless than mine? Nevertheless even because of my weakness, it has pleased You, O Lord, to grant my *little childish desires* and You desire, today, to grant other desires that are *greater* than the universe.

During my meditation, my desires caused me a veritable martyrdom, and I opened the Epistles of St. Paul to find some kind of answer. Chapters 12 and 13 of the First Epistle to the Corinthians fell under my eyes. I read there, in the first of these chapters, that all cannot be apostles, prophets, doctors, etc., that the Church is composed of different members, and that the eye cannot be the hand at one and the same time. The answer was clear, but it did not fulfill my desires and gave me no peace. But just as Mary Magdalene found what she was seeking by always stooping down and looking into the empty tomb, so I, abasing myself to the very depths of my nothingness, raised myself so high that I was able to attain my end. Without becoming discouraged, I continued my reading, and this sentence consoled me: *"Yet strive after THE BETTER GIFTS, and I point out to you* a yet more excellent way." And the Apostle explains how all *the most PERFECT gifts* are nothing without LOVE. That *Charity is the EXCELLENT WAY* that leads most surely to God.

I finally had rest. Considering the mystical body of the Church, I had not recognized myself in any of the members described by St. Paul, or rather I desired to see myself in them *all. Charity* gave me the key to my vocation. I understood that if the Church had a body composed of different members, the most necessary and most noble of all could not be lacking to it, and so I understood that the Church *had a Heart and that this Heart was BURNING WITH LOVE. I understood it was Love alone* that made the Church's members act, that if Love ever became extinct, apostles would not preach the Gospel and martyrs would not shed their blood. I understood that LOVE COMPRISED ALL VOCATIONS, THAT LOVE WAS EVERYTHING, THAT IT EMBRACED ALL TIMES AND PLACES. . . . IN A WORD, THAT IT WAS ETERNAL!

Then, in the excess of my delirious joy, I cried out: O Jesus, my Love. . . . my *vocation*, at last I have found it. . . . MY VOCATION IS LOVE!

Yes, I have found my place in the Church and it is You, O my God, who have given me this place; in the heart of the Church, my

Mother, I shall be *Love*. Thus I shall be everything, and thus my dream will be realized.

Why speak of a delirious joy? No, this expression is not exact, for it was rather the calm and serene peace of the navigator perceiving the beacon which must lead him to the port. . . . O luminous Beacon of love, I know how to reach You, I have found the secret of possessing Your flame.

I am only a child, powerless and weak, and yet it is my weakness that gives me the boldness of offering myself as *VICTIM of Your Love, O Jesus!* In times past, victims, pure and spotless, were the only ones accepted by the Strong and Powerful God. To satisfy Divine *Justice*, perfect victims were necessary, but the *law of Love* has succeeded to the law of fear, and *Love* has chosen me as a holocaust, me, a weak and imperfect creature. Is not this choice worthy of *Love*? Yes, in order that Love be fully satisfied, it is necessary that It lower Itself, and that It lower Itself to nothingness and transform this nothingness into *fire*.

O Jesus, I know it, love is repaid by love alone, and so I searched and I found the way to solace my heart by giving you Love for Love. "Make use of the riches which render one unjust in order to make friends who will receive you into everlasting dwellings" [see Luke 16:9]. Behold, Lord, the counsel You give Your disciples after having told them that "The children of this world, in relation to their own generation, are more prudent than are the children of the light" [see Luke 16:8]. A child of light, I understood that *my desires of being everything*, of embracing all vocations, were the riches that would be able to render me unjust, so I made use of them *to make friends.* Remembering the prayer of Elisha to his Father Elijah when he dared to ask him for HIS DOUBLE SPIRIT [see 2 Kgs 2:9], I presented myself before the angels and saints and I said to them: "I am the smallest of creatures; I know my misery and my feebleness, but I know also how much noble and generous hearts love to do good. I beg you then, O Blessed Inhabitants of heaven, I beg you to ADOPT ME AS YOUR CHILD. *To you alone will be the glory* which you will make me merit, but deign to answer my prayer. It is bold, I know; however, I dare to ask you to obtain for me YOUR TWOFOLD LOVE."

Jesus, I cannot fathom the depths of my request; I would be afraid to find myself overwhelmed under the weight of my bold desires. My excuse is that I am a *child*, and children do not reflect on the meaning of their words; however, their parents, once they are placed upon a throne and possess immense treasures, do not hesitate to satisfy the desires of the *little ones* whom they love as much as they love themselves. To please them they do foolish things, even going to the extent of *becoming weak* for them. Well, I am the *Child of the Church* and the Church is a Queen since she is Your Spouse, O divine King of kings. The heart of a child does not seek riches and glory (even the glory of heaven). She understands that this glory belongs by right to her brothers, the angels and saints. Her own glory will be the reflected glory which shines on her Mother's forehead. What this child asks for is Love. She knows only one thing: to love You, O Jesus. Astounding works are forbidden to her; she cannot preach the Gospel, shed her blood; but what does it matter since her brothers work in her stead and she, *a little child*, stays very close to the *throne* of the King and Queen. She *loves* in her brothers' place while they do the fighting. But how will she prove her *love* since *love* is proved by works? Well, the little child *will strew flowers*, she will perfume the royal throne with their *sweet scents*, and she will sing in her silvery tones the canticle of *Love*.

Yes, my Beloved, this is how my life will be consumed. I have no other means of proving my love for you other than that of strewing flowers, that is, not allowing one little sacrifice to escape, not one look, one word, profiting by all the smallest things and doing them through love. I desire to suffer for love and even to rejoice through love; and in this way I shall strew flowers before Your throne. I shall not come upon one without *unpetalling* it for You. While I am strewing my flowers, I shall sing, for could one cry while doing such a joyous action? I shall sing even when I must gather my flowers in the midst of thorns, and my song will be all the more melodious in proportion to the length and sharpness of the thorns.

O Jesus, of what use will my flowers be to You? Ah! I know very well that this fragrant shower, these fragile, worthless petals, these songs of love from the littlest of hearts will charm You. Yes, these nothings will please You. They will bring a smile to the Church Triumphant. She will gather up my flowers unpetalled *through love* and have them pass through Your own divine hands, O Jesus. And this Church in heaven, desirous of playing with her little child, will cast these flowers, which are now infinitely valuable because of Your divine touch, upon the Church Suffering in order to extinguish its flames and upon the Church Militant in order to gain the victory for it! . . .

How can a soul as imperfect as mine aspire to the possession of the plenitude of *Love*? O Jesus, *my first and only Friend*, You whom

I love UNIQUELY, explain this mystery to me! Why do You not re-serve these great aspirations for great souls, for the *Eagles* that soar in the heights?

I look upon myself as a *weak little bird*, with only a light down as covering. I am not an *eagle*, but I have only an eagle's EYES AND HEART. In spite of my extreme littleness I still dare to gaze upon the Divine Sun, the Sun of Love, and my heart feels within it all the aspirations of an *Eagle*.

The little bird wills *to fly* toward the bright Sun that attracts its eye, imitating its brothers, the eagles, whom it sees climbing up toward the Divine Furnace of the Holy Trinity. But alas! the only thing it can do is *raise its little wings*; to fly is not within its *little* power!

What then will become of it? Will it die of sorrow at seeing itself so weak? Oh no! the little bird will not even be troubled. With bold surrender, it wishes to remain gazing upon its Divine Sun. Nothing will frighten it, neither wind nor rain, and if dark clouds come and hide the Star of Love, the little bird will not change its place because it knows that beyond the clouds its bright Sun still shines on and that its brightness is not eclipsed for a single instant.

At times the little bird's heart is assailed by the storm, and it seems it should believe in the existence of no other thing except the clouds surrounding it; this is the moment of *perfect joy* for the *poor little weak creature*. And what joy it experiences when remaining there just the same! and gazing at the Invisible Light which remains hidden from its faith! . . .

Jesus, I am too little to perform great actions, and my own *folly* is this: to trust that Your Love will accept me as a victim. My *folly* consists in begging the eagles, my brothers, to obtain for me the favor of flying toward the Sun of Love with the *Divine Eagle's own wings*!

As long as You desire it, O my Beloved, Your little bird will remain without strength and without wings and will always stay with its gaze fixed upon You. It wants to be *fascinated* by Your divine glance. It wants to become the *prey* of Your Love. One day I hope that You, the Adorable Eagle, will come to fetch me, Your little bird; and ascending with it to the Furnace of Love, You will plunge it for all eternity into the burning Abyss of this Love to which it has of-fered itself as victim.

O Jesus! why can't I tell all *little souls* how unspeakable is Your condescension? I feel that if You found a soul weaker and littler than mine, which is impossible, You would be pleased to grant it still greater favors, provided it abandoned itself with total confidence to Your Infinite Mercy. But why do I desire to communicate Your secrets of Love, O Jesus, for was it not You alone who taught them to me, and can You not reveal them to others? Yes, I know it, and I beg You to do it. I beg You to cast Your Divine Glance upon a great number of *little* souls. I beg You to choose a legion of *little* Victims worthy of Your LOVE!

The very little Sister Thérèse of the Child Jesus

and the Holy Face, unworthy Carmelite religious.[2]

Elizabeth of the Trinity (1880–1906)

Elizabeth Catez was born in the military camp of Avor, near Bourges (France), on July 18, 1880, after a long and difficult delivery. Her father, Joseph Catez, was a captain in the eighth squadron of the Equipment and Maintenance Corps. In 1882 he was reassigned to Dijon, where a second child, Marguerite (known as "Guite"), was born. Captain Catez died in 1887, leaving his wife Marie to raise their two daughters on a modest military pension.

Normally a good and warmhearted child, the young Elizabeth nevertheless showed a fiery determination to get what she wanted and could throw alarming temper tantrums when frustrated. From the time of her first confession at the age of seven, however, she began applying that same determination toward mastering her lively temperament. The following year she was enrolled for musical studies at the Conservatory, and she eventually developed into an outstanding musician with a promising future as a concert pianist, though the rest of her education was relatively neglected.

Elizabeth made her first communion on August 19, 1891, with a profound awareness of God's presence in the sacrament she had just received. That same evening she also paid her first visit to the Carmel of Dijon, where the prioress explained that her name meant "house of God." Gradually Elizabeth began to focus upon the divine indwelling, which became the hallmark of her spiritual life. Not without great effort, she became more patient and calm.

Her teenage years brought a growing attraction to the contemplative vocation of the Discalced Carmelite nuns, and already at nineteen she was eagerly reading Thérèse's *Story of a Soul*, published only two years earlier. However, at her mother's insistence, Elizabeth postponed entry into religious life and devoted herself instead to the typical activities of a girl of her age and social position: traveling with her mother and sister, going to musical parties with friends, playing games of tennis, participating in the parish choir, helping to run a youth club for the children of workers in a local tobacco factory, and assisting with catechism classes in the parish.

Finally she received permission to enter the Carmel of Dijon at the age of twenty-one, and was given the religious name "Elizabeth of the Trinity," which she came to see as a providential summary of her whole vocation. She devoted herself to the normal routine of the monastery, meanwhile immersing herself in Scripture, in the silent prayer of Carmel, and in pondering the life of the Trinity within her soul and the souls of others. Among her favorite authors were Thérèse of Lisieux, John of the Cross, Ruusbroec, and Paul the Apostle. Her "Prayer to the Trinity," quoted in the *Catechism of the Catholic Church*, was written spontaneously after a sudden inspiration in 1904, and has become one of the most famous prayers of modern times. Other writings from her years in Carmel include two sets of ten-day-retreat notes (one written for her sister Guite), various prayers and verses, and a series of letters written to friends and family.

Though her religious life was outwardly uneventful, the interior peace and joy that had sometimes eluded her as a young child continued to grow. As she wrote to the mother of a friend: "It seems to me that I have found my heaven on earth, since heaven is God, and God is in my soul. The day I understood that, everything became clear to me" (L 122).[1]

In her final years, her focus on the divine indwelling of the Trinity reached new depths as she "rediscovered" the passage from Ephesians about the Christian call to become "praises of God's glory" (see Eph 1:6-14). Elizabeth decided that this was to be her "new name in heaven" (cf. Rev 2:17) and began signing her letters *Laudem gloriae*. After a long and painful struggle with Addison's disease, which she endured with remarkable serenity, she finally succumbed to the illness on November 9, 1906.

Elizabeth's posthumous career was similar to that of her "sister in the Spirit," Thérèse of Lisieux. The usual obituary letter, with selections from Elizabeth's texts, generated such a positive response that the prioress of Dijon Carmel, Mother Germaine, decided to bring out a biography with more extensive selections. Published in October 1909, *Soeur Elisabeth de la Trinité, religieuse Carmélite, 1880–1906: Souvenirs* quickly sold out and was reprinted numerous times; it has since been translated into at least ten languages. In 1939 the noted Dominican author Marie-Michel Philipon published *The Spiritual Doctrine of Elizabeth of the Trinity*, bringing her message to the attention of Catholic scholars. Some years later, one of the great Catholic theologians of the twentieth century, Hans Urs von Balthasar, likewise devoted a major theological study to her, noting her special mission to the modern world, and writing that, in Elizabeth, "contemplative faith expands to its full biblical dimensions."[2] More recently, Elizabeth was beatified by Pope John Paul II on November 25, 1984. Today she is especially appreciated by theologians, spiritual writers, and ordinary Christians who recognize the importance of developing a more explicitly trinitarian spirituality for our times.

For the centenary of her birth in 1980, a critical edition of Elizabeth's writings was prepared by Conrad De Meester, later followed by an up-to-date biography based on a thorough review of all the testimonies and archival materials. These now permit a more complete and balanced picture of this young woman, who was at once thoroughly human and deeply mystical. When asked toward the end of her life if she expected to have a heavenly "mission," like Thérèse, Elizabeth wrote: "I think that in heaven my mission will be to draw souls by helping them to go out of themselves in order to cling to God by a wholly simple and loving movement, and to keep them in this great silence within, which will allow God to communicate himself to them and to transform them into himself" (L 335). The sentiments expressed in her final letter, addressed to her childhood friend Charles Hallo, could as well be directed toward contemporary readers: "Before going to heaven your Elizabeth wants to tell you once more of her deep affection for you and her plan to help you, day by day, until you join her. . . . You will encounter obstacles on the path of life, but do not be discouraged, call me. Yes, call your little sister; in this way you will increase her happiness in heaven; she will be so glad to help you triumph, to remain worthy of God" (L 342).

Selections here include Elizabeth's "Prayer to the Trinity," excerpts from her letters, and a section of her retreat notes, "Heaven in Faith," written for her sister Guite.

"Prayer to the Trinity"

O my God, Trinity whom I adore; help me to forget myself entirely that I may be established in You as still and as peaceful as if my soul were already in eternity. May nothing trouble my peace or make me leave You, O my Unchanging One, but may each minute carry me further into the depths of Your mystery. Give peace to my soul; make it Your heaven, Your beloved dwelling and Your resting place. May I never leave You there alone but be wholly present, my faith wholly vigilant, wholly adoring, and wholly surrendered to Your creative Action.

O my beloved Christ, crucified by love, I wish to be a bride for Your Heart; I wish to cover You with glory; I wish to love You . . . even unto death! But I feel my weakness, and I ask You to "clothe me with Yourself," to identify my soul with all the movements of Your Soul, to overwhelm me, to possess me, to substitute yourself for me that my life may be but a radiance of Your Life. Come into me as Adorer, as Restorer, as Savior. O Eternal Word, Word of my God, I want to spend my life in listening to You, to become wholly teachable that I may learn all from You. Then, through all nights, all voids, all helplessness, I want to gaze on You always and remain in Your great light. O my beloved Star, so fascinate me that I may not withdraw from Your radiance.

O consuming Fire, Spirit of Love, "come upon me," and create in my soul a kind of incarnation of the Word: that I may be another humanity for Him in which He can renew His whole Mystery. And You, O Father, bend lovingly over Your poor little creature; "cover her with Your shadow," seeing in her only the "Beloved in whom You are well pleased."

O my Three, my All, my Beatitude, infinite Solitude, Immensity in which I lose myself, I surrender myself to You as Your prey. Bury Yourself in me that I may bury myself in You until I depart to contemplate in Your light the abyss of Your greatness.[3]

From Letter 123 (June 19, 1902) to a Young Friend, Françoise de Sourdon

Yes, my darling, I am praying for you and I keep you in my soul quite close to God, in that little inner sanctuary where I find Him at every hour of the day and night. I'm never alone: my Christ is always there praying in me, and I pray with Him. You grieve me, my Framboise; I can well see that you're unhappy and I assure you it's your own fault. Be at peace. I don't believe you're crazy yet, just nervous and overexcited, and when you're like that, you make the others suffer too. Ah, if I could teach you the secret of happiness as God has taught it to me. You say I don't have any worries or sufferings; it's true that I'm very happy, but if you only knew that a person can be just as happy even when she is crossed. We must always keep our eyes on God. In the beginning it's necessary to make an effort when we're just boiling inside, but quite gently, with patience and God's help, we get there in the end.

You must build a little cell within your soul as I do. Remember that God is there and enter it from time to time; when you feel nervous or you're unhappy, quickly seek refuge there and tell the Master all about it. Ah, if you got to know Him a little, prayer wouldn't bore you any more; to me it seems to be rest, relaxation. We come quite simply to the One we love, stay close to Him like a little child in the arms of its mother, and we let our heart go. You used to love sitting very close to me and telling me your secrets; that is just how you must go [to] Him; if only you knew how well He understands. . . . You wouldn't suffer any more if you understood that. It is the secret of life in Carmel: the life of a Carmelite is a communion with God from morning to evening, and from evening to morning. If He did not fill our cells and our cloisters, ah! how empty they would be! But through everything, [we] see Him, for we bear Him within us, and our life is an anticipated Heaven. I ask God to teach you all these secrets, and I am keeping you in my little cell; for your part, keep me in yours, and that way we will never be parted. I love you much, my Framboise, and I'd like you to be completely good and completely in the peace of the children of God.

Your Elizabeth of the Trinity[4]

From Letter 133 (August 7, 1902) to a Young Friend, Germaine de Gemeaux

My dear little Germaine,

Thank you for your nice letter; it made me happy. . . . A Carmelite, my darling, is a soul who has *gazed on the Crucified*, who has seen Him offering Himself to His Father as a Victim for souls and, recollecting herself in this great vision of the charity of Christ, has understood the passionate love of His soul, and has wanted to give herself as He did! . . . And on the mountain of Carmel, in silence, in solitude, in prayer that never ends, for it continues through everything, the Carmelite already lives as if in Heaven: "by *God alone*." The same One who will one day be her beatitude and will fully satisfy her in glory is already giving Himself to her. He never leaves her, He dwells within her soul; more than that, the two of them are *but one*. So she *hungers for silence* that she may always listen, penetrate ever deeper into His Infinite Being. She is identified with Him whom she loves, she finds Him everywhere; she sees Him shining through all things! Is this not Heaven on earth! You carry this Heaven within your soul, my little Germaine, you can be a

Carmelite already, for Jesus recognizes the Carmelite from *within*, by her soul. Don't ever leave Him, do everything beneath His divine gaze, and remain wholly joyful in His peace and love, making those around you happy!

A Dieu, my good little Germaine. I've asked our Reverend Mother [the prioress] for a blessing for you, and I'm delighted to send it; our Mother is so good! Like you, she is called Germaine "of Jesus."

Please give my respectful and very affectionate greetings to Monsieur and Madame de Gemeaux. A big kiss to Yvonne, and for you, the best of my soul.

Elizabeth of the Trinity[5]

From "Heaven in Faith," Tenth Day

[First prayer]

38. "Si scires donum Dei . . ." "If you knew the gift of God," Christ said one evening to the Samaritan woman [see John 4:10]. But what is this gift of God if not Himself? And, the beloved disciple tells us: "He came to His own and His own did not accept Him" [see John 1:11]. St. John the Baptist could still say to many souls these words of reproach: "There is one in the midst of you, '*in you*,' whom you do not know" [see John 1:26].

39. "If you knew the gift of God. . . ." There is one who knew this gift of God, one who did not lose one particle of it, one who was so pure, so luminous that she seemed to be the Light itself: "Speculum justitiae" [mirror of justice]. One whose life was so simple, so lost in God that there is hardly anything we can say about it.

"Virgo fidelis," that is, "Faithful Virgin," "who kept all these things in her heart" [see Luke 2:19, 51]. She remained so little, so recollected in God's presence, in the seclusion of the temple, that she drew down upon herself the delight of the Holy Trinity: "Because He has looked upon the lowliness of His servant, henceforth all generations shall call me blessed!" [see Luke 1:48]. The Father bending down to this beautiful creature, who was so unaware of her own beauty, willed that she be the Mother in time of Him whose Father he is in eternity. Then the Spirit of love who presides over all of God's works came upon her: the Virgin said her *fiat*: "Behold the servant of the Lord, be it be done to me according to your word" [see Luke 1:38], and the greatest of mysteries was accomplished. By the descent of the Word in her, Mary became forever God's prey.

40. It seems to me that the attitude of the Virgin during the months that elapsed between the Annunciation and the Nativity is the model for interior souls, those whom God has chosen to live within, in the depths of the bottomless abyss. In what peace, in what recollection Mary lent herself to everything she did! How even the most trivial things were divinized by her! For through it all the Virgin remained the adorer of the gifts of God! This did not prevent her from spending herself outwardly when it was a matter of charity; the Gospel tells us that Mary went in haste to the mountains of Judea to visit her cousin Elizabeth [Luke 1:39-40]. Never did the ineffable vision that she contemplated within herself in any way diminish her outward charity. For, a pious author says, if contemplation "continues towards praise and towards the eternity of its Lord, it possesses unity and will not lose it. If an order from heaven arrives, contemplation turns towards men, sympathizes with their needs, is inclined towards all their miseries; it must cry and be fruitful. It illuminates like fire, and like it, it burns, it absorbs and devours, lifting up to Heaven what it has devoured. And when it has finished its work here below, it rises, burning with its fire, and takes up again the road on high" [quotation from Ruusbroec].

[Second prayer]

41. "We have been predestined by the decree of Him who works all things according to the counsel of His will, so that we may be *the praise of His glory*" [see Eph 1:11-12].

It is St. Paul who tells us this, St. Paul who was instructed by God himself. How do we realize this great dream of the Heart of our God, this immutable will for our souls? In a word, how do we correspond to our vocation and become perfect *Praises of Glory* of the Most Holy Trinity?

42. "In Heaven" each soul is a praise of glory of the Father, the Word, and the Holy Spirit, for each soul is established in pure love and "lives no longer its own life, but the life of God." Then it knows Him, St. Paul says, as it is known by Him [1 Cor 13:12]. In other words "its intellect is the intellect of God, its will the will of God, its love the very love of God. In reality it is the Spirit of love and of strength who transforms the soul, for to Him it has been given to supply what is lacking to the soul," as St. Paul says again [cf. Rom 8:26]. "He works in it this glorious transformation." St. John of the Cross affirms that the "soul surrendered to love, through the strength of the Holy Spirit, is not far from being raised to the degree

of which we have just spoken," even here below! This is what I call a perfect praise of glory!

43. A praise of glory is a soul that lives in God, that loves Him with a pure and disinterested love, without seeking itself in the sweetness of this love; that loves Him beyond all His gifts and desires the good of the Object thus loved. Now how do we *effectively* desire and will good to God if not in accomplishing His will since this will orders everything for His greater glory? Thus the soul must surrender itself to this will completely, passionately, so as to will nothing else but what God wills.

A praise of glory is a soul of silence that remains like a lyre under the mysterious touch of the Holy Spirit so that he may draw from it divine harmonies; it knows that suffering is a string that produces still more beautiful sounds, so it loves to see this string on its instrument that it may more delightfully move the Heart of its God.

A praise of glory is a soul that gazes on God in faith and simplicity; it is a reflector of all that He is; it is like a bottomless abyss into which he can flow and expand; it is also like a crystal through which he can radiate and contemplate all His perfections and His own splendor. A soul which thus permits the divine being to satisfy in itself His need to communicate "all that He is and all that He has," is in reality the praise of glory of all His gifts.

Finally, a praise of glory is one who is always giving thanks. Each of her acts, her movements, her thoughts, her aspirations, at the same time that they are rooting her more deeply in love, are like an echo of the eternal Sanctus.

44. In the heaven of glory the blessed have no rest "day or night, saying: Holy, holy, holy is the Lord God Almighty. . . . They fall down and worship Him who lives forever and ever. . . ."

In the heaven of her soul, the praise of glory has already begun her work of eternity. Her song is uninterrupted, for she is under the action of the Holy Spirit who effects everything in her, and although she is not always aware of it, for the weakness of nature does not allow her to be established in God without distractions, she always sings, she always adores, for she has, so to speak, wholly passed into praise and love in her passion for the glory of her God. In the heaven of our soul let us be praises of glory of the Holy Trinity, praises of love of our Immaculate Mother. One day the veil will fall, we will be introduced into the eternal courts, and there we will sing in the bosom of infinite Love. And God will give us "the new name promised to the Victor" [see Rev 2:17]. What will it be?

LAUDEM GLORIAE[6]

Titus Brandsma (1881–1942)

Anno Sjoerd Brandsma was born in Friesland in northwest Holland on February 23, 1881. His parents, Titus and Tjitsje Brandsma, were farmers and devout Catholics in a largely Protestant region, and passed on their faith to their six children, five of whom eventually entered religious life. At the age of eleven Anno entered the minor seminary of the Franciscans, but because of continual health problems, he was encouraged to seek a less demanding life. After some time at home, he tried religious life once more, this time with the Carmelites of the Ancient Observance at Boxmeer. Here he entered the novitiate on September 17, 1898, and took the religious name of Titus, after his father. He soon discovered within himself a gift for writing, and during his student days was already involved in many literary projects, developing a Carmelite magazine and publishing in a variety of journals. In 1901 he produced his first book, and anthology of texts from St. Teresa of Avila, in whom he developed a lifelong interest.

Titus was ordained to the priesthood on June 17, 1905, but his assignment to Rome for advanced studies was delayed for a year after he annoyed one of his professors during oral examinations. Nevertheless, he graduated from the Pontifical Gregorian University of Rome with a doctorate in philosophy on October 25, 1909, and then returned to the Netherlands to teach. At first he was assigned to teach the Carmelite seminarians in Oss, where he helped reorganize the program of studies. He took an active role in the foundation of the Katholieke Universiteit Nijmegen (now Radboud University) in 1923, the first modern Catholic university in the Netherlands, and was asked to join the faculty as a professor of philosophy and mysticism. He also supervised the nearby construction of a new Carmelite monastery for the friars, where he was assigned and served for a time as superior. Titus had a keen interest in the spirituality of his own country and region, publishing numerous studies and manuscripts of medieval mystics of the Low Countries, and even cofounding a scholarly journal dedicated to this topic. He was also involved in the Apostleship for the Reunion of Eastern Churches and the Catholic Journalists' Association. Yet despite these many commitments and repeated bouts of ill health, he was known as a warm and humble friar who made himself available to anyone who approached him, from the poor to the professors, and always tried to assist them in their needs.

During the academic year 1932–1933, Brandsma was elected to serve as the university's *Rector Magnificus*, and in this position he represented the university in relations with the Dutch government and the Vatican. In 1935 he was invited on a lecture tour in the United States. He was particularly impressed by the grandeur of Niagara Falls, of which he observed, "I see not only the beauty of nature, the immeasurable potentialities of water, but I see God at work in his creation, in his revelation of love."[1] His talks became the basis for his best-known work, *Carmelite Mysticism: Historical Sketches*. He was also asked to write the article on Carmelite spirituality for the *Dictionnaire de Spiritualité*. Both of these texts are among the earliest attempts to present a systematic historical overview of Carmel's spiritual heritage.

Titus was an early and outspoken critic of the ideology of National Socialism. After the Germans invaded the Netherlands in May 1940, they began pressuring newspapers to accept Nazi advertisements and propaganda for publication. The Catholic bishops refused, and as spiritual advisor to the Catholic journalists, Titus was entrusted with the task of conveying this decision to the Catholic editors of Holland. Titus had met with fourteen editors before he was arrested by the Gestapo in January 1942 and sent initially to the prison at Scheveningen, near The Hague. Despite the hardships of his imprisonment, Titus was at peace and found the time for prayer and solitude he had long been seeking. During his seven weeks at Scheveningen, Titus continued his writing, beginning work on a biography of St. Teresa and developing a series of meditations on the Stations of the Cross, among other texts.

On March 12 Titus was transferred with roughly one hundred others to the prison camp of Amersfoort, where the treatment was far more brutal; prisoners were put to work cutting and clearing trees, and many fell sick. Despite prohibitions against priests exercising their ministry, Titus secretly heard confessions, visited the sick, and gave spiritual guidance to many fellow prisoners. Toward the end of April, Titus was sent back to Amersfoort for further questioning, and then on to the infamous Dachau concentration camp, where his health began to decline drastically, due to overwork, meager rations, and constant beatings. Through it all, Titus maintained a serene courage and did what he could to encourage others. Finally he became so sick that he was taken to the camp hospital, where doctors performed horrible experiments on the patients. On July 26, 1942, he was given a lethal injection, just two weeks before Edith Stein was executed at Auschwitz.

Titus Brandsma was beatified as a martyr by John Paul II on November 3, 1985. His example, like that of Edith Stein, continues to inspire many, especially in his native Holland, where in 2005 the residents of Nijmegen chose him as the greatest citizen who had lived there. Numerous churches, schools, and scholarly institutions have been named in his honor. His life clearly demonstrates that Carmelite spirituality and mysticism is entirely compatible with profound scholarship and deep engagement with contemporary social and political issues.

From *Carmelite Mysticism: Historical Sketches*

Lecture X: The Apostolate of Carmelite Mysticism

St. Thérèse Draws the World to Carmel

Now, as never before, the eyes of the world are turned toward Carmel. In its garden a flower has opened its petals, of such ravishing beauty that countless numbers have directed their step hither, wishing to remain in the pleasance where such lovely flowers bloom. They examine anew the secrets of this beauty and once more ask themselves of what the loveliness of Carmel consists. This one flower has in turn drawn attention to so many others that the world has been filled with admiration for life in Carmel and on all sides new convents have been founded in order to fill the world with those sanctuaries in which one may live so saintly a life.

I refer to the flower of Lisieux, Little St. Thérèse of the Child Jesus and of the Holy Face, whose name has flown over the world, whose life's story has been translated into all languages, who is called by God to add new lustre to the glory of Carmel.

Characteristics of Her Life

To describe in a few minutes a life so filled with proofs of intercourse with God, with virtue and abundant infusion of grace, is next to impossible. However, I will try to summarise briefly that which is most characteristic in her life and which at the same time shows her to be one of the loveliest and most eloquent examples of the school of Carmel.

Practice of the Presence of God

In the first place surely, comes her desire to converse with God, to lead a higher life for and through Him. She thoroughly understands that the living God who fills heaven and earth, and at the same time dwells in our innermost heart must be the object of our thoughts and love. Most striking in her life is, therefore, her living in God's presence. She may justly repeat the words of Elias the Prophet: "God lives and I stand before His face." . . .

Her Love of God

As a result of this contemplation of God, love for God wells up in her with irresistible power. Her spirit has been called a spirit of love and so it is. . . . In order to remain firm in our love towards Him, she wants us continually to contemplate God's works and notice the proofs of His love. It is noteworthy that she very eagerly admires Nature and the loveliness of our earthly creation, that she enjoys the magnificence of flowers, the glory of a starry sky, but yet she wishes us to leave all this after a short time in order to mount up through this to God. They are a means, not an end.

Her Humility and Simplicity

From her life before the Face of God, and her love and admiration for His power and majesty a third idea springs forth, fitting remarkably well into the scheme of the Order. I mean the idea of her own nothingness compared with God, her wonderful consciousness of her own smallness and slightness, her humility and her conception of herself as being only a child. This characteristic is often met with in the older saints of the Order, as simplicity and humility are the special hallmarks of the Order. . . . It is so often said by various Carmelite spiritual authors—and it tallies so well with our spirit— that the Order is not called to do great things, to be spoken of, but to make itself loved and attractive by doing ordinary things well, without much talking or noise; to live in a certain seclusion for and with God more than for and with men; to attach value to what God desires more than to what man sets high store by. . . .

Her Conformity to the Will of God

She is quite in the hollow of God's hand and surrenders herself absolutely to what His Providence decrees. She strives after, as perfectly as possible, a conformity to the divine will. . . . The image of the rose shedding its petals had a particular charm for her. She wanted to shed all her leaves, to tear off all her petals and strew them on the path of the Lord. He had to come along that road; she wanted to force Him, as it were, to come and fulfill her desire. . . .

Mary Her Ideal

As a fifth trait in her character I should like to mention that her ideal on the "Little Way" was Our Lady. . . . From her youth she had a fervent, childlike devotion for Our Lady. Her statue stood in front of her in the small room of her paternal home, and it seemed to her as if it smiled down upon her. She entered the Order of Carmel to be her child and to imitate her especially in her union with Our Lord. Just as the life of Our Lady was ordinary and consisted of a series of the most common, everyday acts, so Thérèse wishes her own life to be. . . . Mary surrendered herself unreservedly to God's wishes through her "Behold the handmaid of the Lord. Be it done unto me according to Thy Word." So little Thérèse gave herself unreservedly to God, wishing to please Him only, to trust Him, to be His alone. Like Our Lady, who was not disturbed when St. Joseph did not understand her condition, but left the explanation of this mystery to God, so little Thérèse gave everything into God's hands with a limitless confidence.

. . . She also wanted to taste of union with God with the same delicacy as that with which Mary enjoyed this delight. But just as the descent of God into Our Lady at once incited her to an act of humility, made her go to Elizabeth, Thérèse likewise wanted her union with God, her surrender to Him, to manifest itself in humble acts of charity. . . .

TWO FINAL POINTS

First Point: Her Apostolate of Prayer

Finally, there are two points in the life of little St. Thérèse, deserving special note which stamp her as one of the loveliest representatives of the school of Carmel.

The mysticism of the school of Carmel could not claim to be true mysticism if it were not apostolic in its own peculiar way. St.

Thérèse of Lisieux shows us the true sense of the Apostolate of the school of Carmel. "I would be a missioner," she says, "I should like to have been one from Creation till the end of the world. I should want to preach the Gospel in all continents at once, as far as the farthest isles. Above all I should like martyrdom. One torture would not satisfy me, would not be enough. I should want to undergo them all. Open, O Jesus, the book of life in which the acts of the saints are written down, I should like to have performed them all for You." But then she recollects that God calls her along a different road to the practice of the Apostolate. The Apostolate as a work of God's grace has to be seen as a work of the mystical Body of Christ of which God is the head and the soul, of which we are the members, animated by God. Not all have to fulfill a like duty. Love gave to St. Thérèse the key of the vocation of Carmel in the Apostolate. "I understood," she says, "that if the Church has a body, built up of different organs, the chief, the most necessary organ of all, could not be wanting. I saw that it must have a heart burning with love. I understood that only love sets the limbs in motion, that if love were to be extinguished, the apostles would no longer preach the Gospel, the martyrs would refuse to spill their blood. I understand that love contains all vocations. My vocation is love. I have found my proper place in the Church. I shall be love. In this way I shall be everything. In this way my dream has come true."

Great St. Teresa Practised It Before Her

The vocation which so transported little Thérèse was not hers only, even though hardly anyone has understood it as well as she has. Great St. Teresa of Avila at the foundation of the first convent of her reform had already explained this vocation to her sisters. "Prevented from promoting as I desired the glory of God, I resolved to do the little which lay in my power, viz., to follow the evangelical counsels as perfectly as I was able and to induce the new nuns who are here to do the same, confiding in the great goodness of God Who never fails to assist those who are determined to leave all things for Him; and hoping that all of us being engaged in prayer for the champions of the Church, for the preachers and doctors who defend her, might to the utmost of our power assist my Lord Who has been so much insulted—O my sisters in Christ, help me to entreat Our Lord herein, since for this object He has assembled you here; this is your vocation, these are your employments; these your desires; hither your tears, hither your petitions must tend. . . ."

Here we see that St. Teresa not only has recommended to her sisters the Apostolate of prayer, but has given it to them as a vocation.

Mary Magdalen de' Pazzi: Another Model of Apostolic Prayer

To take an example from the Order of the [Ancient] Observance, I call your attention to the great Italian mystic, Saint Mary Magdalen de' Pazzi, of the convent of Florence. I would I had the occasion to speak longer about her spiritual life and her mystic works, but time does not allow. In this connection I will say, however, that her vocation above all was to pray and do penance in order to obtain the reform of all classes in the Church, religious, priests, laity, and even heretics and pagans. "I desire," she says, "to offer Thee, O my God, all creatures class by class. Would that I had the strength to gather all infidels, to lead them into the bosom of Thy Church. I should pray her to purge them from their unfaithfulness, to give them new life." It is in flashes of fire and with impassioned accents that she pours forth her prayer to God for the salvation of the souls redeemed by the Holy Sacrifice of Calvary.

Contemplative Convents, Aids to Missions

The Little Flower dreamt of conquering the world for God and to realize this dream she entered a convent where she was quite shut off from the world and then cried out, transported with joy, that her dream had come true. Only he can grasp this who has penetrated into the secrets of God's grace; who understands that in praying for grace and in sacrificing our life in union with the Sacrifice of Calvary, God's Grace is obtained. In this the chief part of pastoral care and of missionary work consists. This is the most splendid and intimate joining of the active and contemplative life, not in one person but in the mystical Body of which we are all members. We must be glad that the unity of the mystical Body of Christ recreates even the most secluded life, spent quite shut off from the world and in the service of God, making it a fit soil for missionary work, from which the latter can ever draw new sap of God's grace. This thought has led to the foundations of Carmels in the missionary countries also. Over and above the other sacrifices, these Sisters give up their country and climate and take a lifelong farewell of parents, relations and friends of their own. This idea drew little Thérèse in desire to Indo-China. "Here," she writes, "here I am loved and this affection is very sweet to me. But that is just why I dream of a convent in which I should be unknown, in which I should have to bear the exile of the heart as well. . . ."

Besides, the sight of these convents in the missions keeps alive the idea of the value of the Apostolate of prayer, both for those who practice it and for those who remain outside. It is edifying to see how missionaries themselves vie with each other in founding Carmelite convents: how Popes and Bishops insist on the building of these houses; how the Pope, to further this thought, has made little St. Thérèse to be the patron saint of all mission work as well as the work of the reunion of Churches.

We Should Imitate the Little Flower

This should indue all who are called to the spiritual life of Carmel but especially those who cannot now, or who can no longer, take an active part in the Apostolate of the Church—to regard contemplation as the better part of the Order and should urge them to follow as strictly as possible the contemplative life, calling down the indispensable blessing of God on the activity of the others.

From the small convent of Lisieux St. Thérèse has preached her "Little Way" by sweeping the corridors and washing dishes, cleaning the oratory and working in the garden, by nursing the sick and helping the needy, by studying at the proper time and reading what the mind requires for its development. She has so conquered the world. It is no wonder that this conception of inner life of the school of Carmel, laid down in her *Story of a Soul*, has drawn thousands to Carmel, that in our busy, hurrying time she stands high, like a lighthouse in a churning sea.

Second Point: Her Continued Apostolate After Death

When we look up from the often storm-tossed waves of the Mediterranean to Carmel, lifting its serene height in peerless beauty as a safe haven of refuge, then the image of Little Thérèse beckons us to land there and take our rest; then it is her hand that rings the bells of its silent chapel inviting us to pray with her. . . .

You also are in a gale on your way to the Holy Land, the kingdom of God on earth. I have been allowed to ring the bells of Carmel for you, to make you hear the voices that speak of prayer and apostleship, of prayer on the flanks of that Holy Mountain. Do you also step ashore for a moment to join in this prayer and take back with you the spirit of Carmel, to make it live in the capital of your kingdom, the kingdom of your thoughts, the centre of your lives.

St. Thérèse of Lisieux has said that after death she would strew roses on earth. And of what else is a rose the symbol, if not of love of God, for Whom she wanted to be a rose, a rose shedding its petals on the road of God through the world?

Carmel is the mountain of shrubbery and flowers. With full hands the children of Carmel strew those flowers over the earth. Such a picture of St. Thérèse is widely spread. The Saint scatters widely the flowers which she receives from the hand of Our Lady. . . .

We read in the Carmelite Missal in the Preface for the Feast of Our Lady of Mount Carmel the significance of the little cloud which Elias beheld from Mount Carmel appearing out of the sea. "Who through the small cloud arising out of the sea didst foretell the Immaculate Virgin Mary to the Blessed Elias the Prophet, and didst will that devotion be shown to her by the sons of the prophets." . . . She has her hands filled with flowers and she brings her Divine Son the source of all beauty and grace. On those who pray the first drops of the redeeming rain descend, roses of divine grace.

At the feet of Mary, the Mother of Carmel, I see kneeling in prayer with St. Thérèse the many saintly and blessed women and men who were the very flowers of Carmel during the preceding centuries. The flowers of their example rain down upon us. But they must be transplanted to the garden of our soul.

In our own times St. Thérèse, the "Little Flower," is elected to make that rain more abundant than ever. May she give us from the hand of the Mother of Carmel, from the Holy Mountain, the roses we need for the garden of our soul. The twofold spirit of the Prophet of Carmel will fill the garden of our heart with its sweet odors. And may God walk in its sweetness.

"Blessed are the pure of heart, for they shall see God."[2]

From the Sermons of Titus Brandsma

(Alternate second reading for the Office of Readings for July 27, from *Carmelite Proper of the Liturgy of the Hours*)

You hear it said that we live at a wonderful time, a time of great men and women. It would probably be better to say that we live in an era of decadence in which many, however, feel the need to react and to defend what is most precious and sacred. The desire for the emergence of a strong, capable leader is understandable. But we want such a leader to fight for a holy cause, for an ideal based on divine designs and not merely on human might.

Neo-paganism [as expressed in Nazism] considers the whole of nature as an emanation of the divine: this is what it holds about various races and peoples of the earth. But as star differs from star by reason of its light and brightness, so neo-paganism considers one race more noble and pure than another; to the extent that this one race is held to embody more light within itself, it has the duty of making that life shine and enlighten the world. It is maintained that this is possible only when, eliminating elements foreign to it, it frees itself from all stain. From this notion derives the cult of race and blood, the cult of the heroes of one's own people.

From such an erroneous starting-point, this view can lead to fatal errors! It is sad to see how much enthusiasm and effort are placed at the service of such an erroneous and baseless ideal! However, "we can learn from our enemy"; from his erroneous philosophy we can learn how to purify and better our own ideal: we can learn how to foster a great love for it; how to arouse great enthusiasm, even a willingness to live and die for it; how to build up the courage to incarnate it in ourselves and in others.

We too profess our descendence from God.

We too want what he wants.

But we do not accept the idea of emanation from the divine; we do not divinize ourselves. We admit descendence in dependence. When we speak of and pray for the coming of the kingdom, it is not a prayer for a kingdom based on differences of race and blood but on universal brotherhood. In union with him who makes the sun rise on the good and on the evil, all men are our brothers—even those who hate us and fight us.

We do not want a relapse into the sin of the earthly paradise, into the sin of making ourselves equal to God. We do not wish to begin a cult of heroes based on the divinization of human nature.

We acknowledge the law of God and we submit to it. We do not wish to frustrate—through an unhealthy and heady knowledge of ourselves—our dependence on the Supreme Being who gives us existence. However, even as we acknowledge the law of God within ourselves, we also note another law of desires contrary to the Spirit of God, which wishes to prevail. At times, like St Paul, we experience the desire to act counter to the divine law; we find it difficult to recognize our imperfections; and we act in ways that are destructive to our own nature. We wish to be better than we are, with other talents or a different personality. And sometimes we even think we are what we would like to be.

In our better moments, however, we do recognize our imperfections, and then we understand that there is room for improvement. We are honestly convinced that we could improve if we had more courage. Nothing is accomplished without effort, without struggle. In our better moments, we no longer shed tears over our own weaknesses or over those of others, but we recall what was interiorly said to St Paul: My grace is sufficient for you; in union with me you can do all things.

We live in a world in which love is condemned: it is called weakness, something to be overcome. Some say: never mind love, develop your strengths; let everyone be as strong as possible; let the weak perish. They say that the Christian religion, with its preaching of love, has seen better days and should be substituted for by old Teutonic force. Yes, some proclaim these doctrines, and they find people who willingly adopt them. Love is unknown: "Love is not loved," said St Francis of Assisi in his day; and some centuries later, in Florence, the ecstatic St Mary Magdalene de' Pazzi rang the bells of her Carmelite monastery to let the world know how beautiful love is. Although neo-paganism no longer wants love, history teaches us that, in spite of everything, we will conquer this neo-paganism with love. We shall not give up on love. Love will gain back for us the hearts of these pagans. Nature is stronger than theory: let theory condemn and reject love and call it weakness; the living witness of love will always renew the power which will conquer and capture the hearts of men.[3]

"Before a Picture of Jesus in My Cell"

(Written from Scheveningen Prison, February 1942)

A new awareness of Thy love
Encompasses my heart:
Sweet Jesus, I in Thee and Thou
In me shall never part.

No grief shall fall my way but I
Shall see Thy grief-filled eyes;
The lonely way that Thou once walked
Has made me sorrow-wise.

All trouble is a white-lit joy
That lights my darkest day;

Thy love has turned to brightest light
This night-like way.

If I have Thee alone,
The hours will bless
With still, cold hands of love
My utter loneliness.

Stay with me, Jesus, only stay;
I shall not fear
If, reaching out my hand,
I feel Thee near.

(Tr. Gervaise Toelle, o.carm.)[4]

Edith Stein (1891–1942)

Though they never met in life and came from different branches of the Carmelite family, the names of Titus Brandsma and Edith Stein are often associated in Carmelite literature. Both were noted educators and authors, who spoke out on the issues of the day. Both died in 1942 in Nazi concentration camps of World War II.

The youngest child in a large Jewish family, Edith Stein was born on October 12, 1891—on Yom Kippur, the Jewish "Day of Atonement"—in Breslau (Wroclaw in Polish) in Lower Silesia, then part of Germany but now part of Poland. Her father Siegfried died soon after, and her widowed mother Auguste took charge of the family's struggling lumber business, turning it into a profitable enterprise. Edith was an independent-minded, intellectually precocious, and sometimes temperamental child, who insisted on beginning her education early, yet suddenly decided at age thirteen to leave school. It was at this time also that she made a conscious decision to abandon prayer, despite the fervent Jewish faith of her beloved mother.

Two years later, however, she returned to school with renewed enthusiasm, determined to become a teacher. Her excellent secondary school results qualified her for higher studies, and she entered the University of Breslau in March 1911. Here she started delving into the newly emerging field of psychology, but became disenchanted by what she considered its lack of clarity regarding basic concepts. Deeply impressed by her reading of the *Logical Investigations* of Edmund Husserl, whose phenomenological method seemed to address some of the very issues that psychology ignored, she transferred to the University of Göttingen to begin philosophical studies with "the Master." She became an active member of the "Philosophical Society" gathered around Husserl, a group that at various times had included Adolf Reinach, Max Scheler, Hedwig

Martius, Alexandre Koyré, and other outstanding scholars. Intrigued by Husserl's insistence "that an objective outer world could only be experienced intersubjectively, i.e., through a plurality of individuals who relate in a mutual exchange of information,"[1] she chose "the problem of empathy" (*Einfühlung*) for her dissertation topic, exploring how it is possible for human beings to experience and relate to other individuals as subjects. As she noted, this enabled her to focus on "something which was personally close to my heart and which continually occupied me anew in all later works: the constitution of the human person."[2] After passing her state board examinations "with highest honors," she volunteered for a year of service as a nurse in a Red Cross military hospital for infectious diseases, before following Husserl to his new position at the University of Freiburg. In 1916 she was awarded her doctorate *summa cum laude*, and became Husserl's research assistant, attempting to organize his scattered notes into publishable form. She also continued her own work, writing important essays on the individual and community and on the nature of the state. Despite her outstanding qualifications, however, she was unsuccessful in her efforts to obtain a university position, in part because female professors were still a relative rarity, and in part because of the rising tide of anti-Semitism in Germany.

Meanwhile, Stein had become increasingly sympathetic toward religion, and in 1921 she was converted from her previous atheism upon reading St. Teresa of Avila's *Book of Her Life*. She was baptized on January 1, 1922, and received into the Catholic Church. She felt drawn to the life of the Discalced Carmelite nuns but was told by her spiritual director to wait. From 1923 to 1931, she served as a teacher at the Dominican girls' school of St. Magdalena in Speyer, and became well known internationally as a lecturer on women's issues. She then spent a year as an instructor at the German Institute for Scientific Pedagogy in Münster. Distressed by the persecution of her fellow Jews, Stein wrote a respectful but eloquent letter to Pius XI, urging the church to speak out more forcefully and noting that "responsibility . . . also falls on those who keep silent in the face of such happenings."[3] She also began the autobiographical work known in English as *Life in a Jewish Family*, presenting "a straightforward account of my own experience of Jewish life" as a way of combating racial hatred.

When National Socialist policies against the hiring of Jews made it impossible for her to continue her academic career, she found herself finally at liberty to pursue a religious vocation. She applied to the Carmel of Cologne, where she was admitted in 1933 and given the religious name she had requested, "Sr. Teresa Benedicta of the Cross." Encouraged to resume her scholarly work, she continued her efforts to bring Husserlian phenomenology into dialogue with the scholastic philosophy of Thomas Aquinas.

With violence against Jews in Germany escalating, however, she was transferred for her protection to the Carmel of Echt in Holland at the end of 1938. Any illusion of ultimate safety was soon shattered, however, when Germany invaded the Netherlands in 1940. Efforts to obtain her safe passage to a neutral country proved fruitless, however, in part because she refused to leave without her sister Rosa, who had also converted to Catholicism and had joined her in Echt, serving as portress for the community. As the danger drew nearer, Edith was completing *The Science of the Cross*, a full-length study of St. John of the Cross in honor of the four hundredth anniversary of his birth.

On July 26, 1942, the Catholic bishops of the Netherlands had a pastoral letter read in all their churches denouncing the Nazi persecution of the Jews. Nazi authorities immediately retaliated, ordering the deportation of all Catholics of Jewish descent living in Holland. On August 2, Edith and Rosa Stein were arrested and sent east. From the transit-camps along the way, Edith wrote back to her community reassuringly that "so far I have been able to pray gloriously," yet asking for prayers because "there are so many persons here who need some consolation and they expect it from the Sisters."[4] By August 9 the prisoners had reached Auschwitz, where they were sent to the gas chamber shortly after their arrival.

Because of the confusion of the war and its aftermath, it took some years for the exact circumstances of Stein's death to become known, and for her major manuscripts (mostly unpublished during her lifetime because of laws against works by Jewish authors) to be reassembled and printed. Yet slowly her reputation has grown, and today she is regarded not only as an important thinker but also as one of the great women of the twentieth century. She was beatified in 1987 and canonized in 1998 by Pope John Paul II. The same pontiff declared her copatroness of Europe in 1999, alongside Bridget of Sweden and Catherine of Siena, and presented her as a model philosopher in his encyclical *Fides et Ratio*. Numerous academic societies have been established for the study of her thought, and her works continue to be translated into the major modern languages. Even spiritual seekers who have little interest in philosophy feel drawn to the example of this heroic woman who once wrote that "those who seek the truth are seeking God, whether they know it or not."

From "Fundamental Principles of Women's Education"

In the talk which I gave . . . concerning the foundations of women's education, I tried to draw the picture of woman's soul as it would correspond to the eternal vocation of woman, and I termed its attributes as *expansive, quiet, empty of self, warm, and clear.* Now I am asked to say something regarding how one might come to possess these qualities.

I believe that it is not a matter of a multiplicity of attributes which we can tackle and acquire individually; it is rather a single total condition of the soul, a condition which is envisaged here in these attributes from various aspects. We are not able to attain this condition by willing it, it must be effected through grace. What we can and must do is open ourselves to grace. . . .

The duties and cares of the day ahead crowd about us when we awake in the morning (if they have not already dispelled our night's rest). Now arises the uneasy question: How can all this be accommodated in one day? When will I do this, when that? How shall I start on this and that? Thus agitated, we would like to run around and rush forth. We must then take the reins in hand and say, "Take it easy! Not any of this may touch me now. My first morning's hour belongs to the Lord. I will tackle the day's work which He charges me with, and He will give me the power to accomplish it."

So I will go to the altar of God. Here it is not a question of my minute, petty affairs, but of the great offering of reconciliation. I may participate in that, purify myself and be made happy, and lay myself with all my doings and troubles along with the sacrifice on the altar. And when the Lord comes to me then in Holy Communion, then I may ask Him, "Lord, what do you want of me?" (St. Teresa). And after quiet dialogue, I will go to that which I see as my next duty.

I will still be joyful when I enter into my day's work after this morning's celebration: my soul will be empty of that which could assail and burden it, but it will be filled with holy joy, courage, and energy.

Because my soul has left itself and entered into the divine life, it has become great and expansive. Love burns in it like a composed flame which the Lord has enkindled, and which urges my soul to render love and to inflame love in others. . . . And it sees clearly the next part of the path before it; it does not see very far, but it knows that when it has arrived at that place where the horizon now intersects, a new vista will then be opened.

Now begins the day's work, perhaps the teaching profession— four or five hours, one after the other. That means giving our concentration there. We cannot achieve in each hour what we want, perhaps in none. We must contend with our own fatigue, unforeseen interruptions, shortcomings of the children, diverse vexations, indignities, anxieties. Or perhaps it is office work: give and take with disagreeable supervisors and colleagues, unfulfilled demands, unjust reproaches, human meanness, perhaps also distress of the most distinct kind.

It is the noon hour. We come home exhausted, shattered. New vexations possibly await there. Now where is the soul's morning freshness? The soul would like to seethe and storm again: indignation, chagrin, regret. And there is still so much to do until evening. Should we not go immediately to it? No, not before calm sets in at least for a moment. Each one must know, or get to know, where and how she can find peace. The best way, when it is possible, is to shed all cares again for a short time before the tabernacle. Whoever cannot do that, whoever also possibly requires bodily rest, should take a breathing space in her own room. And when no outer rest whatever is attainable, when there is no place in which to retreat, if pressing duties prohibit a quiet hour, then at least she must for a moment seal off herself inwardly against all other things and take refuge in the Lord. He is indeed there and can give us in a single moment what we need.

Thus the remainder of the day will continue, perhaps in great fatigue and laboriousness, but in peace. And when night comes, and retrospect shows that everything was patchwork and much which one had planned left undone, when so many things rouse shame and regret, then take all as it is, lay it in God's hands, and offer it up to Him. In this way we will be able to rest in Him, actually to rest, and to begin the new day like a new life.

This is only a small indication how the day could take shape in order to make room for God's grace. Each individual will know best how this can be used in her particular circumstances. . . .[5]

From "On the History and Spirit of Carmel"

Until a few years ago, very little from our silent monasteries penetrated into the world. It is different today. People talk a lot about Carmel and want to hear something about life behind the high walls. This is chiefly attributable to the great saints of our time who have captivated the entire Catholic world with amazing speed, for instance, St Thérèse of the Child Jesus. . . .

What does the average Catholic know about Carmel? That it is a very strict, perhaps the strictest penitential Order, and that from it comes the holy habit of the Mother of God, the brown scapular, which unites many of the faithful in the world to us. The whole church celebrates with us the patronal feast of our Order, the feast of the scapular, on July 16. Most people also recognize at least the names of "little" Thérèse and "great" Teresa, whom we call our Holy Mother. She is generally seen as the founder of the Discalced Carmelites. The person who is a little more familiar with the history of the church and monasteries certainly knows that we revere the prophet Elijah as our leader and father. But people consider this a "legend" that does not mean very much. We who live in Carmel and who daily call on our Holy Father Elijah in prayer know that for us he is not a shadowy figure out of the dim past. His spirit is active among us in a vital tradition and determines how we live. Our Holy Mother strenuously denied that she was founding a new Order. She wanted nothing except to reawaken the original spirit of the old Rule [of St. Albert].

Our Holy Father Elijah succinctly says what is most important in the first words of his that the Scriptures give us. He says to King Ahab who worshiped idols (1 Kgs 17:1), "As the Lord the God of Israel lives, before whom I stand, there shall be neither dew nor rain these years, except by my word."

To stand before the face of the living God—that is our vocation. The holy prophet set us an example. He stood before God's face because this was the eternal treasure for whose sake he gave up all earthly goods. He had no house; he lived wherever the Lord directed him from moment to moment: in loneliness beside the brook of Carith, in the little house of the poor widow of Zarephath of Sidon, or in the caves of Mount Carmel. . . . Elijah is not concerned about his daily bread. He lives trusting in the solicitude of the heavenly Father and is marvelously sustained. A raven brings him his daily food while he is in solitude. The miraculously increased provisions of the pious widow nourish him in Zarephath. Prior to the long trek to the holy mountain where the Lord was to appear to him, an angel with heavenly bread strengthens him. So he is for us an example of the gospel poverty that we have vowed, an authentic prototype of the Savior.

Elijah stands before God's face because all of his love belongs to the Lord. He lives outside of all natural human relationships. We hear nothing of his father and mother, nothing of a wife or child. His "relatives" are those who do the will of the Father as he does: Elisha, whom God has designated as his successor, and the "sons of the prophets," who follow him as their leader. Glorifying God is his joy. His zeal to serve him tears him apart: "I am filled with jealous zeal for the Lord, the God of hosts" (1 Kgs 19:10, 14; these words were used as a motto on the shield of the Order). By living penitentially, he atones for the sins of his time. The offense that the misguided people give to the Lord by their manner of worship hurts him so much that he wants to die. And the Lord consoles him only as he consoles his especially chosen ones: He appears to him himself on a lonely mountain, reveals himself in soft rustling after a thunderstorm, and announces his will to him in clear words.

The prophet, who serves the Lord in complete purity of heart and completely stripped of everything earthly, is also a model of obedience. He stands before God's face like the angels before the eternal throne, awaiting his sign, always ready to serve. He has no other will than the will of his Lord. When God bids, he goes before the king and fearlessly risks giving him bad news that must arouse his hatred. When God wills it, he leaves the country at the threat of violence; but he also returns at God's command, though the danger has not disappeared.

Anyone who is so unconditionally faithful to God can also be certain of God's faithfulness. He is permitted to speak "as someone who has power," may open and close heaven, may command the waters to let him walk through and remain dry, may call down fire from heaven to consume his sacrifice, to execute punishment on God's enemies, and may breathe new life into a dead person. We see the Savior's predecessor provided with all the graces that he has promised to his own. And the greatest crown is still in reserve for him: Before the eyes of his true disciple, Elisha, he is carried off in a fiery carriage to a secret place far from all human abodes. According to the testimony of Revelation, he will return near the end of the world to suffer a martyr's death for his Lord in the battle against the Antichrist.

On his feast, which we celebrate on July 20, the priest goes to the altar in red vestments. On this day the monastery of our friars on Mount Carmel, the site of Elijah's grotto, is the goal of mighty bands of pilgrims. Jews, Moslems, and Christians of all denominations vie in honoring the great prophet. We remember him in the liturgy on still another day, in the epistle and preface of the Feast of Mount Carmel, as we usually call the feast of the scapular. On this day we give thanks that our dear Lady has clothed us with the "garment of salvation." The events providing the occasion for this feast did not occur until much later in the Western world. In the year 1251 [according to tradition] the Blessed Virgin appeared to the general of the Order, Simon Stock, an Englishman, and gave him the scapular. But the preface reminds us that it was our dear Lady of Mount Carmel who bestowed this visible sign of her motherly protection on her children far from the original home of the Order. It was she who manifested herself [according to *The Book of the Institution of the First Monks*] to the prophet Elijah in the form of a little rain cloud and for whom the sons of the prophets built the first shrine on Mount Carmel. The legend of the Order tells us that the Mother of God would have liked to remain with the hermit brothers on Mount Carmel. We can certainly understand that she felt drawn to the place where she had been venerated through the ages and where the holy prophet had lived in the same spirit that also filled her from the time her earthly sojourn began. Released from everything earthly, to stand in worship in the presence of God, to love him with her whole heart, to beseech his grace for sinful people, and in atonement to substitute herself for these people, as the maidservant of the Lord to await his beckoning—this was her life.

The hermits of Carmel lived as sons of the great prophet and as "brothers of the Blessed Virgin." . . . [The] spirit which they had received from their predecessors was laid down in our holy Rule. Around 1200, it was given to the Order by St Albert, the patriarch of Jerusalem, and authorized by Pope Innocent IV in 1247. It also condenses the entire meaning of our life in a short statement: "All are to remain in their own cells . . . , meditating on the Law of the Lord day and night and watching in prayer, unless otherwise justly employed." "To watch in prayer"—this is to say the same thing that Elijah said with the words, "to stand before the face of God." Prayer is looking up into the face of the Eternal. We can do this only when the spirit is awake in its innermost depths, freed from all earthly occupations and pleasures that benumb it. Being awake in body does not guarantee this consciousness, nor does rest required by nature interfere. "To meditate on the Law of the Lord"—this can be a form of prayer when we take prayer in its usual broad sense. But if we think of "watching in prayer" as being immersed in God, which is characteristic of contemplation, then meditation on the Law is only a means to contemplation.

What is meant by "the Law of the Lord"? Psalm 118 which we pray every Sunday and on solemnities at Prime, is entirely filled with the command to know the Law and to be led by it through life. The Psalmist was certainly thinking of the Law of the Old Covenant. Knowing it actually did require life-long study and fulfilling it, life-long exertion of the will. But the Lord has freed us from the yoke of this Law. We can consider the Savior's great commandment of love, which he says includes the whole Law and the Prophets, as the Law of the New Covenant. Perfect love of God and of neighbor can certainly be a subject worthy of an entire lifetime of meditation. But we understand the Law of the New Covenant, even better, to be the Lord himself, since he has in fact lived as an example for us of the life we should live. We thus fulfill our Rule when we hold the image of the Lord continually before our eyes in order to make ourselves like him. We can never finish studying the Gospels.

But we have the Savior not only in the form of reports of witnesses to his life. He is present to us in the most Blessed Sacrament. The hours of adoration before the Highest Good and the listening for the voice of the eucharistic God are simultaneously "meditation on the Law of the Lord" and "watching in prayer." But the highest level is reached "when the Law is deep within our hearts" (Ps 40:8), when we are so united with the triune God whose temple we are, that his Spirit rules all we do or do not do. Then it does not mean we are forsaking the Lord when we do the work that obedience requires of us. Work is unavoidable as long as we are subject to nature's laws and to the necessities of life. And, following the word and example of the apostle Paul, our holy Rule commands us to earn our bread by the work of our hands. But for us this work is always merely a means and must never be an end in itself. To stand before the face of God continues to be the real content of our lives.

Islam's conquest of the Holy Land drove the hermit brothers from Carmel. Only for the past 300 years has our Order again had a shrine of the Mother of God on the holy mountain. The transition from solitude into the everyday life of Western culture led to a falsification of the original spirit of the Order. The protective walls of separation, of rigorous penance and of silence fell, and the pleasures and cares of the world pressed through the opened gates. The monastery of the Incarnation in Avila, which our Holy Mother entered in the year 1535, was such a monastery of the mitigated Rule. For decades she endured the conflict between the snares of worldly relationships and the pull of undivided surrender to God. But the Lord allowed her no rest until she let go of everything that bound her and really became serious about recognizing that *God alone suffices.*

The great schism of faith that was tearing Europe apart during her time, the loss of so many souls, aroused in her the passionate desire to stop the harm and to offer the Lord recompense. Whereupon God gave her the idea of taking a little flock of selected souls and founding a monastery according to the original Rule and of serving him there with the greatest perfection. After innumerable battles and difficulties, she was able to found the monastery of St. Joseph in Avila. Her great work of reform grew from there. At her death she left behind 36 monasteries of women and men of the strict observance, the new branch of the Order, the "Discalced" Carmelites. The monasteries of the reform were to be places where the spirit of the ancient Carmel was to live again. The re-established original Rule and the Constitutions drawn up by the saint herself form the fence by means of which she intended to protect her vineyards against the dangers from without. Her writings on prayer, the most complete and most animated presentation of the inner life, are the precious legacy through which her spirit continues to work among us. . . . It is the ancient spirit of Carmel. However, influenced by the battles over faith raging in her time, she gave stronger emphasis than did the primitive Carmel to the thought of reparation and of supporting the servants of the church who withstood the enemy in the front lines.

As our second father and leader, we revere the first male Discalced Carmelite of the reform, St John of the Cross. We find in him the ancient eremitical spirit in its purest form. His life gives an impression as though he had no inner struggles. Just as from his earliest childhood he was under the special protection of the Mother of God, so from the time he reached the age of reason, he was drawn to rigorous penance, solitude, to letting go of everything earthly, and to union with God. He was the instrument chosen to be an example and to teach the reformed Carmel the spirit of Holy Father Elijah. Together with Mother Teresa, he spiritually formed the first generation of male and female Discalced Carmelites, and through his writings, he also illumines for us the way on the "Ascent of Mount Carmel."

The daughters of St Teresa, personally trained by her and Father John, founded the first monasteries of the reform in France and Belgium. From there the Order also soon advanced into the Rhineland. The great French Revolution and the Kulturkampf in Germany tried to suppress it by force. But as soon as the pressure abated, it sprang to life again. It was in this garden that the "little white flower" [i.e., St. Thérèse of Lisieux] bloomed, so quickly captivating hearts far beyond the boundaries of the Order, not only as a worker of miracles for those in need, but also as a director of "little souls" on the path of "spiritual childhood." Many people came to know of this path through her, but very few know that it is not really a new discovery, but the path onto which life in Carmel pushes us.

The greatness of the young saint was that she recognized this path with ingenious deduction and that she followed it with heroic decisiveness to the end. The walls of our monasteries enclose a narrow space. To erect the structure of holiness in it, one must dig deep and build high, must descend into the depths of the dark night of one's own nothingness in order to be raised up high into the sunlight of divine love and compassion.

Not every century produces a work of reform as powerful as that of our Holy Mother. Nor does every age give us a reign of terror during which we have the opportunity to lay our heads on the executioner's block for our faith and for the ideal of our Order as did the 16 Carmelites of Compiègne. But all who enter Carmel must give themselves wholly to the Lord. Only one who values her little place in the choir before the tabernacle more highly than all the splendor of the world can live here, can then truly find a joy that no worldly splendor has to offer.

Our daily schedule ensures us of hours for solitary dialogue with the Lord, and these are the foundation of our life. Together with priests and other ancient Orders of the church, we pray the Liturgy of the Hours, and this Divine Office is for us as for them our first and most sacred duty. But it is not for us the supporting ground. No human eye can see what God does in the soul during hours of inner prayer. It is grace upon grace. And all of life's other hours are our thanks for them.

Carmelites can repay God's love by their everyday lives in no other way than by carrying out their daily duties faithfully in every respect—all the little sacrifices that a regimen structured day after day in all its details demands of an active spirit; all the self-control that living in close proximity with different kinds of people continually requires and that is achieved with a loving smile; letting no opportunity go by for serving others in love. Finally, crowning this is the personal sacrifice that the Lord may impose on the individual soul. This is the "little way," a bouquet of insignificant little blossoms which are daily placed before the Almighty—perhaps a silent, life-long martyrdom that no one suspects and that is at the same time a source of deep peace and hearty joyousness and a fountain of grace that bubbles over everything—we do not know where it goes, and the people whom it reaches do not know from whence it comes.[6]

Jessica Powers (1905–1988)

Agnes Jessica Powers entered the world on February 7, 1905, the third of four children born to Delia and John Powers, descendants of Irish and Scottish immigrants who had settled in rural Wisconsin in the previous century. Jessica was raised on the family farm near Mauston, in an area known to the locals as Cat Tail Valley. Here she developed a lifelong love of nature, but also encountered early experiences of hardship, suffering, and loss. Her beloved older sister Dorothy died of tuberculosis in June 1916, as Jessica was completing her first six years of primary school. During the following two years she attended the Sisters School in Mauston, where one of her teachers, Sr. Lucille Massart, o.p., fostered her appreciation of poetry and encouraged her to write.

In 1922, after completing high school, she enrolled in the school of journalism at Marquette University, since at that time women were not allowed in the school of liberal arts. Lacking funds to continue beyond her first year, she returned briefly to Mauston and then moved for two years (1923–1925) to Chicago, where she worked in the typing pool of a railroad manufacturing company while spending her free time reading books of poetry in the public libraries. In Chicago she joined a literary group that met regularly at the Dominican priory in River Forest to discuss and share poetry. Her early poems began to appear in newspapers and poetry journals.

Diagnosed with symptoms of tuberculosis herself, Jessica returned to Mauston for what she thought would be a short recuperation. Following the death of her mother in September 1925, however, Jessica decided to remain to help her two younger brothers run the family farm. Yet her literary interests never flagged; she continued to publish and became a frequent contributor to "The Percolator," a poetry column in the *Milwaukee Sentinel*.

By 1937 both brothers had married, and Jessica was again free to follow her dreams. She moved to New York City, where she accepted an invitation from the Catholic philosopher Anton Pegis and his wife Jessie to live with them and help care for their children. New York was the center of the Catholic Revival of the 1930s, and Jessica became an active member of the Catholic Poetry Society of America, founded a few years earlier. Her first book of poetry, *The Lantern Burns*, was published in 1939, to favorable reviews. Her reputation as an important Catholic poet was growing.

Meanwhile, she was growing spiritually as well. Jessica attended Mass daily, set aside regular times for personal prayer, and became a Franciscan tertiary. Already at Marquette she had been introduced to the poetry of John of the Cross, and a later reading of St. Thérèse's *Story of a Soul* had moved her deeply. Without knowing much about the Order itself, she began to feel a growing attraction to Carmel, though she assumed at first that her age, health, and limited financial resources would be an obstacle to joining. Still, with the encouragement of a retreat director, she began contacting Carmelite monasteries, only to be told that they were already full, until she learned of a new community being established in her home state of Wisconsin. She applied and was accepted.

Jessica entered the Carmel of the Mother of God in Milwaukee on June 24, 1941, as a postulant. Despite a recurrence of tuberculosis symptoms that required some time in a sanitarium, on April 25 of the following year she received the habit and the religious name "Sr. Miriam of the Holy Spirit," well suited to her special love for the Third Person of the Trinity. Until the end of her life she remained with this community as a Discalced Carmelite nun.

Sr. Miriam had been prepared to set aside her writing career upon entering the monastery, but her superiors encouraged her to continue. Her second book, *The Place of Splendor*, was published in 1946, the year of her final vows, and contained poems composed both before and after her entry into Carmel.

Yet finding time for poetry amid the demands of community life proved difficult. Except for *The Little Alphabet*, a children's book published in 1955, no new collection of her poems would appear for another twenty-six years. She served two successive three-year terms as prioress, from 1955 to 1961, which meant overseeing all the details of the transfer of the community to a new property in Pewaukee, on the outskirts of Milwaukee, in 1958. She was elected again for one more term from 1964 to 1967, a particularly challenging period as religious communities struggled to respond to the Second Vatican Council's call for renewal. She felt ill-equipped for administrative duties and her literary output fell, but she accepted the will of her sisters in a spirit of generous service.

Later years brought a renewed attention to her writings. In 1972 the Carmel of Reno, Nevada, printed *Mountain Sparrow*, a booklet of ten of her poems accompanied by the artwork of Sr. Marie Celeste of the Reno Carmel. A small collection of Christmas poems, *Journey to Bethlehem*, came out in 1980, and her own community privately printed *The House at Rest* in 1984. An Italian translation of *The Place of Splendor* was published in 1981, and a French translation in 1989. Shortly before her death on July 9, 1988, she reviewed and approved the final manuscript of *The Selected Poetry of Jessica Powers*, coedited by Sr. Regina Siegfried, A.S.C. (a longtime student of her works), and Bishop Robert F. Morneau (who for many years had used her poems in his retreats and conferences). The numerous popular and scholarly books and articles on Jessica Powers that have appeared since her death confirm her status as a major religious poet of our time.

As an artist and poet, Jessica Powers stands within a long Carmelite tradition; for Carmelites, after silence itself, symbol and image are the privileged means of conveying some small glimpse of what takes place in the human-divine encounter. Many Carmelites—Teresa of Avila, the Martyrs of Compiègne, Thérèse of Lisieux, Elizabeth of the Trinity, Edith Stein, Titus Brandsma, and countless others—have felt moved to express their contemplative experiences in verse, sometimes with mixed results. However, like the poetry of her spiritual mentor St. John of the Cross, the best of Jessica Powers's poems have been recognized not only for their spiritual depth but also for their outstanding literary quality. Here we have chosen a few poems representing some of her characteristic themes: the thirst for beauty, the longing for God, journey and rest, suffering and joy, emptiness and fulfillment, God's love and mercy, the Holy Spirit and Blessed Virgin, and the wonders of nature (especially birds, both in themselves and as metaphors of spiritual realities).

The early poem "Robin at Dusk," published when she was twenty-two, expresses the youthful poet's desire "that a song of mine could burn / the air with beauty." "Letter of Departure" and "The Little Nation" reveal something of Powers's critical view of her times as she entered Carmel in 1941, a few months before the attack on Pearl Harbor that brought the United States into World War II. Like Thomas Merton and so many others, however, she found that contemplative religious life, rather than separating her from "the world," drew her ever more profoundly into its deepest joys and sorrows. Poems such as "Counsel for Silence" (with its allusion to Elijah's sojourn in the *wadi* Cherith), "The House at Rest" (inspired by John of the Cross's "Dark Night"), "This Paltry Love," "Take Your Only Son," and "God Is a Strange Lover" speak of the struggles and purifications of the spiritual journey, the encounter with our own nothingness before God, and the heartbreak of surrendering everything we hold dear—even what we *think* we know of God, the world, and ourselves—to the all-consuming divine love. "The Pool of God" presents Mary as the model of that transparency to God that spiritual seekers long for.

Other poems, however, speak of the consoling light discovered within and beyond the pain and darkness. During her time in New York, our author once had a memorable discussion with an editor friend, who maintained that truth was the primary attribute of God, while Jessica argued for beauty. Later in life she concluded that they were both wrong, and that God's most important quality is mercy. "The Mercy of God" reflects this insight, and echoes St. Thérèse's theme of utter dependence on the God of Merciful Love. In "To Live with the Spirit" she adds that one must become a listener and a lover, casting "down forever . . . the compass of the whither and the why" and learning to walk in "waylessness" and "unknowing." "The Ledge of Light" finds the poet enjoying a foretaste of the spiritual goal, but still yearning for its complete fulfillment. The final poem here ends with a ringing affirmation of our eternal destiny as "a measureless sheer / beatitude of yes."

"Robin at Dusk"[1]

> I can go starved the whole day long,
> draining a stone, eating a husk,
> and never hunger till a song
> breaks from a robin's throat at dusk.
>
> I am reminded only then
> how far from day and human speech,
> how far from the loud world of men
> lies the bright dream I strain to reach.
>
> Oh, that a song of mine could burn
> the air with beauty so intense,
> sung with a robin's unconcern
> for any mortal audience!

Perhaps I shall learn presently
his secret when the shadows stir,
and I shall make one song and be
aware of but one Listener.[2]

"Letter of Departure"

"There is nothing in the valley, or home, or street
                              worth turning back for—
nothing!" you write. O bitter words and true
to seed the heart and grow to this green answer:
let it be nothing to us that we knew
streets where the leaves gave sparsely of the sun
or white small rested houses and the air
strung with the sounds of living everywhere.
The mystery of God lies before and beyond us,
so bright the sight is dark, and if we halt
to look back once upon the burning city,
we shall be paralyzed by rage or pity,
either of which can turn the blood to salt.

We knew too much of the knowable dark world,
its secret and its sin,
too little of God. And now we rise to see
that even our pledges to humanity
were false, since love must out of Love begin.
Here where we walk the fire-strafed road and thirst
for the great face of love, the blinding vision,
our wills grow steadfast in the heart's decision
to keep the first commandment always first.
We vow that nothing now shall give us cause
to stop and flounder in our tears again,
that nothing—fire or dark or persecution—
or the last human knowledge of all pain—
shall turn us from our goal.

With but the bare necessities of soul—
no cloak or purse or scrip—let us go forth
and up the rocky passes of the earth,
crying, "Lord, Lord," and certain presently
(when in the last recesses of the will
and in the meshes of the intellect
the quivering last sounds of earth are still)

to hear an answer that becomes a call.
Love, the divine, Love, the antiphonal,
speaks only to love,
for only love could learn that liturgy,
since only love is erudite to master
the molten language of eternity.[3]

"The Little Nation"

Having no gift of strategy or arms,
no secret weapon and no walled defense,
I shall become a citizen of Love,
that little nation with blood-stained sod,
where even the slain have power, the only country
that sends forth an ambassador to God.
Renouncing self and crying out to evil
to end its wars, I seek a land that lies
all unprotected like a sleeping child;
nor is my journey reckless and unwise.
Who doubts that love is an effective weapon
may meet with a surprise.[4]

"Counsel for Silence"

Go without ceremony of departure
and shade no subtlest word with your farewell.
Let the air speak the mystery of your absence,
and the discerning have their minor feast
on savory possible or probable.
Seeing the body present, they will wonder
where went the secret soul, by then secure
out past your grief beside some torrent's pure
refreshment. Do not wait to copy down
the name, much less the address, of who might need you.
Here you are pilgrim with no ties of earth.
Walk out alone and make the never-told
your healing distance and your anchorhold.
And let the ravens feed you.[5]

"The House at Rest"

On a dark night
Kindled in love with yearnings—

Oh, happy chance!—
I went forth unobserved,
My house being now at rest.

—St. John of the Cross

How does one hush one's house,
each proud possessive wall, each sighing rafter,
the rooms made restless with remembered laughter
or wounding echoes, the permissive doors,
the stairs that vacillate from up to down,
windows that bring in color and event
from countryside or town,
oppressive ceilings and complaining floors?

The house must first of all accept the night.
Let it erase the walls and their display,
impoverish the rooms till they are filled
with humble silences; let clocks be stilled
and all the selfish urgencies of day.

Midnight is not the time to greet a guest.
Caution the doors against both foes and friends,
and try to make the windows understand
their unimportance when the daylight ends.
Persuade the stairs to patience, and deny
the passages their aimless to and fro.
Virtue it is that puts a house at rest.
How well repaid that tenant is, how blest
who, when the call is heard,
is free to take his kindled heart and go.[6]

"This Paltry Love"

I love you, God, with a penny match of love
that I strike when the big and bullying dark of need
chases my startled sunset over the hills
and in the walls of my house small terrors move.
It is the sight of this paltry love that fills
my deepest pits with seething purgatory,
that thus I love you, God—*God*—who would sow
my heights and depths with recklessness of glory,
who hold back light-oceans straining to spill on me, on *me*,
stifling here in the dungeon of my ill.

This puny spark I scorn, I who had dreamed
of fire that would race to land's end, shouting your worth,
of sun that would fall to earth with a mortal wound
and rise and run, streaming with light like blood,
splattering the sky,
soaking the ocean itself, and all the earth.[7]

"Take Your Only Son"

None guessed our nearness to the land of vision,
not even our two companions to the mount.
That you bore wood and I, by grave decision,
fire and a sword, they judged of small account.

Speech might leap wide to what were best unspoken
and so we plodded, silent, through the dust.
I turned my gaze lest the heart be twice broken
when innocence looked up to smile its trust.

O love far deeper than a lone begotten,
how grievingly I let your words be lost
when a shy question guessed I had forgotten
a thing so vital as the holocaust.

Hope may shout promise of reward unending
and faith buy bells to ring its gladness thrice,
but these do not preclude earth's tragic ending
and the heart shattered in its sacrifice.

Not beside Abram does my story set me.
I built the altar, laid the wood for flame.
I stayed my sword as long as duty let me,
and then alas, alas, no angel came.[8]

"God Is a Strange Lover"

God is the strangest of all lovers; His ways are past
    explaining.
He sets His heart on a soul; He says to Himself, "Here will I rest
    my love."
But He does not woo her with flowers or jewels or words that
    are set to music,
no names endearing, no kindled praise His heart's direction
    prove.

His jealousy is an infinite thing. He stalks the soul with
   sorrows;
He tramples the bloom; He blots the sun that could make her
   vision dim.
He robs and breaks and destroys—there is nothing at the last
   but her own shame, her own affliction,
and then He comes and there is nothing in the vast world but
   Him and her love of Him.
Not till the great rebellions die and her will is safe in His hands
   forever
does He open the door of light and His tendernesses fall,
and then for what is seen in the soul's virgin places,
for what is heard in the heart, there is no speech at all.

God is a strange lover; the story of His love is most
   surprising.
There is no proud queen in her cloth of gold; over and over
   again
there is only, deep in the soul, a poor disheveled woman
   weeping . . .
for us who have need of a picture and words: the Magdalen.[9]

"The Pool of God"

There was nothing in the Virgin's soul
that belonged to the Virgin—
no word, no thought, no image, no intent.
She was a pure, transparent pool reflecting
God, only God.
She held His burnished day; she held His night
of planet-glow or shade inscrutable.
God was her sky and she who mirrored Him
became His firmament.

When I so much as turn my thoughts toward her
my spirit is enisled in her repose.
And when I gaze into her selfless depths
an anguish in me grows
to hold such blueness and to hold such fire.
I pray to hollow out my earth and be
filled with these waters of transparency.
I think that one could die of this desire,

seeing oneself dry earth or stubborn sod.
Oh, to become a pure pool like the Virgin,
water that lost the semblances of water
and was a sky like God.[10]

"The Mercy of God"

I am copying down in a book from my heart's archives
the day that I ceased to fear God with a shadowy fear.
Would you name it the day that I measured my column of
　　virtue
and sighted through windows of merit a crown that was near?
Ah, no, it was rather the day I began to see truly
that I came forth from nothing and ever toward nothingness
　　tend,
that the works of my hands are a foolishness wrought in the
　　presence
of the worthiest king in a kingdom that never shall end.
I rose up from the acres of self that I tended with passion
and defended with flurries of pride;
I walked out of myself and went into the woods of God's mercy,
and here I abide.
There is greenness and calmness and coolness, a soft leafy
　　covering
from the judgment of sun overhead,
and the hush of His peace, and the moss of His mercy to tread.
I have naught but my will seeking God; even love burning in
　　me
is a fragment of infinite loving and never my own.
And I fear God no more; I go forward to wander forever
in the wilderness made of His infinite mercy alone.[11]

"To Live with the Spirit"

To live with the Spirit of God is to be a listener.
It is to keep the vigil of mystery,
earthless and still.
One leans to catch the stirring of the Spirit,
strange as the wind's will.

The soul that walks where the wind of the Spirit blows
turns like a wandering weather-vane toward love.

It may lament like Job or Jeremiah,
echo the wounded hart, the mateless dove.
It may rejoice in spaciousness of meadow
that emulates the freedom of the sky.
Always it walks in waylessness, unknowing;
it has cast down forever from its hand
the compass of the whither and the why.

To live with the Spirit of God is to be a lover.
It is becoming love, and like to Him
toward Whom we strain with metaphors of creatures:
fire-sweep and water-rush and the wind's whim.
The soul is all activity, all silence;
and though it surges Godward to its goal,
it holds, as moving earth holds sleeping noonday,
the peace that is the listening of the soul.[12]

"The Ledge of Light"

I have climbed up out of a narrow darkness
on to a ledge of light.
I am of God; I was not made for night.

Here there is room to lift my arms and sing.
Oh, God is vast! With Him all space can come
to hole or corner or *cubiculum.*

Though once I prayed, "O closed Hand holding me . . ."
I know Love, not a vise. I see aright,
set free in morning on this ledge of light.

Yet not all truth I see. Since I am not
yet one of God's partakers,
I visualize Him now: a thousand acres.

God is a thousand acres to me now
of high sweet-smelling April and the flow
of windy light across a wide plateau.

Ah, but when love grows unitive I know
joy will upsoar, my heart sing, far more free,
having come home to God's infinity.[13]

"Yes"

Yes to one   is often no to another
here walks my grief   and here has often been
my peak of anguish   yes is the one need
of my whole life   but time and time again
law forces no   up through my heart and lips
spiked leaden ball   rending as it arises
leaving its blood and pain   yes is the soft
unfolding of petals   delicate with surprises
curve and caress   and billowing delight
out to the one or many   I would guess
heaven for me   will be an infinite
flowering of one species   a measureless sheer
beatitude of yes[14]

Recent Voices

Over the past fifty years, the face of Carmel, like that of the church itself, has changed dramatically. The Second Vatican Council's call for renewal brought both blessings and challenges. Along with other religious families, Carmelites in the post–Vatican II era were encouraged to distinguish their perennial values from certain historical forms and expressions that might need to be modified according to "the signs of the times." Constitutions and customs were updated, though not without difficulties (especially for the Discalced Carmelite nuns). New expressions of the Carmelite way of life continued to emerge; today there are approximately one hundred congregations and secular institutes formally "aggregated" or linked to Carmelite and Discalced Carmelite friars, as well as countless groups of all sorts that incorporate various aspects of Carmel's saints and spirituality among the elements of their own vocation in the church.

Most important, Carmelites everywhere have returned to their roots, recommitting themselves to the essential elements of their Carmelite vocation and "rereading" their rich heritage in the light of today's needs. In the English-speaking world, new initiatives—such as the Institute of Carmelite Studies, the Carmelite Forum, the Carmelite Institute, associations formed by the Carmelite nuns, national secretariats established for the Lay Carmelites (belonging to the O.Carms.) and the Secular Carmelites (belonging to the OCDs), and countless other developments—are fostering greater dialogue and collaboration within the Carmelite family while making the Carmelite tradition more accessible to contemporary audiences.

At the same time, as confidence in religious institutions seems to have declined in the West, popular interest in spirituality and mysticism has blossomed. Increasing numbers of ordinary Christians feel drawn to contemplative prayer, once thought to be restricted to monks and nuns, and they turn to the Carmelite tradition for assistance. More and more spiritual seekers of other faith traditions look to Teresa, John of the Cross, Thérèse, and other Carmelite figures as wise guides and companions on their spiritual journeys. Many of those with no denominational affiliation, who might describe themselves as "spiritual but not religious," are nevertheless eager to learn from Carmel's spiritual masters. John of the Cross's expression "dark night," later expanded to "dark night of the soul," has become a part of popular culture. Even secular academicians are intrigued by the literary accomplishments and psychological insights of the Carmelite saints.

All of this has given today's members of the Carmelite family an unprecedented opportunity to share with people across the religious and social spectrum in a common dialogue on the deepest issues of human existence. Also, as they reclaim their Elijan roots, contemporary Carmelites recognize more than ever that their commitment to prayer, silence, and solitude must deepen, rather than diminish, their concern for the great social issues of our day. They realize that the contemplative and prophetic dimensions of the Carmelite vocation must always go together. Carmelites today are involved in ministries and apostolic prayer and service of all sorts, and now have NGO status with the United Nations.

Though predictions are inherently risky, certain trends are clear and seem likely to continue. Carmelite women and laity are gradually assuming roles of greater responsibility and working alongside the friars as equal partners in prayer and ministry. The Lay and Secular Carmelites are now the fastest growing part of the Carmelite family. Among the Carmelite friars and nuns, new vocations are most plentiful in the developing world—in India, Korea, Indonesia, and parts of Africa and Latin America, for example. All of these trends present new challenges and opportunities. One of the most important tasks for Carmelites in the years ahead will be to explore how their great heritage can be authentically inculturated in new places and social contexts, in ways that will enrich all of us.

The final selections of this anthology, from three contemporary American Carmelites, are meant to reflect some of these changes and challenges as Carmel moves toward the future. The late Peggy Wilkinson (1929–2009) was a much-loved figure among Secular Carmelites in the United States. She made her profession as a Secular Carmelite in 1967, and for over forty years served as a teacher, formator, artist, author, and mentor for others while continuing to care for her husband and children. In the excerpt here from *Finding the Mystic Within You*, she speaks of integrating her Carmelite vocation with the responsibilities of a wife and mother, and encountering the living God at the center of domestic life.

Sr. Lois Ann Wetzel, O.CARM., belongs to the Carmelite Sisters for the Aged and Infirm, one of the congregations aggregated to the Carmelite Order. She has held various nursing positions in the facilities operated by her community. She is a past board member of the Carmelite Institute and currently serves on the Carmelite Heritage committee and the Mission Effectiveness committee of her own congregation. Her contribution here was presented as part of a panel discussion at the Carmelite Forum Conference held at Saint Mary's College in South Bend, Indiana, in June 2010, on the theme of "Carmel's Quest for the Living God: A Future to Hope In."

For six years, William J. Harry, O.CARM., served as delegate to the Carmelite NGO with the United Nations, as part of his responsibilities as a general councilor for the Carmelite Order. He is currently the west commissary provincial for the Most Pure Heart of Mary Province in the United States as well as communications director for the Carmelite NGO. His essay discusses Carmel's presence with the United Nations and what Carmelites can contribute to the shared human struggle to build a better world.

Peggy Wilkinson, *Finding the Mystic Within You*

In the late fifties, before Vatican II, when the Mass was still in Latin, and "meditation" was not yet a household word, I began to feel the need for a "something more" in my spiritual life. Unsure of what I was seeking, but confident that it was there in the deeper levels of my faith, I began looking for guidance. Most of the help I received came from books, for at the time, there were not many spiritual programs available at the parish level. (Fortunately, this has changed since Vatican II.) Every book that was either by a Carmelite or about a Carmelite seemed to speak my language and answer the need that I was unable to put into words. During the sixties, the Discalced Carmelite Monastery in Washington, D.C., held Colloquia. In 1965 my husband Tom, my brother Jim Dimond, and I attended a series, and I discovered that there was a "Third Order" for lay people. Although I have been a Catholic all of my life, I did not remember ever hearing about "Third Orders." I found that the First Order consists of priests and brothers, the Second Order of nuns, and the Third Order of those in the world, married or single, who continue their spiritual development in the spirit or charism of the parent order. Today, [some of these] Third Orders are called [Lay or] Secular Orders. In addition to Carmelites there are Dominican, Franciscan, . . . etc.

When I found the Carmelite Secular Order it was like being led to an oasis after wandering alone in the desert for years, and I couldn't wait to attend meetings. My husband was somewhat bothered at what I was doing, thinking I was "trying to escape the humdrum (or hectic) house and family" (we have eight children) and reminding me that I did not have that much spare time for additional commitments. I could not accurately explain to him what it was I found in Carmel, but knew that for me it was my spiritual lifeblood.

Since my husband was a little wary, I thought it important not to let the path I had chosen cause any obvious change in our usual routine. I reassured him that my becoming a Carmelite would not interfere with our family life, and I would not expect everyone else to follow my spiritual path. I kept a low profile, and made my prayer life as unobtrusive as possible. I was professed on Trinity Sunday, 1967.

The basic Carmelite rule of life [for the Secular Carmelites] consists of a half-hour daily meditation and the Liturgy of the Hours. I said my office while feeding the baby her bottle. Since Tom worked shift work, he often came home as the children left for school; or the children would come in from school as he left for work. On those days my husband's dinner would be prepared in the middle of the day so that he could have his main meal before he left, and take a lunch to work. This meant that dinner had to be prepared again in the evening for the children. They were often a little "unruly" when Dad wasn't present at the table, and we can all laugh about it now, even me.

There was not too much in the way of "silence and solitude" in those days, and I rearranged my time for contemplative prayer daily according to the home schedule. (It is much better to be able to establish a regular time for contemplative prayer.) Eventually, an interior silence develops and establishes an inner grounding of peace, which is an immense help in the center of constant noise and activity, or as Tom sometimes described it, "the eye of the hurricane." That was how it sounded on rainy days, when he had worked all night and was trying to sleep, and children, their friends, and pets were "just playing" in the house.

Interior silence is even better than exterior silence, for it can usually be depended upon. It is like a firm foundation upon which, over a lifetime, the waves of problems and illnesses, crises or disasters may crash but not crush, may shake but not shatter.

Our children are not only very active, but very loving, and I was able to see many spiritual truths clarified by just observing them, especially when they were unaware. I won't embarrass them by mentioning any of the cute things they used to do, but I keep records.

With meals, laundry, dental and doctor's appointments, homework assistance, etc., I did not have a great deal of free time. When the evening meal, homework, and children's baths were over, my bath was frequently the only available quiet space and time for my meditation. As the children grew older, of course, it became much easier, and eventually I was even able to attend an occasional weekend retreat. Getting away from the routine for an extended time is not only refreshing, but spiritually enriching.

A few years later it was discovered that my mother was becoming senile, and she came to live with us. It was like having a baby again, as she could not be left alone. My husband and the children were wonderful and loving, but it was a very difficult time. As we heard about Alzheimer's disease, and saw some of its victims on television documentaries, we recognized the similar behavior. I resolved to keep Mother out of an institution as long as she could still recognize us, for she would become fearful if she did not at all times see a familiar face. Mother could still laugh and would enjoy herself with the children, and they would dance with her and include her in their games. I bought adult diapers and would have to shower and dress her. If I was not home my husband attended to her, for she was like an infant, completely unaware. After a few years, when her health worsened, we had to put Mother in a nursing home, but I was grateful that by this time she was beyond caring about where she was.

It has been a busy and active life, and I could not have made it without God's help, I am certain of that. The spiritual strength I received from my prayer relationship helped me to do things I never thought I would be able to do, not that I did them perfectly. Sometimes, it is enough just to endure. I often wondered how people could get through the difficulties of life that everyone encounters without inner support from God, even though they may have family support. Contemplative prayer and the Carmelite community were for me absolute necessities. Over the years, as my husband got to know many of the Carmelites, he understood why it was so important to me. As I became familiar with the writings of Teresa of Avila and John of the Cross I could see that the spiritual journey they describe, each in his own way, is for everyone. I wondered why their writings were not more widespread. . . .

The spirit of Carmel is love and contemplation. It is founded on the spirit of Elijah, who waited on the mountain in silence and solitude and found God, not in the earthshaking events of storm, wind, and fire, but in the everyday, often overlooked or taken for granted, "gentle breeze." The contemplative spirit requires not so much a change of life as a change of awareness, an interior change. It is not the outward circumstances of life that make a contemplative, but the inner intention of the soul.

The Order of Carmel is dedicated to Mary, who "kept the words of the Lord and pondered them in her heart." The first hermits on Mt. Carmel were called "the Brothers of Our Lady of Mt. Carmel." When they were driven out of the Holy Land because of wars, they settled in Europe.

. . . Because Teresa [of Avila] and John [of the Cross] wrote the first and most complete accounts of the various stages of the spiritual journey, their approach is usually called the "Carmelite way." Actually, it is more universal, for if the Apostles had described their own spiritual journeys, they would probably have had similar accounts, since they, too, were brought to divine transformation or "spiritual marriage." The basic spiritual journey is the same, but the experiences along the way will be different for each soul.

At the end of the Song of Songs in the Old Testament there is a conversation. St. John of the Cross writes that it is between the persons of the Trinity. "What shall we do for our 'sister' on the day she is betrothed?" They are speaking of the soul. Each soul is the "sister" . . . of God, of His very "Be"-ing. Each soul comes forth from God and is meant to return to God as a bride after it is spiritually prepared.

This spiritual preparation is the basis of the spiritual journey, and contemplative prayer is an essential part of the soul's development. We are all mystics, lovers and contemplatives. Love and contemplation are the language and activity of heaven; and earth is the soul's apprenticeship for heaven. Contemplative prayer helps to develop an awareness of who we are as children of God, why we are here, and the divine destiny to which we are called.

Teresa of Avila considered prayer more as a "relationship" than "recitation," and described it as a "friendship with the Lord that grows into love." Since friendship and love are intrinsic to human nature, Teresa believed that contemplative prayer was possible for everyone willing to make the necessary preparations.

Contemplative prayer awakens inner vision. . . . Inner awareness enables the soul to see the world in a new way—the way that God sees it. As the unmistakable presence of the Indwelling God becomes clearer, prayerful souls recognize the divine in the eyes of all of their brothers and sisters, and "see" (experience) God always at work in the world beneath ordinary surface appearances.

In this Age of the Laity the Carmelite teachings are particularly relevant, especially for the current younger generation. . . . From infancy this generation has been interiorly prepared like fertile ground, open and receptive, but for many of them there was no forthcoming spiritual seed. Their conditioning has developed a singular capacity for the Divine, and only a personal, in-depth relationship with God, a Divine Intimacy, will satisfy their spiritual hunger.

God comes to each soul as it is and we, as brothers and sisters of the same family, can love, respect, affirm, and encourage each other in our spiritual efforts, united in the same goal—if not in the same approach. As any intimate relationship is unique to the persons involved, the relationship of each soul and its Beloved is special and deeply personal. We can benefit from each other's experiences. . . .[1]

Lois Ann Wetzel, from the 2010 Panel Discussion "Carmel's Quest for the Living God: A Future to Hope In"

When I was asked to speak on this panel my immediate response was: "What could I possibly say among such lights of the Order as are represented here? I am just an everyday working Carmelite doing her everyday things in ordinary ways." But then I thought, that really describes all of us here in one way or the other.

When I consider my hope for Carmel's future I keep finding myself returning first of all to her roots. Elijah's declaration to Ahab in Chapter 17 of the first Book of Kings—"The Lord lives, I stand in his presence"—has been a favorite passage of mine for years. It speaks to me of the fundamental Carmelite stance before God. It has helped form my own interior Carmelite attitude and helped inform my outward choices.

"The Lord lives, I stand in his presence." What a beautifully intimate expression! The Carmelite stands before the presence of the living God in an intimate encounter. And in this intimate experience of coming into the presence of the Lord, the Carmelite becomes more and more who he or she was created to be by this same loving Lord. The "I" of the encounter becomes more and more the authentic "I," the "real me" if you will, the me who is called into existence by God and precedes every role or position the person has. In standing before the Lord, every attitude, assumption and inclination must be examined and surrendered to the fire of the Divine Presence until the Carmelite is able to stand before his God in purity of heart.

Of course this does not take place because we decide it will. It does not take place in any particular time frame. As we all know, it is the work of a lifetime. And it is God's work. We just need to show up with hearts open to the encounter, with the awareness that, indeed, the Lord *does* live and, indeed, I stand in his presence, and with a willingness to allow him to do his work in us. The implications are profound.

How often do we mix up the proper order? How often does our interior stance imply to the Lord "*I* live, you stand in *my* presence"? Some translations render the passage as "The Lord lives whom I serve." How often have our attitudes or behavior said to others, "I live whom *you* serve"? Elijah's declaration to Ahab offers us a healthy dose of reality. The *Lord* lives and we stand in *his* presence.

To be effective in the world now and in the future we must bring this basic Carmelite awareness into every situation in which we find ourselves. The Lord lives and we stand in his presence in every time and place. We stand in his presence with the elderly: we stand in his presence with the immigrant, with the poor, with the dispossessed, with our families, our communities and so on.

Our service to our brothers and sisters must be more than social action. It must be more than our own plans and agendas, however enlightened they may be. We must carry our awareness of the Lord's presence with us and pray for eyes and hearts to recognize him among the people we serve and in the circumstances in which we find ourselves.

By living in the awareness of God's presence and striving to respond authentically to him, Carmelites have the opportunity to give the world what it desperately needs; reassurance that our God is with us. He is present and at work in the multitudinous social and human needs that cry to heaven for relief, from every corner of our battered world.

Carmelites of the future must be there to meet these needs. They must be there to serve him whom they love and in whose presence they stand, wherever they find him. By being faithful to the tradition that formed them, Carmelites of the future will find new and creative ways to respond to and help shape a world where Isaiah's vision is realized: "The blind see, cripples walk, lepers are cured, the deaf hear and the dead are raised to life."[2]

William J. Harry, "Do We Have a Place at the Table?"

The idea of the Carmelites becoming an official Non-Governmental Organization (NGO) has left some asking, "Why?" They cannot make the link between our Carmelite journey and the road provided by an organization such as the United Nations. Initially I could not understand why we would seek a role at the UN myself.

The Carmelite NGO is now a reality, primarily through the good efforts of members of the Congregation of Our Lady of Mt. Carmel in Louisiana. However, participation has gradually expanded to make the project one which is more of the Carmelite Family as was the original intent. But the question about its connection to our mission as a religious family continues to be heard. Weekly I am asked "What exactly are we Carmelites doing there?"

It is a fair question. Are Carmelites not supposed to be focused on proclaiming the Gospel? Have we not discovered that our uniqueness is in being prophetic in the tradition of Elijah and in following the example of Mary? For centuries have Carmelites not usually waited for the people in our churches, schools, retreat centers and behind monastic walls? Definitely so!

But there is also a part of our Carmelite tradition that calls us to be present in the market place—where there is a good chance we will encounter people who do not share our love of God. A market place will likely provide us an opportunity to brush up against people who do not understand or even know our Carmelite traditions. It might also be the place where we can prove to be most prophetic. Does not our Carmelite tradition ask us to seek our God in places and events which may be non-traditional? Are we not called to rely on that mysterious Spirit that blows where it will? Could not this new market place be more receptive to and need Carmelite spirituality more than we might first think?

At the 2002 UN NGO Conference, on the topic of "Rebuilding Societies Emerging from Conflict: A Shared Responsibility," the opening session took place in the impressive General Assembly Hall, the most familiar venue at the United Nations. The keynote speaker was Mary Robinson, both much admired and much hated for her outspokenness against injustices as United Nations Commissioner for Human Rights. She stood at the same podium where presidents, prime ministers, two popes, dictators, and an endless procession of ambassadors have spoken on behalf of the people of the world governments for the last half century. The Carmelites who were present took seats usually reserved for ambassadors and their staffs, our first few steps into this particular marketplace.

I expected to hear about the need for money, the value of the peacekeeping forces, the fostering of better communication between governments as ways to make sure societies emerge from wars. Ms. Robinson never once mentioned any of those tried and tired solutions. She spoke about conflict being overcome by forgiveness and reconciliation, the transformation of the people from warriors to people focused on the good in each other.

If we needed an answer to the often asked question about the purpose of our presence at the UN, Ms. Robinson gave it to us, loud and clear. She said that nothing is really going to change on the world scene until the world's peoples experience the very things that we seek in our own lives as Carmelites—forgiveness, reconciliation, and transformation of the human person.

It struck me that after 800 years of practice we certainly have a few suggestions on how this might occur in the various cultures and situations around the world. Carmelites have never come out of one mold. We "do" our charism in a variety of ways. We learn from our saints that there are a variety of ways to approach our God. But each approach requires that the human person change. Only then is . . . any real communion with our God and neighbor possible.

 . . . Yes. Carmelites belong in the churches, the schools, the retreat centers, and the monasteries. But we also belong in the larger marketplace. Carmelites belong anywhere people will benefit from Carmelite spirituality. The United Nations just happens to be one more of the untested marketplaces in our world today. But it is available to us now. I heard that marketplace clearly asking for us to come forward and teach what we know about the Gospel value of transformation. We have been asked to become a part of the world's healing process and to help build the human community. Why would we not take the opportunity to serve God and God's people in this way?[3]

Notes

Introduction

1. Thomas Merton, *Disputed Questions* (New York: Farrar, Straus and Cudahy, 1960), 242.

2. Hans Urs von Balthasar, *Two Sisters in the Spirit: Thérèse of Lisieux and Elizabeth of the Trinity* (San Francisco: Ignatius Press, 1992).

The Carmelite Tradition

1. This translation of the *Rubrica prima* is found in Jane Ackerman, *Elijah: Prophet of Carmel* (Washington, DC: ICS Publications, 2003), 123.

2. Translations of Teresa's works, here and elsewhere in this anthology, are taken from *The Collected Works of St. Teresa of Avila*, trans. Kieran Kavanaugh and Otilio Rodriguez, 3 vols. (Washington, DC: ICS Publications, 1976–1985). Reference numbers refer to the chapter and section of the work cited.

The Carmelite Rule (ca. 1207)

1. Translation by Fr. Bede Edwards, originally published in *The Rule of Saint Albert*, ed. Hugh Clarke and Bede Edwards (Aylesford and Kensington: n.p., 1973), 79–93.

Ignea Sagitta (*The Flaming Arrow*) (ca. 1270)

1. Thomas Merton, *Disputed Questions* (New York: Farrar, Straus and Cudahy, 1960), 238.

2. Excerpts from Nicholas of Narbonne, *The Flaming Arrow (Ignea Sagitta)*, trans. and introduced by Michael Edwards, from the critical edition by Adrian Staring, Vineyard Series #2 (Durham: Teresian Press, 1985), 15–51. Originally published in Nicholas of Narbonne, "The Flaming Arrow," trans. Bede Edwards, *Sword* 39 (1979): 3–52.

The Book of the Institution of the First Monks (ca. 1380)

1. Felip Ribot, o.carm., *The Ten Books on the Way of Life and Great Deeds of the Carmelites (including The Book of the First Monks)*, translated by Richard Copsey, *Early Carmelite Spirituality* Series, 1 (Faversham: Saint Albert's Press; Rome: Edizioni Carmelitane, 2005, 2nd ed. 2007), 8–10.

Teresa of Avila (1515–1582)

1. Translations of Teresa's works are taken from *The Collected Works of St. Teresa of Avila*, trans. Kieran Kavanaugh and Otilio Rodriguez, 3 vols. (Washington, DC: ICS Publications, 1976–1985). Reference numbers refer to the chapter and section of the work cited.

2. Excerpts are taken from Kavanaugh and Rodriguez, *Collected Works of St. Teresa of Avila*, 3 vols. *The Book of Her Life* is found in the first volume, while *The Way of Perfection* and *The Interior Castle* appear in the second.

3. "Efficacy of Patience," Kavanaugh and Rodriguez, *Collected Works of St. Teresa of Avila*, vol. 3, p. 386. The image is a reconstruction of the bookmark based on examples of her handwriting.

John of the Cross (1542–1591)

1. Teresa of Avila, *The Book of Her Foundations*, in *The Collected Works of St. Teresa of Avila*, trans. Kieran Kavanaugh and Otilio Rodriguez, vol. 3 (Washington, DC: ICS Publications, 1985). Reference numbers refer to the chapter and section of the work cited.

2. John Paul II, *Master in the Faith: Apostolic Letter on the Occasion of the Fourth Centenary of the Death of Saint John of the Cross* (December 14, 1990), 14. This particular translation from the original Spanish appeared in *Catholic International* 2 (March 1–14, 1991): 207.

3. Excerpts are taken from *The Collected Works of St. John of the Cross*, trans. Kieran Kavanaugh and Otilio Rodriguez, rev. ed. (Washington, DC: ICS Publications, 1991). The *Sayings* are numbered according to this edition. In references to *The Ascent of Mount Carmel* and *The Dark Night*, the numbers indicate the book, chapter, and section quoted. In references to *The Spiritual Canticle* and *The Living Flame of Love* prose commentaries, the first number indicates the stanza being commented upon, while the second number indicates the section quoted.

Jerome Gracián (1545–1614)

1. Joseph F. Chorpenning, *Christophorus Blancus' Engravings for Jerónimo Gracián's Summary of the Excellencies of St. Joseph (1597)* (Philadelphia: Saint Joseph's University Press, 1996), 5.

2. These excerpts are taken from Michael Dodd, "Jerome Gratian's *Constituciones del Cerro*: An Example of Teresian Humor," in *A Better Wine: Essays Celebrating Kieran Kavanaugh, O.C.D.*, ed. Kevin Culligan, *Carmelite Studies* 10 (Washington, DC: ICS Publications, 2007), 97–102, 109–10, 114, 129–30, 132–33.

Mary Magdalen de' Pazzi (1566–1607)

1. Letter of His Holiness Benedict XVI to the Archbishop of Florence on the Occasion of the Fourth Centenary of the Death of Mary Magdalene de' Pazzi, April 29, 2007.

2. *The Complete Works of Saint Mary Magdalen de' Pazzi, Carmelite and Mystic (1566–1607)*, trans. Gabriel N. Pausback, Vol. I: "The Forty Days," "The Renovation of the Church," Letters–Teachings (Aylesford, England: Carmelite Fathers, 1971), 17–19.

3. She writes of Pentecost ("feast of the Holy Spirit") and Trinity Sunday ("the morning of the Most Holy Trinity").

4. From *Complete Works of Saint Mary Magdalen de' Pazzi*, Vol. IV: *"Revelations and Enlightenments"* (or *"The Eight Days of the Holy Spirit"*), *"The Probation"* I, 11–12, 19–21, 24–26.

John of St. Samson (1571–1636)

1. Redemptus Maria Valabek, *Prayer Life in Carmel: Historical Sketches* (Rome: Carmel in the World Paperbacks, 1982), 98.

2. Critical edition by Hein Blommestijn, O.CARM., *Oeuvres Complètes* 1 (Rome/ Paris, 1992). English translation by Maurice Cummings, O.CARM., forthcoming in the collection *Fiery Arrow* (Leuven: Peeters, 2011).

Lawrence of the Resurrection (1614–1691)

1. Quotations are identified by section and page number, as found in Lawrence of the Resurrection, *Writings and Conversations on the Practice of the Presence of God*, critical edition by Conrad De Meester, trans. Salvatore Sciurba (Washington, DC: ICS Publications, 1994).

2. Excerpts are from De Meester and Sciurba, *Writings and Conversations on the Practice of the Presence of God*. The headings and numbering of paragraphs are taken from this edition.

Michael of St. Augustine (1621–1684) and Maria Petyt (1623–1677)

1. Mary Petyt is quoted from *Union with Our Lady: Marian Writings of the Venerable Mary Petyt of St. Teresa*, T.O.CARM., trans. and arranged by Thomas E. McGinnis (New York: Scapular Press, 1954). The numbering of the sections is according to this work.

2. The selections are from Michael of St. Augustine, *Life with Mary: A Treatise on the Marian Life*, trans. and arranged by Thomas McGinnis (New York: Scapular Press, 1953). The numbering of the sections is according to this edition.

Martyrs of Compiègne (d. 1794)

1. Terrye Newkirk, *The Mantle of Elijah: The Martyrs of Compiègne as Prophets of the Modern Age* (Washington, DC: ICS Publications, 1995), 44.

2. Ibid., 42–43.

3. William Bush, *To Quell the Terror: The Mystery of the Vocation of the Sixteen Carmelites of Compiègne Guillotined July 17, 1794* (Washington, DC: ICS Publications, 1999), 199–202, 203–4, 208–15, 221–22, 224, 230–33.

Thérèse of Lisieux (1873–1897)

1. Thérèse of Lisieux, *Story of a Soul: The Autobiography of Saint Thérèse of Lisieux*, trans. John Clarke, 3rd ed. (Washington, DC: ICS Publications, 1996), 207–8.

2. Ibid., 190–98, 200.

Elizabeth of the Trinity (1880–1906)

1. Quotations from Elizabeth's letters (here indicated by "L" and the letter number) are from Elizabeth of the Trinity, *Complete Works,* Vol. 2: *Letters from Carmel,* trans. Anne Englund Nash (Washington, DC: ICS Publications, 1995).

2. Hans Urs von Balthasar, *Two Sisters in the Spirit: Thérèse of Lisieux and Elizabeth of the Trinity,* trans. Donald Nichols and Anne Elizabeth Englund (San Francisco: Ignatius Press, 1992), 11.

3. Prayer quoted from Elizabeth of the Trinity, *I Have Found God, Complete Works,* Vol. 1: *Major Spiritual Writings,* trans. Aletheia Kane (Washington, DC: ICS Publications, 1984), 183–84.

4. Englund Nash, *Complete Works,* Vol. 2: *Letters from Carmel,* 51–52.

5. Ibid., 61–62.

6. "Heaven in Faith," quoted from Kane, trans., *I Have Found God,* Vol. 1: *Major Spiritual Writings,* 110–13.

Titus Brandsma (1881–1942)

1. Redemptus Maria Valabek, *Prayer Life in Carmel: Historical Sketches* (Rome: Carmel in the World Paperbacks, 1982), 181–82.

2. Titus Brandsma, *Carmelite Mysticism: Historical Sketches* (Darien, IL: Carmelite Press, 2002), 75–85.

3. Second Reading (Alternative 2) for July 27, from the sermons of Titus Brandsma, in *Proper of the Liturgy of the Hours of the Order of the Brothers of the Blessed Virgin Mary of Mount Carmel and of the Order of the Discalced Carmelites* (Rome: Institutum Carmelitanum, 1993), 224–27.

4. Ibid., 455–56.

Edith Stein (1891–1942)

1. Edith Stein, *Life in a Jewish Family,* trans. Josephine Koeppel (Washington, DC: ICS Publications, 1986), 269.

2. Ibid., 397.

3. See "Text of Stein's 1933 Letter to the Pope," in *Inside the Vatican* (March 2003): 27. The text is accompanied by an article by William Doino, "Edith Stein's Letter," exploring the context and significance of this correspondence.

4. Letters 341 and 342 in *Edith Stein, Self-Portrait in Letters: 1916–1942,* trans. Josephine Koeppel (Washington, DC: ICS Publications, 1993), 352–53.

5. From "Fundamental Principles of Women's Education," in Edith Stein, *Essays on Woman,* trans. Freda Mary Oben, 2nd ed., rev. (Washington, DC: ICS Publications, 1996), 143–45.

6. "On the History and Spirit of Carmel," from Edith Stein, *The Hidden Life: Hagiographic Essays, Meditations, Spiritual Texts,* trans. Waltraut Stein (Washington, DC: ICS Publications, 1992), 1–6.

Jessica Powers (1905–1988)

1. All poems are taken from *The Selected Poetry of Jessica Powers,* ed. Regina Siegfried and Robert F. Morneau (Washington, DC: ICS Publications, 1999).

2. Ibid., 187.
3. Ibid., 43–44.
4. Ibid., 39.
5. Ibid., 85.
6. Ibid., 122.
7. Ibid., 48.
8. Ibid., 153.
9. Ibid., 16.
10. Ibid., 63.
11. Ibid., 1.
12. Ibid., 38.
13. Ibid., 22.
14. Ibid., 137.

Recent Voices

1. Peggy Wilkinson, *Finding the Mystic Within You* (Washington, DC: ICS Publications, 1999), 5–11.
2. Lois Ann Wetzel, contributor to "Carmel's Quest for the Living God: A Future to Hope In," a panel discussion at the Carmelite Forum Conference, June 16–20, 2010, Saint Mary's College, South Bend, Indiana.
3. William J. Harry, "Do We Have a Place at the Table?" *CITOC (Centrum Informationis Totius Ordinis Carmelitarum)* (October–December 2004): no. 4.

Selected Bibliography

General Introductions

Boaga, Emanuele, and Luigi Borriello, eds. *Dizionario Carmelitano*. Rome: Città Nuova, 2008.

Egan, Keith. "Carmelite Spirituality." In *The New Dictionary of Catholic Spirituality*. Edited by Michael Downey, 117–25. Collegeville, MN: Liturgical Press, 1993.

———. "The Spirituality of the Carmelites." In *Christian Spirituality, Vol. 2: High Middle Ages and Reformation*. Edited by Jill Raitt, 50–62. New York: Crossroad, 1987.

McGreal, Wilfrid. *At the Fountain of Elijah: The Carmelite Tradition*. Traditions of Christian Spirituality Series. Maryknoll, NY: Orbis Books, 1999.

Paul-Marie of the Cross. *Carmelite Spirituality in the Teresian Tradition*. Translated by Kathryn Sullivan. Edited by Steven Payne. Washington, DC: ICS Publications, 1997.

Rohrbach, Peter Thomas. *Journey to Carith: The Sources and Story of the Discalced Carmelites*. 1966. Reprint. Washington, DC: ICS Publications, 2005.

Saggi, Louis, ed. *Saints of Carmel*. Translated by Gabriel N. Pausback. Rome, Italy: Carmelite Institute, 1972.

Smet, Joachim. *The Carmelites: A History of the Brothers of Our Lady of Mount Carmel*. 4 vols. Darien, IL: Carmelite Spiritual Center, 1975–85.

Valabek, Redemptus Maria. *Prayer Life in Carmel*. Rome: Institutum Carmelitanum, 1982.

Welch, John. *The Carmelite Way: An Ancient Path for Today's Pilgrim*. New York: Paulist Press, 1996.

Origins and the Carmelite Rule

The Carmelite Rule (1207–2007): Proceedings of the Lisieux Conference, 4–7 July 2005. Edited by Evaldo Xavier Gomes, Patrick McMahon, Simon Nolan, and Vincenzo Mosca. Textus et Studia Historica Carmelitana, 28. Edizioni Carmelitane, 2008.

Cicconetti, Carlo. *La Regola del Carmelo: Origine, Natura, Significato.* Textus et Studia Historica Carmelitana, 12. Rome: Institutum Carmelitanum, 1973.

―――. *The Rule of Carmel.* Translated by Gabriel Pausback. Edited and abridged by Paul Hoban. Darien, IL: Carmelite Spiritual Center, 1984.

Edwards, Bede, trans. *The Rule of St. Albert.* Aylesford and Kensington: Carmelite Press, 1973.

Friedman, Elias. *The Latin Hermits of Mount Carmel: A Study in Carmelite Origins.* Rome: Teresianum, 1979.

Giordano, Silvano, ed. *Carmel in the Holy Land: From Its Beginnings to the Present Day.* Arenzano, Italy: Il Messaggero di Gesù Bambino, 1995.

Griffin, Eltin, ed. *Ascending the Mountain: The Carmelite Rule Today.* Dublin: Columba Press, 2004.

Mulhall, Michael, ed. *Albert's Way: First North American Congress on the Carmelite Rule.* Rome: Institutum Carmelitanum, 1989.

The Rule of Carmel: New Horizons. Rome: Editrice "Il Calamo," 2000.

Secondin, Bruno. *La Regola del Carmelo: Per una nuova interpretatione.* Rome: Edizioni Carmelitane, 1982.

―――, ed. *La Regola del Carmelo Oggi.* Rome: Institutum Carmelitanum, 1983.

Waaijman, Kees. *The Mystical Space of Carmel: A Commentary on the Carmelite Rule.* Fiery Arrow Series. Leuven: Peeters, 1999.

Mary and Elijah in the Carmelite Tradition

Ackerman, Jane. *Elijah: Prophet of Carmel.* Washington, DC: ICS Publications, 2003.

Boaga, Emanuele. *The Lady of the Place: Mary in the History and in the Life of Carmel.* Rome: Edizioni Carmelitane, 2001.

Buggert, Donald W., et al. *Mother, Behold Your Son: Essays in Honor of Eamon R. Carroll, O.CARM.* Washington, DC: Carmelite Institute, 2001.

Chandler, Paul, ed. *A Journey with Elijah: Carmelite Seminar on the Prophet Elijah.* Rome: Institutum Carmelitanum, 1991.

McCaffrey, James. *The Carmelite Charism: Exploring the Biblical Roots.* Dublin: Veritas, 2004.

The Scapular of Our Lady of Mount Carmel: Catechesis and Ritual. Prepared under the direction of the North American Provincials of the Carmelite Orders. Distributed by ICS Publications, 2131 Lincoln Road, NE, Washington, DC, 20002.

Valabek, Redemptus Maria. *Mary, Mother of Carmel: Our Lady and the Saints of Carmel.* 2 vols. Rome: Institutum Carmelitanum, Carmel in the World Paperbacks, 1988.

Welch, John F., ed. *Carmel and Mary: Theology and History of a Devotion.* Washington, DC: Carmelite Institute, 2002.

Medieval Period

Including Ignea Sagitta *and* Book of the Institution of the First Monks

Andrews, Frances. *The Other Friars: Carmelite, Augustinian, Sack and Pied Friars.* Woodbridge, Suffolk: Boydell Press, 2006.

Copsey, Richard, trans. and ed. *The Ten Books on the Way of Life and Great Deeds of the Carmelites (including The Book of the First Monks).* By Felip Ribot. Rome: Edizioni Carmelitane, 2005.

Edwards, Bede, trans. *The Book of the Institution of the First Monks (Chapters 1 to 9).* Boars Hill, Oxford: Teresian Press, 1969.

Jotischky, Andrew. *The Carmelites and Antiquity: Mendicants and Their Past in the Middle Ages.* New York: Oxford University Press, 2002.

Merton, Thomas. "The Primitive Carmelite Ideal." In *Disputed Questions.* New York: Farrar, Straus and Cudahy, 1960.

Nicholas of Narbonne. *The Flaming Arrow (Ignea Sagitta).* Translated by Michael Edwards. Vineyard Series 2. Durham, England: Teresian Press, 1985. Originally published in "The Flaming Arrow." Translated by Bede Edwards. *Sword* 39 (1979): 3–52.

Staring, Adrian, ed. *Medieval Carmelite Heritage: Early Reflections on the Nature of the Order.* Rome: Institutum Carmelitanum, 1989.

Teresa and the Teresian Reform

Ahlgren, Gillian T. W. *Entering Teresa of Avila's* Interior Castle: *A Reader's Companion.* New York: Paulist Press, 2005.

Alvarez, Tomas (of the Cross). "The Carmelite School: St. Teresa and St. John of the Cross." In *Jesus in Christian Devotion and Contemplation.* Translated by Paul Oligny, 86–101, 111–13. St. Meinrad, IN: Abbey Press, 1974.

———, ed. *Diccionario de Santa Teresa.* Burgos, Spain: Editorial Monte Carmelo, 2002.

Alvarez, Tomas, and Fernando Domingo. *Saint Teresa of Avila: A Spiritual Adventure.* Translated by Christopher O'Mahoney. Washington, DC: ICS Publications, 1982.

Astigarraga, Juan Luis, and Agustí Borrell, eds. *Concordancias de los escritos de Santa Teresa de Jesús.* 2 vols. Rome: Teresianum, 2000.

Bilinkoff, Jodi. *The Avila of St. Teresa.* Ithaca, NY: Cornell University Press, 1989.

Burrows, Ruth. *Interior Castle Explored.* London: Sheed & Ward, 1982.

Clissold, Stephen. *St. Teresa of Avila.* New York: Seabury Press, 1982.

Dicken, E. W. Trueman. *The Crucible of Love: A Study of the Mysticism of St. Teresa of Jesus and St. John of the Cross.* New York: Sheed & Ward, 1963.

Dubay, Thomas. *Fire Within: St. Teresa of Avila, St. John of the Cross and the Gospel on Prayer.* San Francisco: Ignatius Press, 1989.

Du Boulay, Shirley. *Teresa of Avila: An Extraordinary Life.* New York: Blue-Bridge, 2004.

Efrén de la Madre de Dios, and Otger Steggink. *Tiempo y vida de Santa Teresa.* Biblioteca de Autores Cristianos. 3rd ed. Madrid: Editorial Católica, 1996.

Egido, Teofanes. "The Historical Setting of St. Teresa's Life." Translated by Michael Dodd and Steven Payne. *Carmelite Studies*, vol. 1. Edited by John Sullivan, 122–82. Washington, DC: ICS Publications, 1980.

Galilea, Segundo. *The Future of Our Past: The Spanish Mystics Speak to Contemporary Spirituality.* Notre Dame, IN: Ave Maria Press, 1985.

Kavanaugh, Kieran. "St. Teresa and the Spirituality of Sixteenth Century Spain." In *The Spirituality of Western Christendom*, Vol. 2: *The Roots of the Modern Christian Tradition.* Edited by E. Rozanne Elder. Kalamazoo, MI: Cistercian Publications, 1984.

———. "Spanish Sixteenth Century: Carmel and Surrounding Movements." In *Christian Spirituality, Vol. 3: Post-Reformation and Modern.* Edited by Louis Dupré and Don E. Saliers, 69–92. New York: Crossroad, 1991.

Marie-Eugene. *I Want to See God* and *I Am a Daughter of the Church.* Westminster, MD: Christian Classics, 1982.

Moriones, Ildefonso. *The Teresian Charism: A Study of the Origins.* Translated by Christopher O'Mahony. Rome: Teresianum, 1968.

O'Donoghue, Noel Dermot. *Mystics for Our Time: Carmelite Meditations for a New Age.* Collegeville, MN: Liturgical Press, 1989.

Rodriguez, Otilio. *A History of the Teresian Carmel.* Darlington, n.d.

Sanchez, Manuel Diego. *Bibliografía sistemática de Santa Teresa de Jesus.* Madrid: Editorial de Espiritualidad, 2008.

Sullivan, John, ed. *Centenary of St. Teresa (Catholic University Symposium—October 15–17, 1982).* Carmelite Studies, 3. Washington, DC: ICS Publications, 1984.

Teresa of Jesus, St. *The Collected Letters of St. Teresa of Avila.* Translated by Kieran Kavanaugh. 2 vols. Washington, DC: ICS Publications, 2001–7.

———. *The Collected Works of St. Teresa of Avila.* Translated by Kieran Kavanaugh and Otilio Rodriguez. 3 vols. Washington, DC: ICS Publications, 1976–85.

Weber, Alison. *Teresa of Avila and the Rhetoric of Femininity.* Princeton, NJ: Princeton University Press, 1990.

Welch, John. *Spiritual Pilgrims: Carl Jung and Teresa of Avila.* Mahwah, NJ: Paulist Press, 1982.

Williams, Rowan. *Teresa of Avila.* Wilton, CT: Morehouse Publishing, 1992.

John of the Cross

Astigarraga, Juan Luis, Agustí Borrell, and F. Javier Martín de Lucas, eds. *Concordancias de los escritos de San Juan de la Cruz.* Rome: Teresianum, 1990.

Bruno de Jesus-Marie. *Saint John of the Cross.* New York: Sheed & Ward, 1932.

Burrows, Ruth. *Ascent to Love: The Spiritual Teaching of St John of the Cross.* Denville, NJ: Dimension Books, 1987.

Collings, Ross. *John of the Cross.* The Way of the Christian Mystics Series, 10. Collegeville, MN: Liturgical Press, 1990.

Crisógono de Jesús Sacramentado. *The Life of St. John of the Cross.* Translated by Kathleen Pond. London: Longmans, Green & Co., 1958.

Culligan, Kevin. *Saint John of the Cross and Spiritual Direction.* Dublin: Carmelite Centre of Spirituality, 1983.

Doohan, Leonard. *The Contemporary Challenge of John of the Cross: An Introduction to His Life and Teaching.* Washington, DC: ICS Publications, 1995.

FitzGerald, Constance. "From Impasse to Prophetic Hope: Crisis of Memory." In *CTSA Proceedings* 64 (2009): 21–42.

———. "Impasse and Dark Night." In *Living With Apocalypse: Spiritual Resources for Social Compassion.* Edited by Tilden Edwards, 93–116. San Francisco: Harper & Row, 1984.

Graviss, Dennis. *Portrait of the Spiritual Director in the Writings of St. John of the Cross.* Rome: Institutum Carmelitanum, 1983.

Hardy, Richard P. *John of the Cross: Man and Mystic.* Boston: Pauline, 2004.

Howells, Edward. *John of the Cross and Teresa of Avila: Mystical Knowing and Selfhood.* New York: Crossroad, 2002.

John of the Cross. *The Collected Works of St. John of the Cross.* Translated by Kieran Kavanaugh and Otilio Rodriguez. Rev. ed. by Kieran Kavanaugh. Washington, DC: ICS Publications, 1991.

Kavanaugh, Kieran. *John of the Cross: Doctor of Light and Love.* Spiritual Legacy Series. New York: Crossroad, 1999.

Matthew, Iain. *The Impact of God: Soundings from St John of the Cross.* London: Hodder & Stoughton, 1995.

McGowan, John, ed. *A Fresh Approach to St John of the Cross.* Kildare, Ireland: St Pauls, 1993.

Merton, Thomas. *The Ascent to Truth.* New York: Harcourt, Brace & Co., 1951.

———. "Light in Darkness: The Ascetical Doctrine of St. John of the Cross." In *Disputed Questions,* 208–17. New York: Farrar, Straus & Giroux, 1960.

Muto, Susan. *John of the Cross for Today: The Ascent.* Notre Dame, IN: Ave Maria Press, 1991.

———. *John of the Cross for Today: The Dark Night.* Notre Dame, IN: Ave Maria Press, 1994.

Nemick, Francis Kelly, and Marie Theresa Coombs. *O Blessed Night: Recovering from Addiction, Codependency and Attachment Based on the Insights of St. John of the Cross and Pierre Teilhard de Chardin.* Staten Island, NY: Alba House, 1991.

Payne, Steven. *John of the Cross and the Cognitive Value of Mysticism.* Norwell, MA: Kluwer Academic Publishers, 1990.

Payne, Steven, ed. *John of the Cross: Conferences and Essays by Members of the Institute of Carmelite Studies and Others.* Carmelite Studies, 6. Washington, DC: ICS Publications, 1992.

Ruiz, Federico, ed. *God Speaks in the Night: The Life, Times, and Teaching of St. John of the Cross.* Translated by Kieran Kavanaugh. Washington, DC: ICS Publications, 1991.

Sanchez, Manuel Diego. *Bibliografía sistemática de San Juan de la Cruz.* Madrid: Editorial de Espiritualidad, 2000.

Tavard, George. *Poetry and Contemplation in St. John of the Cross.* Athens, OH: Ohio University Press, 1988.

Thompson, Colin. *The Poet and the Mystic: A Study of the Cántico Espiritual of San Juan de la Cruz.* Oxford, England: Oxford University Press, 1977.

————. *St. John of the Cross: Songs in the Night.* London: SPCK, 2002.

Thompson, William M. *Fire and Light: On Consulting the Saints, Mystics and Martyrs in Theology.* Mahwah, NJ: Paulist Press, 1987.

Tyler, Peter M. *St John of the Cross.* London: Continuum, 2010.

von Balthasar, Hans Urs. *The Glory of the Lord: A Theological Aesthetics*, Vol. III: *Studies in Theological Style: Lay Styles,* 105–71. Translated by Andrew Louth et al. San Francisco: Ignatius Press, 1986.

Welch, John. *When Gods Die: An Introduction to John of the Cross.* Mahwah, NJ: Paulist Press, 1990.

Wojtyla, Karol. *Faith According to Saint John of the Cross.* San Francisco: Ignatius Press, 1981.

Jerome Gracián and the Early Discalced Carmelites

Ana de San Agustín. *The Visionary Life of Madre Ana de San Agustín.* Edited by Teresa Howe. Suffolk, England: Tamesis Press, 2004.

Ana de San Bartolomé. *Autobiography and Other Writings.* Translated and edited by Darcy Donahue. Chicago: University of Chicago Press, 2008.

Gracián, Jerome. "Constituciones of the Cerro, or Treatise on Melancholy." Translated by Michael Dodd. In *A Better Wine: Essays Celebrating Kieran Kavanaugh, O.C.D.* Edited by Kevin Culligan, 95–135. Carmelite Studies, 10. Washington, DC: ICS Publications, 2007.

————. *Just Man, Husband of Mary, Guardian of Christ: An Anthology of Readings from Jerónimo Gracián's* Summary of the Excellencies of St. Joseph (1597). Philadelphia: St. Joseph's University Press, 1993.

————. *Obras.* Edited by Silverio de Santa Teresa. Burgos: El Monte Carmelo, 1932–33.

————. *Peregrinación de Anastasio.* Edited by Juan Luis Astigarraga. Rome: Institutum Historicum Carmelitanum, 2001.

María de San José Salazar. *Book for the Hour of Recreation.* Introduction and notes by Alison Weber. Translated by Amanda Powell. Chicago: University of Chicago Press, 2002.

Nevin, Winifred. *Heirs of St. Teresa of Avila.* Milwaukee, WI: Bruce, 1959.

Wilson, Christopher, ed. *The Heirs of St. Teresa of Avila.* Carmelite Studies, 9. Washington, DC: ICS Publications, 2006.

Mary Magdalen de' Pazzi

de' Pazzi, Mary Magdalen. *The Complete Works.* Translated by Gabriel Pausback. 5 vols. Fatima: Casa Beata Nuno, 1969–75.

————. *Maria Maddalena De' Pazzi: Selected Revelations.* Translated by Armando Maggi. Classics of Western Spirituality Series. New York: Paulist Press, 2000.

Larkin, Ernest. "The Ecstasies of the Forty Days of St. Mary Magdalene de' Pazzi." *Carmelus* 1 (1954): 29–71.

Maggi, Armando. *Uttering the Word: The Mystical Performances of Maria Maddalena de' Pazzi, a Renaissance Visionary.* Albany, NY: SUNY Press, 1998.

Secondin, Bruno. *Santa Maria Maddalena de' Pazzi: Esperienze e dottrina.* Rome: Edizioni Carmelitane, 2007.

Thor-Salviat, Salvator. *Secrets of a Seraph: The Spiritual Doctrine of Saint Mary Magdalene de' Pazzi.* Translated by Gabriel N. Pausback. Downers Grove, IL: Carmelite Third Order Press, Aylesford Priory, 1961.

John of Saint Samson

Jean de Saint-Samson. *Oeuvres Complètes 1: L'éguillon, les flammes, les flèches, et le miroir de l'amour de Dieu, propres pour enamourer l'ame de Dieu en Dieu mesme.* Edited by Hein Blommestijn. Rome: Institutum Carmelitanum, 1992.

————. *Oeuvres Complètes 2: Méditations et Soliloques 1.* Edited by Hein Blommestijn. Rome: Institutum Carmelitanum, 1993.

————. *Oeuvres Complètes 3: Méditations et Soliloques 2—L'exercice des esprits amoureux xolitaires en leurs solitudes.* Edited by Hein Blommestijn. Rome: Edizione Carmelitane, 2000.

McGreal, Wilfrid. *John of St. Samson.* Saints of Carmel Series, 1. Faversham, Kent: The Carmelite Press, 1962, 1978.

Poslusney, Venard, trans. and ed. *Prayer, Aspiration and Contemplation: From the Writings of John of St. Samson.* Staten Island, NY: Alba House, 1975.

Stefanotti, Robert. *The Phoenix of Rennes: The Life and Poetry of John of St. Samson, 1571–1636.* Medieval and Early Modern Mysticism Series. New York: Peter Lang, 1994.

Lawrence of the Resurrection

Freer, Harold Wiley. *God Meets Us Where We Are: An Interpretation of Brother Lawrence.* Nashville, TN: Abingdon Press, 1967.

Lawrence of the Resurrection. *The Practice of the Presence of God.* Translated with an introduction by John J. Delaney. Foreword by Henri J. M. Nouwen. New York: Image Books, Doubleday, 1977.

———. *Writings and Conversations on the Practice of the Presence of God.* Critical edition by Conrad De Meester. Translated by Salvatore Sciurba. Washington, DC: ICS Publications, 1994.

Maas, Robin. "Practicing the Presence of God: Recollection in the Carmelite Tradition." *Spiritual Life* 36 (1990): 99–107.

May, Gerald G. *The Awakened Heart: Opening Yourself to the Love You Need.* San Francisco: Harper San Francisco, 1991.

Michael of St. Augustine and Maria Petyt

Faesen, Robert, ed. *Albert Deblaere, S.J. (1916–1994): Essays on Mystical Literature.* Leuven: Peeters, 2004.

Michael of St. Augustine. *Life with Mary: A Treatise on the Marian Life.* Translated and edited by Thomas McGinnis. New York: Scapular Press, 1953.

Petyt, Maria. *Union with Our Lady: Marian Writings.* Translated and edited by Thomas McGinnis. New York: Scapular Press, 1954.

Martyrs of Compiègne

Bernanos, Georges. "Dialogues of the Carmelites." Translated by Michael Legat. In *The Heroic Face of Innocence: Three Stories by Georges Bernanos.* Grand Rapids, MI: Eerdmans, 1999.

Bush, William. *Gertrud von Le Fort, Bernanos, and the Historical Sources of "Die Letzte am Schafott."* Carmel de Compiègne, 1991.

———, ed. "Literature and Martyrdom" issue of *Renascence: Essays on Values in Literature* 48 (Fall 1995).

————. *To Quell the Terror: The Mystery of the Vocation of the Sixteen Carmelites of Compiègne Guillotined July 17, 1794*. Washington, DC: ICS Publications, 1999.

Le Fort, Gertrud von. *The Song at the Scaffold*. Translated by Olga Marx. New York: Sheed & Ward, 1933.

Newkirk, Terrye. *The Mantle of Elijah: The Martyrs of Compiègne as Prophets of the Modern Age*. With a Pastoral Letter by His Excellency Adolphe-Marie Hardy, Bishop of Beauvais, Noyon, and Senlis (France), for the Bicentenary of the Martyrdom of the Sixteen Blessed Carmelites of Compiègne. Washington, DC: ICS Publications, 1995.

Poulenc, Francis. *Dialogues of the Carmelites*. English version by Joseph Machlis. Ricordi's Collection of Opera Librettos. London: G. Ricordi & Co., 1993.

Thérèse of Lisieux

Ahern, Patrick V. *Maurice and Thérèse: The Story of a Love*. New York: Doubleday, 1998.

De Meester, Conrad, ed. *Saint Thérèse of Lisieux: Her Life, Times, and Teaching*. Washington, DC: ICS Publications, 1997.

————. *The Power of Confidence: Genesis and Structure of the "Way of Spiritual Childhood" of St. Thérèse of Lisieux*. Translated by Susan Conroy. Staten Island, NY: Alba House, 1998.

————. *With Empty Hands: The Message of St. Thérèse of Lisieux*. Washington, DC: ICS Publications, 2002.

Descouvemont, Pierre, and Helmuth Nils Loose. *Thérèse and Lisieux*. Grand Rapids, MI: Eerdmans, 1996.

Foley, Marc. *The Love that Keeps Us Sane: Living the Little Way of St. Thérèse of Lisieux*. Mahwah, NJ: Paulist Press, 2000.

Gaucher, Guy. *The Passion of Thérèse of Lisieux*. Translated by Anne Marie Brennan. New York: Crossroad, 1990.

————. *The Story of a Life: St. Thérèse of Lisieux*. First paperback ed. San Francisco: HarperSanFrancisco, 1993.

O'Donnell, Christopher. *Love in the Heart of the Church: The Mission of Thérèse of Lisieux*. Dublin: Veritas, 1997.

O'Mahony, Christopher, ed. and trans. *St Thérèse of Lisieux by Those Who Knew Her: Testimonies from the Process of Beatification*. Dublin: Veritas, 1975.

Payne, Steven. *Saint Thérèse of Lisieux: Doctor of the Universal Church*. New York: St Pauls, 2002.

Schmidt, Joseph F. *Everything is Grace: The Life and Way of Thérèse of Lisieux*. Ijamsville, MD: The Word Among Us Press, 2007.

Thérèse of Lisieux. *General Correspondence*. Translated by John Clarke. 2 vols. Washington, DC: ICS Publications, 1982–88.

————. *Her Last Conversations*. Translated by John Clarke. Washington, DC: ICS Publications, 1977.

————. *The Plays of St. Thérèse of Lisieux*. Translated by Susan Conroy and David J. Dwyer. Washington, DC: ICS Publications, 2008.

————. *The Poetry of Saint Thérèse of Lisieux*. Translated by Donald Kinney. Washington, DC: ICS Publications, 1996.

————. *The Prayers of Saint Thérèse of Lisieux*. Translated by Aletheia Kane. Washington, DC: ICS Publications, 1997.

————. *Story of a Soul: The Autobiography of St. Thérèse of Lisieux*. Translated by John Clarke. 3rd edition. Washington, DC: ICS Publications, 1996.

von Balthasar, Hans Urs. *Two Sisters in the Spirit: Thérèse of Lisieux and Elizabeth of the Trinity*. Translated by Donald Nichols, Anne Elizabeth Englund, and Dennis Martin. San Francisco: Ignatius Press, 1992.

Elizabeth of the Trinity

Borriello, Luigi. *Spiritual Doctrine of Elizabeth of the Trinity*. Staten Island, NY: Alba House, 1986.

De Meester, Conrad. *Élisabeth de la Trinité: Biographie*. Paris: Presses de la Renaissance, 2006.

————. *Élisabeth de la Trinité vue et entendu par les témoins*. Toulouse: Éditions du Carmel, 2007.

————, ed. *Elizabeth of the Trinity—Light Love Life: A Look at a Face and a Heart*. Translated by Aletheia Kane. Washington, DC: ICS Publications, 1987.

Elizabeth of the Trinity. *Complete Works*, Vol. 1: *General Introduction, Major Spiritual Writings*. Translated by Aletheia Kane. Washington, DC: ICS Publications, 1984.

————. *Complete Works*, Vol. 2: *Letters from Carmel*. Translated by Anne Englund Nash. Washington, DC: ICS Publications, 1995.

Lafrance, Jean. *Elizabeth of the Trinity: The Charism of Her Prayer*. Adapted from the French by a Nun of the Carmel du Pater Noster, Jerusalem. Darlington, England: Darlington Carmel, 1983.

Moorcroft, Jennifer. *He Is My Heaven: The Life of Elizabeth of the Trinity*. Washington, DC: ICS Publications, 2001.

Philipon, M. M. *The Spiritual Doctrine of Elizabeth of the Trinity*. Translated by a Benedictine of Stanbrook Abbey. Reprint ed. Westminster, MD: Newman Bookshop, 1947; Washington, DC: Teresian Charism Press, 1985.

Tomás-Fernández, Simeone della S. Famiglia. *Bibliografia della Serva di Dio Elisabetta della Trinità*. Rome: Postulazione Generale O.C.D., 1974.

von Balthasar, Hans Urs. *Two Sisters in the Spirit: Thérèse of Lisieux and Elizabeth of the Trinity*. Translated by Donald Nichols, Anne Elizabeth Englund, and Dennis Martin. San Francisco: Ignatius Press, 1992.

Titus Brandsma

Brandsma, Titus. *Carmelite Mysticism: Historical Sketches.* Darien, IL: Carmelite Press, 2002.

Brandsma, Titus, Albert Servaes, and Jos Huls. *Ecce Homo: Schouwen van de weg van Liefde/Contemplating the Way of Love.* Leuven: Peeters, 2003.

Dölle, Constant. *Encountering God in the Abyss: Titus Brandsma's Spiritual Journey.* Fiery Arrow Series, 5. Leuven: Peeters, 2002.

Gluckert, Leopold. *Titus Brandsma: Friar against Fascism.* Darien, IL: Carmelite Press, 1985.

Malham, Joseph M. *By Fire into Light: Four Catholic Martyrs of the Nazi Camps.* Fiery Arrow Series, 4. Leuven: Peeters, 2002.

Rees, Joseph. *Titus Brandsma: A Modern Martyr.* London: Sidgwick and Jackson, 1971.

Valabek, Redemptus Maria, ed. *The Beatification of Father Titus Brandsma, Carmelite (1881–1942): Martyr in Dachau.* Rome: Institutum Carmelitanum, 1986.

———, ed. *Essays on Titus Brandsma: Carmelite Educator, Journalist, Martyr.* Rome: Institutum Carmelitanum, 1985.

Edith Stein

Neyer, Maria Amata. *Edith Stein: Her Life in Photos and Documents.* Translated by Waltraut Stein. Washington, DC: ICS Publications, 1999.

Posselt, Teresia Renata. *Edith Stein: The Life of a Philosopher and Carmelite.* Edited by Suzanne M. Batzdorff, Josephine Koeppel, and John Sullivan. Washington, DC: ICS Publications, 2005.

Stein, Edith. *Essays on Woman.* Translated by Freda Mary Oben. 2nd ed., rev. Washington, DC: ICS Publications, 1996.

———. *Finite and Eternal Being: An Attempt at an Ascent to the Meaning of Being.* Translated by Kurt F. Reinhardt. Washington, DC: ICS Publications, 2002.

———. *The Hidden Life: Hagiographic Essays, Meditations, Spiritual Texts.* Translated by Waltraut Stein. Washington, DC: ICS Publications, 1992.

———. *Knowledge and Faith.* Translated by Walter Redmond. Washington, DC: ICS Publications, 2000.

———. *Life in a Jewish Family.* Translated by Josephine Koeppel. Washington, DC: ICS Publications, 1986.

———. *On the Problem of Empathy.* Translated by Waltraut Stein. 3rd rev. ed. Washington, DC: ICS Publications, 1989.

———. *Science of the Cross.* Translated by Josephine Koeppel. Washington, DC: ICS Publications, 2003.

Sullivan, John, ed. *Edith Stein: Essential Writings*. Modern Spiritual Masters Series. Maryknoll, NY: Orbis Books, 2002.

Jessica Powers

Kappes, Marcianne. *Track of the Mystic: The Spirituality of Jessica Powers*. Kansas City, MO: Sheed & Ward, 1994.

Leckey, Dolores R. *Winter Music: A Life of Jessica Powers*. Kansas City, MO: Sheed & Ward, 1993.

Morneau, Robert F. *Songs Out of Silence: 99 Sayings by Jessica Powers*. Hyde Park, NY: New City Press, 2010.

Powers, Jessica. *The Selected Poetry of Jessica Powers*. Edited by Regina Siegfried and Robert F. Morneau. Washington, DC: ICS Publications, 1999.

Other Post-Teresian Discalced Carmelite Figures

Teresa Margaret Redi (1747–1770), Francisco Palau (1811–1872), Mary of Jesus Crucified (1846–1878), Teresa of the Andes (1900–1920), Père Jacques Bunel (1900–1945)

Brunot, Amédée. *Mariam the Little Arab: Sister Mary of Jesus Crucified (1846–1878)*. Translated by Jeanne Dumais and Miriam of Jesus. Eugene, OR: Carmel of Maria Regina, 1984.

Gabriel of St. Mary Magdalene. *From the Sacred Heart to the Trinity: The Spiritual Itinerary of Saint Teresa Margaret of the Sacred Heart, O.C.D.* Translated by Sebastian Ramge. Reprint ed. Washington, DC: ICS Publications, 2006.

Griffin, Michael, trans. *God the Joy of My Life: A Biography of Saint Teresa of the Andes, with the Saint's Spiritual Diary*. 2nd ed. Hubertus, WI: Teresian Charism Press, 1994.

———, comp. *A New Hymn to God: Saint Teresa of the Andes*. Washington, DC: Teresian Charism Press, 1993.

———, comp. and trans. *Testimonies to Saint Teresa of the Andes*. Washington, DC: Teresian Charism Press, 1995.

Murphy, Francis J. *Père Jacques: Resplendent in Victory*. Washington, DC: ICS Publications, 1998.

Pacho, Eulogio. *Francisco Palau y Quer: A Passion for the Church*. Translated by David J. Centner. 3rd ed. Rome: Carmelite Missionaries, 2004.

Palau y Quer, Francisco. *My Relations with the Church*. Edited by Eulogio Pacho. Translated by Nora Birch and Maria Elena Pampliega. Rome: Carmelite Missionaries, 2000.

Other Recent Voices and Developments

Caterine, Darryl V. *Conservative Catholicism and the Carmelites: Identity, Ethnicity, and Tradition in the Modern Church.* Bloomington, IN: Indiana University Press, 2001.

Deeney, Aloysius. *Welcome to the Secular Order of Discalced Carmelites.* Washington, DC: ICS Publications, 2009.

Dent, Barbara. *The Marriage of All and Nothing.* Edited by Mary Freiberger. Washington, DC: ICS Publications, 2002.

Egan, Keith J., ed. *Carmelite Prayer: A Tradition for the 21st Century.* New York: Paulist Press, 2003.

Malley, John, Camilo Maccise, and Joseph Chalmers. *In Obsequio Jesus Christi: The Letters of the Superiors General O.Carm. and O.C.D., 1992–2002.* Rome: Edizioni OCD, 2003.

Mark, Kevin, ed. *Towards a Prophetic Brotherhood: Documents of the Carmelite Order, 1972–1982.* Melbourne: The Carmelite Centre, 1984.

Weaver, Mary Jo. *Cloister and Community: Life within a Carmelite Monastery.* Bloomington, IN: Indiana University Press, 2002.

Wilkinson, Peggy. *Finding the Mystic Within You.* Washington, DC: ICS Publications, 1999.

Williams, Joan. *Growing Free: A Carmelite Remembers.* New York: Alba House, 1988.